Dyslexia

Dyslexia

Developing the Debate

JULIAN ELLIOTT AND ROD NICOLSON

Edited by Andrew Davis

Bloomsbury Academic
An imprint of Bloomsbury Publishing Plc

B L O O M S B U R Y

LONDON · OXFORD · NEW YORK · NEW DELHI · SYDNEY

Bloomsbury Academic

An imprint of Bloomsbury Publishing Plc

50 Bedford Square	1385 Broadway
London	New York
WC1B 3DP	NY 10018
UK	USA

www.bloomsbury.com

BLOOMSBURY and the Diana logo are trademarks of Bloomsbury Publishing Plc

First published 2016

British Library Cataloguing-in-Publication Data
A catalogue record for this book is available from the British Library.

ISBN:	PB:	978-1-4742-3375-0
	ePDF:	978-1-4742-3374-3
	ePub:	978-1-4742-3373-6

Library of Congress Cataloging-in-Publication Data
A catalogue record for this book is available from the Library of Congress.

Typeset by Fakenham Prepress Solutions, Fakenham, Norfolk NR21 8NN
Printed and bound in Great Britain

Contents

Notes on contributors

Andrew Davis is an Honorary Research Fellow in the School of Education, Durham University, UK. After eight years teaching in primary schools, specializing in early years, he taught philosophy of education, maths for primary teachers and information technology at Cambridge University, UK, before moving to Durham University in 1990. His roles at Durham included Director of the Primary PGCE course and Convenor of Primary Mathematics Courses. His extensive publications in educational assessment draw on his academic discipline of analytical philosophy. He co-authored (with Suggate and Goulding) the best-selling *Mathematical Knowledge for Primary Teachers*, currently in its fourth edition. In 2014 his short book *To Read or Not to Read: Decoding Synthetic Phonics* attracted widespread media coverage and controversy. He is currently writing a monograph on educational research and the teaching of reading.

Julian Elliott is Professor of Educational Psychology, at Durham University, UK and Principal of Collingwood College, Durham University. Initially, a teacher of children with special educational needs, he subsequently practised as an educational psychologist, before becoming a university lecturer in 1990. A Fellow of the Academy of Social Sciences, a Chartered Psychologist, and an Associate Fellow of the British Psychological Society, he is registered to engage in clinical practice as an educational psychologist by the Health Professions Council. His research primarily operates at the interface of educational psychology as both a discipline and a profession. His book, *The Dyslexia Debate*, co-authored with Elena Grigorenko (Yale University) was published in 2014.

Rod Nicolson is Professor of Psychology at the University of Sheffield, UK. His area of specialism is human learning, and he has published over 100 scientific articles and books in the field. Working with Angela Fawcett for over two decades, he has a leading international role in dyslexia research, theory and practice. Their book *Dyslexia, Learning and the Brain* (2007) created a unique and comprehensive framework for understanding the causes of dyslexia in terms of reading, learning and neural circuitry. Recently he has been working on the strengths of dyslexia, with his book *Positive Dyslexia* (2015) providing a complete blueprint for success in life as a dyslexic person.

Series editor's preface: Key debates in educational policy

Christopher Winch

IMPACT pamphlets were launched in 1999 as an initiative of the Philosophy of Education Society of Great Britain. Their aim was to bring philosophical perspectives to bear on UK education policy and they have been written by leading general philosophers or philosophers of education. There are now more than twenty volumes.

They dealt with a variety of issues relating to policy within the field of education. Some have focused on controversial aspects of current government policy such as those by Andrew Davis on assessment, Harry Brighouse on disparities in secondary education, Mary Warnock on changes in provision for pupils with special educational needs, and Colin Richards on school inspection. Others, such as those by Michael Luntley on performance-related pay and by Chris Winch on vocational education and training, have been critical of new policy initiatives. Yet others have been concerned with the organization and content of the school curriculum. These have included pamphlets by Kevin Williams on the teaching of foreign languages, Steve Bramall and John White on Curriculum 2000, David Archard on Sex Education, Stephen Johnson on thinking skills, Graham Haydon on Personal, Social and Health Education, and John Gingell on the Visual Arts.

The launch of each pamphlet has been accompanied by a symposium for policymakers and others at which issues raised in the pamphlets have been further explored. These have been attended by government ministers, opposition spokespersons, other MPs, representatives from the Qualifications and Curriculum Authority, employers' organizations, trade unions and teachers' professional organizations as well as members of think tanks, academics and journalists.

Some of the original pamphlets have made a lasting impression on the world of education policy and have, in addition, sparked debates in both the policy and academic worlds. They have revealed a hunger for dealing with certain topics in a philosophically oriented way because it has been felt that the original pamphlet initiated a debate that needs and deserves to be taken a lot further. The Key Debates in Educational Policy series aimed to take some of these debates further by selecting from those original IMPACT pamphlets whose influence continues to be keenly felt and either reproducing or expanding them to take account of the most recent developments in the area with which they deal. In addition, each of the original pamphlets receives a lengthy reply by a distinguished figure in the area who takes issue with the main arguments of the original pamphlet. Each of the Key Debates volumes also contained a substantial foreword and/or afterword by an academic with strong interests in the area under discussion, which gave the context and provided extensive commentary on the questions under discussion and the arguments of the original author and his/her respondent.

There are a number of reasons for this. Philosophical techniques applied to policy issues can be a very powerful tool clarifying questions and developing arguments based on ethical, aesthetic, political and epistemological positions. Philosophical argumentation is, however, by its nature, controversial and contested. There is rarely, if ever, one side to a philosophical question. The fact that the IMPACT pamphlets have often aroused lively debate and controversy is testament to this. There has been a hunger for a more rounded version of the debate to be presented in a format accessible to those who do not have a formal philosophical background but who find philosophical argumentation about educational issues to be useful in developing their own ideas. This series aimed to cater for this audience while also presenting rigorous argumentation that can also appeal to a more specialist audience. The current volume is a departure from past practice as the treatment given to the topic is not overtly philosophical. Instead detailed psychological arguments are deployed for and against the existence of dyslexia. However, this volume also illustrates the importance of conceptual clarity within scientific enquiry, as a large element of the dyslexia debate concerns whether and how such a condition, if it exists, can be best understood. In this sense therefore there is a strong continuity between this volume and its predecessors.

It was hoped that each volume in this series would provide an introduction and set the scene to each topic and give the readership a splendid example of philosophical argumentation over a complex and important educational issue.

Introduction

Andrew Davis

This book differs in some ways from previous volumes in the Key Debates in Educational Policy series. The latter have explored policy debates from a philosophical perspective, and most of the contributors have written directly from a philosophy of education vantage point. The present offering shares the series aim of examining education policy issues philosophically. However, on this occasion, the main contributors are social science researchers with significant expertise in empirical approaches. Much of the book is given over to their contrasting explorations of current dyslexia research.

Many readers will be familiar with controversies about learning disabilities such as dyslexia and ADHD. The associated arguments show little sign of being settled in the near future. One of the reasons for this, I believe, is that underlying the discussions are several ontological, epistemological and normative complexities. When empirical evidence is used to support particular positions in the debates, important non-empirical assumptions are sometimes needed in addition to complete the arguments concerned. The Afterword selects a subset of these issues from the main contributors' exchanges, and comments on them from the perspective of philosophy and philosophy of education.

Julian Elliott and Rod Nicolson have debated the status of dyslexia for many years. Their exchanges have taken place as a result of TV programmes such as *The Dyslexia Myth* and at an academic level that includes conferences with titles such as *The Death of Dyslexia*. It is hardly surprising that headings such as these have stirred passions. People with a range of apparently conflicting perspectives all really care about the welfare of students with difficulties. Needless to say, both Elliott and Nicolson share these strong moral commitments, while approaching the debates from differing standpoints.

Their disagreements are not about whether some students experience significant challenges when learning to read and when dealing with other language-related problems. Elliott acknowledges that 'there is a long and detailed history of accounts of people who have struggled with literacy' (this volume). He quotes from Rice and Brooks (this volume p. 76) to sum up his perspective on dyslexia's status. It is his answer to the question 'whether dyslexic people differ from other poor readers'. He goes as far as saying that challenging the notion of dyslexia 'should not concern the spurious question as to whether such a condition exists' (this volume p. 74). He recognizes that there are many different understandings of the disorder and outlines them systematically. He proceeds to argue that none of these survives scientific scrutiny.

Nicolson's position is complex. As I understand him, his response to Rice and Brooks is that dyslexic people do differ from other poor readers. He distinguishes between dyslexia as a specific learning difficulty and what he calls its 'behavioural manifestation in the reading domain' (this volume p. 8). He dubs the latter a 'reading disability'. He devotes significant attention to the brains of dyslexics, and is quite explicit that neurological features distinguish them from non-dyslexics. Nicolson makes what is for me is a disturbing observation about the position of US researchers: federal support is contingent on a developmental disorder being 'intrinsic (that is, brain-based) rather than produced by the environment' (p. 124). It looks as though a particular view is taken in the US about what it is for a disorder to be 'real'. I will devote much attention to the 'reality' issue in the Afterword.

Nicolson refers to the 'strong heritability' of dyslexia (this volume p. 14). That is the kind of point often made by those who want to emphasize the biological basis of a condition. However, given his attention to social and emotional factors in his treatment of dyslexia as a reading disability, his perspective cannot be simplistically characterized as a 'medical' model. I understand the latter to be, broadly speaking, a model postulating a disorder with a biological base. He writes poignantly about stress, anxiety and learning, claiming that these can lead to 'learned helplessness', this in turn giving rise to 'impairments' at the brain level (this volume p. 61)

His 'Delayed Neural Commitment' hypothesis in connection with dyslexia as a specific learning difficulty points to delays in brain developments that are needed for reading. Nevertheless, he is clear that appropriate provision for very young children can help to build 'the skills and neural circuitry needed to underpin classroom readiness and reading readiness' (this volume p. 72).

Elliott also accepts that research has established that 'we can identify certain areas and functions of the brain that are associated with reading disability' (this volume p. 95), but insists that this is compatible with the denial that it can provide guidance on differentiating interventions between dyslexics and others with decoding problems.

In the Afterword I explore some ethical and conceptual questions stimulated by the Nicolson-Elliott exchanges. Many suffer frustration and misery at school, and indeed throughout their lives because of problems with aspects of language, especially reading. It is this reality with which Nicolson and Elliott are deeply concerned. The results of empirical research into dyslexia very obviously have important practical implications. I will try to show that a philosophical scrutiny of the status and fairness of the dyslexia label can also bear on practice. I raise a number of issues in the course of my contribution, and make no apology for refraining from offering definitive answers or solutions. There are complexities and uncertainties here, and to brush over them will do no service to those experiencing learning problems, or to their teachers.

I offer no verdicts on the actual exchanges between Nicolson and Elliott. That is not the aim of the Afterword. Their contributions can speak for themselves. Nicolson understandably sees this book as representing his and Elliott's 'attempt to identify areas of agreement and disagreement, with a view to trying to find a successful way forward' (this volume p. 6).

1

Developmental dyslexia: The bigger picture

Rod Nicolson

Introduction

Developmental dyslexia is a highly prevalent, socially important, and individually traumatic condition. Estimates of prevalence vary depending on the definition used, but a typical suggestion is around 5 to 10 per cent (Lyon 1996). This yields an estimate of 3 to 6 million dyslexic people in the UK. It is socially important because most western countries have legislation requiring that individuals with disabilities (including dyslexia) are entitled to additional support. It is traumatic to the dyslexic individuals and to their families especially in the school years. It is a modern disability because until relatively recently most societies were functionally illiterate, with only a few scholars able to master the art of reading.

In this first part of the book, I set out what I consider to be the most promising ways to approach dyslexia – from the point of view of theory, of education, and of the individual. These are separate lines of enquiry, but in an ideal world all three perspectives would cohere so as to provide a solution that somehow optimizes the overall approach to be taken. I have called this part Developmental Dyslexia: The Bigger Picture to indicate that it is necessary to 'decentre' from narrow views of dyslexia, and to consider the issues from all angles, but there is a great need to find synergy between the many different scientific, educational and political forces involved.

I will start with two anecdotes that highlight the complexity of the problem.

The first anecdote relates to my wife Margaret, a highly experienced school teacher who was providing one-to-two mathematics support as part of the UK government 'Pupil Premium' initiative for ten-year-old disadvantaged children. Both children in one pair had diagnoses of dyslexia. Child A, who was in fact the better reader, took the diagnosis as excusing his failure to learn, and refused to engage with the opportunities available. Child B, by contrast, said that his mother had explained that because he was dyslexic he had to try harder to learn, but would learn if he tried hard. Not surprisingly, Child B benefited much more from the support. Margaret identified where his major problems lay. These were derived from lack of knowledge of the standard rules of number and number bonds, allied to a complete lack of self-belief. She introduced a simple support programme, boosting both knowledge and self-belief, with a high proportion of successful learning episodes. This led to a transformation in self-belief and self-efficacy, which led to systematic and steady progress over the next few years, and considerable success in secondary school. By contrast, Child A neither flourished nor succeeded at school.

I will use this anecdote to make the obvious but necessary point that a diagnosis by itself is neither good nor bad. It depends upon the use to which it is put. A more subtle point, however, relates to Child A. What has happened to prevent him from even trying to learn at school? And how can we avoid this personal disaster?

The second anecdote relates to my partner/protagonist in this book, Julian Elliott. I have known Elliott for many years in his role of 'dyslexia devil's advocate' asking the awkward questions that the 'dyslexia industry' would rather not answer. I respect this role highly, and indeed, my career has been somewhat similar, also asking theoretical questions that are problematic for the 'mainstream' dyslexia theorists. Not surprisingly, given our track records of dissent, Elliott and I also disagree with each other, and this book represents our attempt to identify areas of agreement and disagreement, with a view to trying to find a successful way to move forward.

The anecdote relates to the International Dyslexia Association conference in New Orleans in November 2013. I had convened a symposium on Positive Dyslexia, for which the theme was 'Find and Follow your Strengths', and this was followed by a session from Elliott, where he gave a talk on the 'dyslexia debate'.

Elliott gave a bravura performance, providing his side of the debate. He examined the definition of dyslexia, the theories for dyslexia, the assessment of dyslexia, the treatment of dyslexia, the genetics of dyslexia, providing a welter of information, which he expertly demonstrated was contradictory, incoherent, flawed, or worse. At the end of each examination of the evidence, he concluded sorrowfully 'Doesn't stack up'.

The core problem Elliott described is as follows. Before he became an academic, as a practising educational psychologist, Elliott was often required to assess a child for dyslexia. This is a time-consuming and problematic task. The general 'best practice' approach to dyslexia assessment in, say, a nine-year-old child would be to administer an IQ test, usually the Wechsler Intelligence Scale for Children (Wechsler 2003), deriving the full scale IQ together with the four indexes Working Memory Index, Processing Speed Index, Perceptual Organization Index and Verbal Comprehension Index. Then arrange literacy-related tests, including single word reading, spelling, comprehension, phonology, working memory, writing speed, and perhaps rapid naming. If the IQ is, say, over a standard score of 90, and literacy performance is less than 90, for example, the diagnosis might be 'dyslexia'.

The recommendation to support will then lead to a systematic, comprehensive phonics support reading programme, which is considered best practice. However, exactly the same recommendation for support is also considered best practice for any child with poor literacy, irrespective of discrepancy with IQ.

One can see Elliott's dilemma. He has to undertake lengthy assessment procedures, for which at least two-thirds of the time is taken with an IQ test which he considers to be of doubtful validity, to derive a diagnosis which he considers questionable, all of which is then ignored subsequently. Why doesn't he just omit the IQ based discrepancy tests?

Of course Elliott is well able to provide a fully supported version of his analysis, and will do so in this book. This is why I have referred to my memory of the occasion as an anecdote, highlighting that the event made a lasting impression on me (but that my memory may not be wholly accurate). Elliott's analysis inspired me to co-author this book, so as to further explore these issues, and to provide another side of the debate.

In this first part, I set myself some stiff challenges, to answer four questions implicit in Elliott's analysis. What is dyslexia? Why does dyslexia lead to reading disability? What is the most cost-effective solution to reading support for all, and what is the role of an educational psychologist in dyslexia support? My solution combines science with sense, and appears to be completely novel.

My overall plan is as follows. First I provide a brief history of dyslexia research over the past forty years, because it is impossible to understand the currents and eddies of research without an appreciation of the scientific, academic and political tides that drove them. This analysis explains why researchers chose to focus on phonological deficits and to downplay other difficulties known to be strongly associated with dyslexia.

This motivates a core distinction that I will make between dyslexia as a specific learning difficulty (SpLD), which is the intrinsic brain difference characteristic of dyslexia, and reading disability (RD), which is its behavioural manifestation in the reading domain.

Following a brief listing of the many theories of SpLD and RD, I consider first SpLD, and go back to first principles, taking dyslexia as a Developmental, Learning, Disability specific to reading, and present some of the necessary background to understanding of each of these four theoretical constructions.

I then focus on dyslexia as a specific learning difficulty, and reveal by means of evidence from my research programme with Angela Fawcett, just what these specific learning difficulties comprise. This leads to our 'procedural learning deficit' framework, and the more recent, broader framework 'Delayed Neural Commitment' (DNC) which holds that there are delays not only in skill learning but also in the creation of the neural circuits that underpin reading readiness.

This theoretical analysis of the causes of SpLD provides one of the two major foundations of my analysis of RD. Why is there a disability in reading acquisition? DNC leads to delays in the acquisition of the reading sub-skills (phonology, letter knowledge, eye fixation), perseverance of prior habits that interfere with the new learning, and delay in the creation of the neural circuits needed for efficient processing and executive control (speed of processing, working memory, response inhibition, goal maintenance, control of anxiety and aggression) and which are taken for granted by formal class teaching methods.

Mismatch between reading readiness, classroom readiness and teaching method leads to consistent and traumatic cognitive and social failure, which is exacerbated by the 'remedial reading group' approach. This leads to chronic levels of stress and anxiety in reading-related situations (akin to maths anxiety). The stress/anxiety has catastrophic effects on the learning capabilities, basically diverting all brain resources from the flexible, declarative learning circuits to the fixed 'fight, flee or freeze' procedural systems. The 'mental abscesses' caused are long-lasting and cognitively debilitating, essentially disabling learning in the classroom reading context.

This analysis underpins my concluding answers to the four challenging questions implicit in Elliott's analysis.

However, I don't expect anyone (least of all Elliott!) to take this on trust. What is the evidence for this startling series of claims!?

Dyslexia: A developmental learning disorder specific to reading

This section provides an overview of the background: a brief history (scientific and political), then a summary of areas of agreement, followed by a more detailed analysis of the components of dyslexia – development, learning, disorder, and reading. This background knowledge provides the foundation for my brief description of the range of explanatory theories for dyslexia.

Dyslexia: A short history

The first systematic approach to identification and support of dyslexia was by the neurologist, Samuel Orton (1937), who believed that the underlying problem was visual. He called the problem 'strephosymbolia' to indicate that the visual representations of letters were twisted. The first international approach to dyslexia resulted in the classic definition by the World Federation of Neurology in 1968, 'a disorder in children who, despite conventional classroom experience, fail to attain the language skills of reading, writing and spelling commensurate with their intellectual abilities'.

In the 1970s there was a range of theoretical and applied approaches to dyslexia and other learning disabilities, and it is worth highlighting that there was a very different approach to developmental disabilities during this period, in that they were considered primarily in terms of commonalities rather than differences. In the UK the standard diagnosis was in terms of minimal brain dysfunction (Wender 1978) or 'soft neurological signs' (Touwen and Sporrel 1979). This definition was used as an umbrella term for childhood learning difficulties ranging from clumsiness to speech problems.

The 1980s were, by contrast, the decade of differentiation. Representative organizations were set up, often via parents, for each of the developmental disorders. In order to gain a distinctive voice, advocates of each developmental learning difference attempted to differentiate it from the others, developing a unique niche, organization and pressure group to better support the individuals with each disability. Less tangibly, there were also tides of professional power at work. The educationalists had created a new discipline which explicitly rejected many of the traditional psychology concepts, from behaviourism to psychometrics to Piaget. Psychology, Medicine and Speech Therapy each determined to establish a clear role in developmental disorders, with the medical profession annexing ADHD, the psychologists Developmental Coordination Disorder and autism, and the speech therapists Specific Language Impairment. Dyslexia was there for the taking, with several groups vying to gain the ascendancy.

By the mid-1980s there was a burgeoning interest in dyslexia. Each profession was able to propose both theoretical and practical methods of support. The two major professions involved initially were the kinesiologists, who argued that there were intrinsic difficulties with co-ordinated, fluent movements, and the optometrists, who argued that there were visual differences.

Difficulties in motor co-ordination were long established. Of course, one of the most evident signs of abnormality in dyslexia is the often quite atrocious quality of handwriting (Miles 1983). There is also evidence that young dyslexic children up to the age of 8 have difficulty in tying shoelaces (Miles 1983). Deficits have also been noted in young dyslexic children in copying (Rudel 1985). In an extensive longitudinal study, the British Births Cohort study (Haslum 1989) examined aspects of health in a cohort of 12,905 children at each age. Two motor skills tasks emerged among the six variables significantly associated with dyslexia at age ten, namely failure to throw a ball up, clap several times and catch the ball, and failure to walk backwards in a straight line for six steps.

There was already strong evidence that soft neurological signs were implicated in the motor skill deficits associated with dyslexia. These included a deficit in speed of tapping, heel–toe placement, rapid successive finger opposition and accuracy in copying (Denckla 1985; Rudel 1985). Dyslexic children, Denckla suggested, are characterized by a 'non-specific developmental awkwardness', so that even those dyslexic children who show reasonable athletic ability are poorly co-ordinated. This awkwardness is typically outgrown by puberty (Rudel 1985). Interestingly, a recent meta-analysis of the incidence of motor difficulties in SLI, ASD, DCD and typical development (Leonard and Hill 2014) identified forty-three studies, many of which highlighted a significant relationship between motor skills and the development of social cognition, language and social interactions, thereby highlighting the pervasive role of motor skills in non-physical domains.

There was also a range of approaches to visual problems in dyslexia. As noted earlier, Orton and his followers had considered that dyslexia was strongly linked to visual problems, and the major thrust of the Orton-Gillingham remediation programme (Gillingham and Stillman 1960; Orton 1966) was to scaffold the links between vision, letter knowledge and sensory-motor processing by means of multi-sensory stimulation. Most recently, the magnocellular deficit hypotheses hold that problems in dyslexia are attributable to abnormal sensory pathways in vision (Stein and Walsh 1997) or audition (Tallal et al. 1993). I discuss the theories in somewhat more detail in the later section on theories of dyslexia.

In direct opposition to these sensorimotor approaches, in his seminal book Vellutino (1979) argued that the problem was actually in language. This was a rather startling assertion at the time, because the language skills of dyslexic children do appear to be relatively unimpaired, which is why the difficulties in learning to read are unexpected. However, Vellutino demonstrated that, although dyslexic children did have problems in cross-modality learning (that is combining visual and auditory processing) these occurred specifically when verbal processing was required, and he provided evidence that the problem was specifically because of difficulties in the level of verbal working memory, which he claimed to be a linguistic system.

Taken in conjunction with the then new evidence that kindergarten children with weak phonological awareness were likely to develop reading difficulties, and that teaching of phonological skills at kindergarten level did reduce the subsequent reading problems (Bradley and Bryant 1983; Lundberg et al. 1980), this provided the platform for a bold and innovative scientific, educational and political initiative that transformed the dyslexia landscape.

The key (and incontrovertible) argument was that if dyslexia experts each proposed and advocated a different theory and different methods of support, this would destroy the credibility of dyslexia research and practice in the view of the politicians and would thereby prevent systematic funding initiatives. In a far-sighted initiative, the US dyslexia theorists and practitioners joined forces with the educationalists who advocated phonics support and in conjunction with the Orton Dyslexia Society they provided a coherent targeted research programme that captured the imagination of the politicians in control of research funding at that time. Their central vision was that reading problems were one of the greatest costs to US education and to US industry; the reading problems were attributable to reading disability, and that the reading disabilities could be alleviated if not wholly eliminated by the appropriate use of phonics-based support.

This multi-disciplinary consensus view led directly to the desired outcomes in the USA. Dyslexia was relabelled 'reading disability' (RD) to highlight the core problem, and RD was given the status of a learning disability, and dyslexic children were therefore entitled to a range of support. The National Institute of Child Health and Human Development funded an ambitious multi-site research programme (which continues to the present day) into the causes and remediation of reading disability. Researchers were required to support the RD approach or to take the consequences. Research based on the wider perspective established by Orton and Geschwind was not funded.

The initial optimism was quickly doused by the real world, in that the interventions proved to be very much less effective than hoped, and the scientific research aimed at establishing the causes of the fundamental problems in the 'phonological module' proved to be frustratingly inconclusive. For example, a 'definitive' article by international proponents of the phonological deficit hypothesis (Vellutino et al. 2004) was unable to provide any explanation at all of how the phonological deficits arise, and also significantly weakened the hypothesis by claiming that there were essentially three related problems, phonology, working memory and 'critical timing capabilities'.

In the face of these difficulties, the RD researchers proclaimed that the problems lay in the failure to fully understand the reading processes, and were once more successful in persuading the US Congress to provide huge funding for an extensive research programme aimed at gathering the evidence needed to identify and introduce the most effective methods of teaching reading. This led to major initiatives over the 1990s and 2000s, with the formation of the Society for the Scientific Study of Reading (SSSR) in the early 1990s, and the National Reading Panel report (2000) providing an impressive empirical and statistical analysis of what methods were effective and at what age. This was followed by the 'No Child Left Behind' initiatives, which led in turn to the concept of 'Response To Intervention', as discussed in the later section on learning to read.

From my own perspective, despite the excellence of the research undertaken within the reading domain, the most disconcerting aspect from a scientific perspective was the 'closed world' assumption – the implicit viewpoint that reading was in some way such a 'special' skill that only reading-related research was relevant to understanding reading disability. That is, evidence and theories derived from different perspectives and approaches were somehow deemed inadmissible. This reminded me forcefully of the dogmatic (and doomed) rejection by the behaviourists in the early nineteenth century of any theoretical evidence that was outside their stimulus-response framework.

Areas of agreement

There is no doubt that dyslexia is highly prevalent in the population, with the general consensus being a prevalence of 5–10 per cent as noted earlier. There is no doubt that there is a strong heritability for dyslexia, with the son of a dyslexic parent having at least a 50 per cent chance of also having dyslexia (Pennington et al. 1991). There is no doubt that dyslexic children suffer from a clear phonological deficit in early school years (Shaywitz 1996; Stanovich 1988). There is no doubt that there is also a plethora of further symptoms of dyslexia, both positive and negative (Menghini et al. 2010; Miles 1983; Nicolson and Fawcett 1995).

There is also no doubt that, even with the very best reading support, a high proportion of dyslexic children fail to learn to read fluently enough to read for pleasure and frequently leave school with barely adequate levels of reading. There is indeed a high incidence of dyslexia among young offenders and prisoners, with a recent project (Hewitt-Main 2012) diagnosing dyslexia in 53 per cent of the 2,029 prisoners at Chelmsford Prison during the project.

There is also no doubt that supporting dyslexic children has taken funds from the educational system that could have been put to a range of alternative good uses. On the other hand, there is no doubt that 'a stitch in time can save nine', and that failure to intervene appropriately has escalating costs, financially and emotionally throughout the following years. A recent Dutch study demonstrated that well-targeted reading support approaches can lead to substantial prospective cost savings and improvements in quality of life (Regtvoort et al. 2013).

There is finally no doubt that UK and US schools are not being as effective as hoped in remediating reading failure. The PISA (Programme for International Student Assessment) (OECD 2010), ranked the UK twenty-fifth for reading, a considerable fall from the 2006 ratings. Notably, the UK and the USA were the two lowest performing of all OECD English-speaking countries.

There is also substantial agreement that dyslexia is a heterogeneous 'syndrome', not only with differing symptoms away from the core problem of reading, but also with overlaps to other developmental disorders. Subtypes of developmental dyslexia were first proposed by Boder (1973) who distinguished between visual and auditory subtypes. Further subtypes may be seen in terms of overlaps between different developmental disorders. One of the most remarkable aspects is the very high comorbidity between developmental dyslexia and other developmental disabilities. Comorbidity between dyslexia and ADHD is long established (Willcutt and Pennington 2000). As Gilger and Kaplan (2001) argue, 'in developmental disorders comorbidity is the rule not the exception'.

Unfortunately, as Elliott has demonstrated, consensus and clarity become elusive if one tries to dig deeper, to 'explain' dyslexia or to 'remediate' the reading problems. For this, one needs to think more carefully, and more deeply.

Dyslexia: A developmental learning disorder for reading

The obvious approach to understanding a disability that is defined in terms of 'development', 'learning', 'disorder' and 'reading' is to undertake 'due diligence' on each of these labels. It becomes clear that the scientific fields corresponding to each are not only complex and ever-progressing, but also that there is remarkably little overlap between research concepts from each field. I will take each in turn.

Developmental

Piaget
Jean Piaget was the central figure in mid-twentieth-century psychology, having a major role in creating the sciences of developmental psychology and cognitive psychology in his books on cognitive development, which were in turn based on acute observation of his own children's development.

His framework of four developmental stages – sensorimotor to two years, pre-operational to five years, concrete operations to around ten years and then formal operations – remains the major attempt to classify the development of a child's cognitive processing ability and has been immensely influential. In addition, he emphasized the fact that without action there is no learning.

His most evocative idea for me, though, is that of 'bricolage' which is a French term which means something like 'cobbling a solution together from whatever is to hand'. So the child creates new ideas and skills by adapting the existing ones. For me, though, the key point that he stressed is that the form of learning has to be appropriate to the child's stage of development. It is counter-productive to use abstract teaching methods if a child has not reached the formal operations stage (Inhelder and Piaget 1958).

Piaget's approach has become much less influential in recent decades. For psychologists the information-processing approach provided a new metaphor for understanding cognition, as I note below, and the early information-processing theorists were not interested in the development of cognitive processing. For educationalists, Piaget's approach was too abstract, and theorists such as Flavell (1977) gained greater influence.

Information processing

'Human Information Processing' rapidly gained hegemony in psychology in the 1960s. The central idea was that any organism needs to be able to make sense of its environment – to identify whether a novel event represents an opportunity or a threat – and is therefore continually processing 'information' from its environment. The more efficiently it processes the information, the better are its chances of survival. Within this framework, concepts such as 'the central executive', 'working memory' and 'processing speed' took centre stage.

Unfortunately, because computers do not actually develop, the treatment of development in information-processing approaches was very limited. Interestingly, the recent work on the development of executive functions, which I discuss in a later section may be seen as bridging the gap between the Piagetian and the information-processing frameworks.

Progressive modularization

In the 1980s, theorists such as Fodor (1983) had argued that the brain should be viewed as a collection of independent 'modules' that worked autonomously, and that analysis of cognition could be seen in terms of the modules contained. The phonological deficit hypothesis reflects this theoretical framework, suggesting that there is some problem with the 'phonological module'. Fodor's hypothesis is certainly justifiable for adult cognition. There do appear to be relatively independent, encapsulated modules for a range of skills from language to mathematics to vision, with modules within modules within modules.

Unfortunately, the framework is particularly weak in terms of explaining how the modules arise. Fodor's initial position, that many modules reflect innate predispositions, is clearly inadequate and has led to major misconceptions in the literature. Current approaches adopt the 'progressive modularization' framework (Karmiloff-Smith 1995) where processing starts off in a non-modular framework, but becomes modularized through extensive practice. This framework has many commonalities with the automatization framework I present in the following section.

Learning

Learning was at the heart of the behaviourist paradigm, and the behaviourists made great progress in the understanding of how animals learn and how best to facilitate this learning. Established and effective teaching approaches in the mid-twentieth century such as rote learning, overlearning, consolidation, distributed practice, instrumental conditioning, and reward formed the basis for much instruction.

Following the fall of behaviourism, learning slipped out of the mainstream in psychology (where it was replaced by 'memory') and in education (where it was replaced by 'attainment'). Both approaches commit the extraordinary category error of confusing a product (attainment or memory) with the process that leads to that product (learning). However, there has been substantial recent progress in the understanding of learning, in terms of the types, timescales, neuroscience and conditions of learning. It is necessary to provide a brief overview of these issues. In my view, learning provides the framework that unifies dyslexia, education and psychology.

Controlled processing and automatic processing

Consider the skill of learning to drive in a non-automatic car. A major blocker is the skill of clutch control. In order to start, it is necessary to slowly release the clutch until the engine starts to 'bite', such that the drive starts to be transferred to the wheels. Then release the clutch pedal slowly and press the accelerator pedal to allow a smooth drive-away. This is a relatively simple task on the flat, but is very challenging on an uphill start. It is necessary to use the handbrake to prevent the car slipping backwards and so the trick is to find the bite point, while simultaneously releasing the clutch pedal with the left foot, depressing the accelerator pedal with the right foot and releasing the handbrake with the left (or right) hand, a nightmare process!

To take a more cognitive task, one on which I have had thousands of hours practice, without acquiring fluency, consider typing. I am able to type (badly) at about twenty words per minute, using both hands and most fingers, but this involves visually monitoring the position of my fingers on the keys. I have tried repeatedly to learn to touch type, but have also repeatedly given up, because my typing speed plummeted as a consequence. This indicates the difficulties of unlearning bad habits. It can take longer to unlearn a bad habit than to learn the good habit from scratch!

These everyday examples highlight key learning concepts: knowledge and skill, procedural ('how') versus declarative ('what') knowledge, habit learning, stress reducing the amount of resources available, together with unlearning and competition for resources.

Anderson's three stage model of learning

The above analysis highlights one of the fundamental distinctions (Schneider and Shiffrin 1977) in cognitive psychology, that between controlled processing, which requires attentional control, uses up working memory capacity and is often serial, and automatic processing, which, once learned in long-term memory, operates independently of the participant's control and uses no working memory resources.

This distinction is central to the major model of cognitive learning (Anderson 1982), which has been shown to apply not only to acquisition of physical skills but also mental skills. It distinguishes between three stages of skill acquisition: the declarative stage where one works out what to do, the procedural stage where one works out how to do it and the tuning stage where one gradually becomes more expert and automatic.

Declarative processing is the means by which controlled processing works. It uses conscious, attentional resources (often, but not always language-based) to work out a 'high level' method of doing the task. 'Take the gearstick, move it to second', and so on. It has the advantage of flexibility and variety, but has two major drawbacks: first it is far too slow and second, it clogs up the controlled processing, in that one can only concentrate on one thing at a time.

By contrast, procedural processing is 'low level', fast and takes up little conscious capacity. Basically it is a series of precisely timed instructions (often in parallel) to the muscles involved, 'Muscle A contract by amount B at time C for duration D ...' and is not available to conscious awareness.

A key difficulty therefore is 'proceduralization', going from the declarative stage to the procedural stage. Whereas declarative processing is easy to set up (but easily forgotten), procedural processing takes extensive practice over many days, as revealed by Shiffrin and Schneider. The neural circuits for declarative and procedural processing are completely different (Squire 1987), and therefore one of the major problems in proceduralization is how to communicate between the two systems, and this is commonly achieved by extended trial-and-error learning.

It is important to note that Anderson's formulation only applies to children over the age where they can respond reasonably well to instruction. For younger ages, infants and toddlers have very little declarative or controlled processing ability, and learn by the natural learning processes of imitation, play, and trial and error.

Three fundamental forms of human learning

This analysis is now supported by the cognitive neuroscience of learning, In fact it is possible to distinguish three fundamentally different types: procedural learning, which includes three subtypes (statistical learning, reward-based learning and trial-and-error learning), which is basically for the acquisition of skills; declarative learning (which is for knowledge); and neural circuit building (which is for getting the bigger picture). The three procedural forms are a legacy of the many-million-years-old vertebrate machinery, the 'primitive' types that we have inherited from the first vertebrates, fish, crocodiles, lizards. Declarative learning is much more recent, a human speciality, more dependent on thought. And neural circuit building is the unsung and under-explored basis for human development (and reading). As with everything else in the brain, these learning systems combine (or sometimes compete). I will take them in turn.

(i) Procedural learning

Statistical learning (also known as unsupervised learning) occurs automatically via repeated exposure. It is a consequence of the ability of networks of neurons to 'self-organize', that is automatically to adjust the 'weights' (that is the connectivities) between elements to identify objects despite changes in size, angle, lighting, and so on, in vision, and to identify phonemes despite changes in pitch, emphasis, loudness of speech, and to automatically link visual objects with simultaneously occurring auditory information.

In reinforcement learning an action results in a reward (and hence is 're-inforced' in behaviourist terms). A reward is anything that improves the animal's state – food when hungry, water when thirsty, and so on – the carrot rather than the stick. Any organism that can optimize its ratio of reward to effort will have a competitive advantage, and therefore most animals have specialized neural machinery designed to identify just what actions or context (or both) led to the reward. Unlike statistical learning, this machinery is designed to gain the maximum possible out of even a single reward, and vertebrates have specialized neural circuits, running via the basal ganglia, for reward-based processing.

Trial-and-error learning occurs when the animal knows what it is trying to achieve and gets an 'error signal' to indicate how close the action was to achieving the planned outcome – for example, a child trying to imitate an adult's action or speech. There are two forms, imitation when one is trying to get started and then tuning as the actions get more fluent.

All regions of the brain support statistical learning. Only the basal ganglia support reinforcement-based learning, the success-based learning. Only the cerebellum supports trial-and-error learning, where there is a target and an error signal. And hence the brain regions need to work together through networks. If error-based learning is required, then it is necessary to involve the cerebellum as part of the circuit, along with the other parts of the brain involved.

(ii) Declarative (consciously accessible) learning

Declarative learning is one of the ways that we use our knowledge of the world to improve our memory and performance. The most obvious form of declarative learning is 'learning by being told' rather than 'learning by doing' or 'learning by observing'.

The key structure for declarative learning is the hippocampus, and it is generally considered that, in the same way as the procedural learning circuits need to involve the basal ganglia and/or cerebellum, declarative processing needs to involve the hippocampus.

As I shall emphasize later, an issue that I consider to be central to the process of learning to read (which is difficult for everyone, but particularly difficult for dyslexic children) is the process of getting cross-talk between the declarative and procedural system, so that one can proceduralize the knowledge that is gained declaratively (through being told rather than by doing).

(iii) Neural circuit building

Automatization tends to build smaller but more efficient systems. By contrast, there is a further level of neural circuit, which Anderson (1983) refers to as the 'architecture' of the information-processing system – the way that the various parts of neural processing combine to produce a highly efficient system. When discussing development (above) I noted the Piagetian framework, which highlights the way that the child builds more and more sophisticated operating systems over a period of ten or more years. I also noted the information processing and cognitive viewpoints that highlight the development of processing efficiency, executive function, working memory and response inhibition. It is difficult for adults to appreciate that these are major accomplishments, because adults have completed the task and have therefore changed their way of processing information to exploit the new circuitry, with the result that they cannot imagine any other way of doing it!

As we shall see, these changes are particularly obvious in reading, in that the circuitry involved in the early phonological stage of reading is radically different from the efficient sight word reading of later years.

Disorder

The implicit assumption in referring to 'disorder' is that there is some underlying brain difference that is intrinsic, and therefore unlikely to be alleviated just by normal maturation and experience. In the case of reading, there has been considerable discussion as to how one might distinguish delay from disorder. A reasonable principle was posited by Bryant and Goswami (1986), who argued that it is good practice when assessing performance of dyslexic children to have a control group of the same Chronological Age (CA) and also, to control for reading experience, a group of the same reading age (RA).

Reading

I will defer issues relating to reading to the section on learning to read.

Theories of dyslexia

There are many theories for the causes of dyslexia. And the focus of much of the research and advocacy for dyslexia over the past thirty years has been aimed at establishing dyslexia as a disability. This of course has led to major progress and to a range of important theories from many eminent researchers internationally. It is beyond the scope of this section to give even a summary of the individual theories. Accessible overviews of a range of theories were given in Demonet et al. (2004) and also in Nicolson and Fawcett (2008). A recent phonology-centric overview is provided in Peterson and Pennington (2012).

When talking about theories it is useful to distinguish three levels of explanation (Morton and Frith 1995): the behaviour level (which can be observed directly, like reading), the cognitive level (which gives a description of how the brain works overall for things like memory, language, learning) and the brain level (which looks at the components of the brain). And now there is also the genetic level.

Cognitive level

In terms of theories, at the behavioural level, the problem is reading. Many theories have attempted to explain this deficit at the next deeper level, namely the cognitive level, thereby providing a causal explanation.

The dominant theory is of course the phonological deficit hypothesis (Stanovich 1988), as discussed earlier. The hypothesis proposes that the reading difficulties are attributable to problems in phonological processing, that is breaking a word down into its constituent sounds. These difficulties cause problems in sound segmentation and also in word blending, both of which are critical for the development of reading and spelling. There has been extensive research on phonological deficit.

However, phonological deficit is by no means the only relevant theory. There are actually many other cognitive level theories, some narrower, some broader. I provide representative examples below. Each one of them has merit – supportive evidence and also successful remediation studies.

The double-deficit hypothesis (Wolf and Bowers 1999) holds that there are two risk factors for reading acquisition: phonological deficit and processing speed deficit (as revealed by slow performance on a rapid naming task, where, for example, one is required to say the names of forty pictures of everyday objects as fast as possible). Children who suffer from a 'double deficit' were shown to have much higher risk of reading problems than children with only one. As noted earlier, phonological deficit theorists argue that this is best seen as a variant of the phonological deficit hypothesis.

A related but more specific approach, the speech rhythm deficit hypothesis, (Goswami et al. 2002) holds that the phonological problems arise from difficulties in perceiving the onset of the amplitude envelope which forms the basis of determining the prosody of an utterance (and hence identifying syllable boundaries). The authors provided evidence that 25 per cent of the variance in reading could be predicted from this ability.

The visuo-spatial attention deficit hypothesis (Facoetti et al. 2003) holds that reading-related deficits may be attributable at least partly to difficulties in 'covert orienting' that is, preparing to switch attention to a new specific location while still concentrating on the current location. This is a process required for skilled reading in that the reader is covertly attending to the next words while reading the currently fixated one. The authors demonstrated that training in covert attention by stimulating the user with peripheral stimuli was highly effective for visuo-spatial attention and also led to marked reading gains. In a subsequent study (Franceschini et al. 2013) they demonstrated that the effects could be achieved naturally by means of a 'shoot em up' computer game in which the user had to covertly attend to where the bad rabbits were likely to emerge! A related hypothesis (Bosse et al. 2007) holds that visual attention span is reduced in dyslexia.

Further visual hypotheses relate to fixation accuracy and stability, together with saccadic accuracy. As noted earlier Stein and his colleagues identified eye movement differences (Eden et al. 1994; Stein 1989), and more recently several authors have reported disadvantages with visual crowding or advantages for reading with larger fonts (Moores et al. 2011; Schneps et al. 2013).

An independent approach to auditory processing (Tallal et al. 1993) proposed that, in common with children with Specific Language Impairment, dyslexic children have specific problems in rapid auditory processing. Furthermore, Tallal and her colleagues developed a complete and commercial remediation system, Fast ForWord, that addressed both auditory processing problems and reading needs within an integrated game-based approach. A range of positive findings has been reported by researchers linked to the programme (Lajiness-O'Neill et al. 2007) but meta-analyses of large-scale studies have found no clear evidence of benefit (Stevens et al. 2008).

Finally, two hypotheses address the learning processes in dyslexia. A series of studies by Blomert and his colleagues (Froyen et al. 2011) strongly criticizes the phonological deficit account as being a description rather than explanation, and provides evidence that dyslexic children have specific difficulties in integrating the visual letters with their sounds (that is, the visual-auditory cross-modality links are not made automatically). This echoes the original Vellutino studies indicating cross-modality difficulties. It may also be seen as a specific instance of the automatization deficit hypothesis (Nicolson and Fawcett 1990), applied to the reading domain. I address the automatization deficit framework at length shortly.

Brain level

Theories framed at the brain level typically attempt to explain cognitive level deficits in terms of the brain structures that cause them.

The most prevalent brain-level hypothesis is in terms of sensory processing, and in particular what is known (probably inaccurately) as the magnocellular deficit hypothesis. There is extensive, albeit inconsistent, evidence of specific visual problems relating to detection of low contrast moving visual gratings (Eden et al. 1996), which was attributed to impaired function in the visual magnocellular system.

In an attempt to integrate both visual and auditory magnocellular approaches (Stein 2001) has suggested that they may be a pan-sensory-motor abnormality in the magnocellular systems for audition, vision and action.

An alternative brain-level theory is the cerebellar deficit hypothesis (Nicolson et al. 1995, 2001). The authors argued that the framework was able to subsume all the above accounts (automatization deficit, phonological deficit and speed deficit) at the cognitive level, while providing a causal link to the underlying brain structures and mechanisms. I address this framework, and the subsequent procedural learning deficit framework in the following section.

Genetic level

There is clear evidence of genetic transmission of dyslexia. A male child with a dyslexic parent or sibling has a 50 per cent chance of being dyslexic (Pennington et al. 1991). There has been very extensive genetic research over the past ten years. Unfortunately, the lack of progress contrasts markedly with the transformation in genetics techniques over that period, and the extensive research that has taken place (Carrion-Castillo et al. 2013).

In short, dyslexia is both polygenic (the result of many genes) and multifactorial (resulting from interactions between genes). A range of gene locations on the chromosomes has been found, labelled DYX1 to DYX9, together with a range of possible candidate genes within these locations. Following Wagner (2005), it is clear that the weak link is 'the uncertain phenotype', the difficulty in identifying which reading symptoms are important. As I have argued, it is necessary to find a symptom in between the behaviour level and the genetic level, an 'endophenotype' at the cognitive level or the brain level (or a level in between). For this we need a theoretical understanding of dyslexia at all levels from brain to behaviour. This is precisely what I develop in the following section.

Dyslexia as specific learning difficulties

In the UK the 'correct' description of dyslexia is 'specific learning difficulty' and in the US 'Specific Learning Disability', so in my research with Angela Fawcett it seemed natural to start our investigations with the hypothesis that dyslexia is some general deficit in learning and for some reason it is difficult for dyslexic children to become 'expert' in a task.

Nicolson and Fawcett Research Phase 1: Dyslexia and learning

My expertise is in human learning, and I was convinced that any solution must involve analysis of the underlying learning differences in dyslexia. Our general initial hypothesis was that there must be some problem somewhere in the learning processes. Given the commonality between motor learning and cognitive learning, we proposed the strong form of the hypothesis that the problems should be evident in both types, whether the task is a cognitive task or a motor task.

This learning framework led directly to what remains as the simplest and most complete framework for understanding dyslexia – the Dyslexic Automatization Deficit hypothesis (Nicolson and

Fawcett 1990). The hypothesis states that dyslexic children have problems making skills automatic and therefore need to 'consciously compensate' even for simple skills. So if a task is not too difficult, dyslexic children might well be able to perform within the normal range, but they would be doing it by explicitly concentrating hard on it, whereas a non-dyslexic child would just 'download' the task to some unconscious automatic mechanism.

One can make the analogy of listening to someone speaking with an unusual accent. One can follow it, but needs to concentrate hard. Or, perhaps more accurately, because it involves the co-ordination of physical, mental and spatial skills, coping with dyslexia might be like driving in a foreign country, where it is possible to cope but at the expense of greater concentration, more effort, more stress and greater tiredness. Unfortunately, for a dyslexic child, there is no 'home' accent and no 'home country'.

This hypothesis was welcomed by large numbers of dyslexic individuals, who all said that seemed to capture their difficulties extremely well. But of course we needed to do the science.

The logic behind our research approach was as follows: dyslexia theories are designed to handle the reading-related deficits, and so reading-related tests will not discriminate between the theories. Hence what was needed to discriminate between the theories was a test in a domain where they make different predictions, ideally domains where some theories predict there should be no deficit. This was again a departure from established wisdom in the field. For many researchers into RD it seemed unthinkable to look outside of the reading domain when trying to find the cause of reading disability.

From a learning perspective, however, there is nothing special about reading. It is not wired into the brain like language might be. There are no special reading-acquisition-devices in our heads. Historically there have been many illiterate societies.

In my view the processes of learning to read are similar to the processes of learning to play chess, learning to type, or learning to drive: a combination of cognitive and physical skills that are slowly built up by experience.

So for me it made perfect sense to look outside the reading box. Indeed it seemed to me to be completely against scientific principles NOT to!

Study 1: Balance and dyslexia

Our key study was on the gross motor skill of balance. We took balance because it was the motor skill that everyone has practised endlessly and for which there was solid evidence, in 1989 when we started, that dyslexic children over the age of nine balanced within the normal range. We used the 'one foot in front of the other' Romberg task, which assesses side-to-side balance. We did it with thirteen-year-old dyslexic and control adolescents matched for IQ and age.

The critical test for automaticity is what is known as the 'dual task' setup, where the participant not only does the primary task (balance) but also has to undertake another (secondary) task that takes up controlled processing resources. If the primary task is achieved automatically, it should be possible to perform the dual task with little or no interference, whereas if it too requires controlled processing there will be a substantial decrement.

We got our participants to balance for 30 seconds and we measured the number of wobbles. There were two conditions, the 'single task' where they just balanced, and the 'dual task' where they balanced and counted at the same time. It turned out we had to make the counting task individually calibrated so that each participant could comfortably count once per 2 seconds.

For the single task condition there was no difference between the two groups. Participants made very few wobbles, as predicted from the literature.

But for the dual task there was a dissociation. The control participants' balance was unimpaired, whereas the dyslexic participants wobbled a lot more.

In short, under optimal conditions the dyslexic children could balance as well as the controls. But the controls were balancing automatically, whereas the dyslexic children were not. There seemed to be automatization problems even for balance. We also checked these results with different balance tasks, including a blindfold balance task, designed to make sure that they could not visually compensate for any balance problems. We got the same results (Fawcett and Nicolson 1992) in that the dyslexic children had balance deficits when blindfolded and thus unable to use visual cues.

This was strong evidence for an automatization deficit account. It was completely contrary to the predictions of the Phonological Deficit Hypothesis, and indeed counter to the predictions of almost every theory I have just outlined. In our view, therefore, this study by itself falsified all the competing frameworks, although other theorists queried or dismissed this inconvenient finding as being irrelevant to reading.

In fact, there were several attempts to replicate the findings over the next few years. The consensus of these replications was that, given a sensitive age-appropriate design, many dyslexic children, at least half, do show balance difficulties compared with children of the same age (Ramus et al. 2003) but that these are not causal with regard to the reading difficulties (Rochelle and Talcott 2006).

Study 2: Skill, development and dyslexia

In our literature reviews around 1990, we were struck by the fact that each research group provided convincing evidence that dyslexic children were impaired on the tests that they administered. The phonologists found phonological deficits. The optometrists found visual deficits, the kinesiologists motor deficits, the information-processing theorists working memory and speed deficits. But they rarely looked for deficits outside their own field. This was a clear case of confirmation bias.

So we resolved to test matched dyslexic and control children at three age levels on a wide range of skills covering most of these theories. In order to avoid confusion, we took a stringent criterion for dyslexia, namely an IQ of at least 90 (to eliminate generalized learning deficit) and a reading age at least eighteen months behind that expected. We used this definition in all the studies we undertook.

Note that this is not the discrepancy definition (which would allow the inclusion of participants with an IQ of 120 and standard score for reading of 100). Nor is it the 'no discrepancy' criterion (which would include participants with an IQ of 85 and a reading standard score of 85). Furthermore, we screened all our dyslexic participants for attention deficit, eliminating any with scores indicating a 'comorbidity' between dyslexia and ADHD. The criteria we used were intended to eliminate children with 'borderline' diagnostic characteristics in the expectation that this would lead to 'cleaner' data.

We developed a research design that included six groups of children: three groups of dyslexic children at ages 8, 11 and 15 years, together with three groups of normally achieving children matched for age and IQ. Furthermore, the two older groups of dyslexic children were also matched for reading age with the two younger groups of controls (Dys 15 with Cont 11, Dys 11 with Cont 8). This design allows a number of different analyses to be performed, and provides a method of investigating the effects of maturation on the skills involved.

The specific issues addressed in the research programme were: first, what proportion of dyslexic children showed each type of deficit; second, whether there is some deficit which is the 'primary' one, which underlies the other deficits; and third, whether it is possible to identify different subtypes of dyslexia, such that each subtype has discriminably different characteristics.

In an attempt to minimize confounding factors arising from differences in experience together with use of compensatory strategies, we decided to test 'primitive' skills in the major modalities, skills that are not normally trained explicitly, and are not easily subject to compensatory strategies. In addition to psychometric tests of IQ and literacy, four types of test were used, namely tests of phonological skill, working memory, information processing speed, and motor skill (Fawcett and Nicolson 1995).

In order to make it easier to compare between tests, the results for each test have been converted to the age-equivalent scores, taking the data from our control groups together with control data from other studies where possible (Figure 1.1).

The figure bears detailed analysis. First, inspecting the left-hand set of six columns (reading age) the scores are as expected. The Cont 15 (fifteen-year-old controls) group have a reading age of around 15, the Dys 15 and Cont 11 groups have a reading age around eleven years, confirming that the Cont 11 group are a RA match for the Dys 15 group. Similarly the Dys 11 and Cont 8 groups are matched with RA around eight years. The Dys 8 group have RA around six years (hence, hardly started on reading) as do the Mild 11 group. The results are similar but slightly more pronounced for spelling.

As expected, there were severe difficulties for the phonological skills – phonological discrimination and segmentation, though not for nonsense-word repetition, which is generally considered

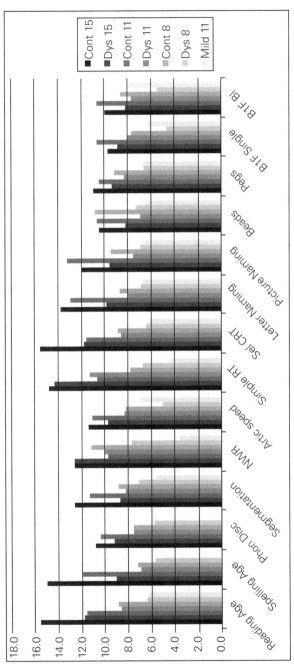

FIGURE 1.1 *Age-equivalent scores across the range of primitive skills*

a phonology/memory task. Articulation speed was also severely delayed, significantly worse than the RA controls, indicating a disorder. Letter naming and picture naming were also significantly worse than the RA controls, indicating a disorder. Finally, inspection of the four physical co-ordination tasks (bead threading, pegboard, balance on one foot and balance on one foot blindfold) indicates that there is also a disorder for these, with performance worse than the RA controls. See Nicolson and Fawcett (1994) for detailed analysis.

Inspection of the data for the 11-year-children with mild cognitive impairment (poor readers with IQ between 80 and 90) suggests that their overall scores were comparable to those for the eight-year-old dyslexic group (and hence very severely impaired) for all the measures except balance.

Study 3: Blending of procedural skills

The next study was actually a very simple one, in terms of blending procedural skills. It was published in 2000, although we did it in 1992. It is one of the few direct tests of learning in the literature and we obtained stunning results (Nicolson and Fawcett 2000).

For scientific clarity we needed a skill away from reading or phonology, and we hit on the issue of skill blending. In the studies reported above, we had discovered that dyslexic children performed within the normal range on simple reactions but that they were significantly slower on a choice reaction.

So we decided to train them on a choice-reaction task and see what happens in terms of the learning curves. It may be seen on the left-hand side of Figure 1.2 that the dyslexic participants were slower but not significantly slower than the controls on the simple reaction task (SRT). Both sets of participants were slower on the choice reaction (CRT) than on the simple reaction, as one would expect. However, the dyslexic children were more adversely affected than the controls, as may be seen from the mean first trial on the choice reaction. A key issue, however, is how fast they then learned to complete the task efficiently. It may be seen that participants undertook 2,500 trials in repeated sessions over the next four weeks.

The controls (the lower curve) improved their performance, getting steadily faster. For the dyslexics, there was much less of a

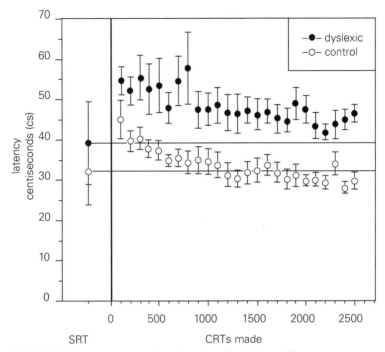

FIGURE 1.2 *Procedural learning: blending of primitive skill*

learning effect. Looking at the first 100 trials, it may be seen that the controls learned rapidly, whereas the dyslexics appeared to make no progress. And, at the asymptote, the performance after many trials, the controls were actually better than their simple reactions whereas the dyslexic children were worse.

Hence the dyslexic children had more problems with the initial blending of the two responses into one. They did make more errors, which are not shown on this chart. They had slower final performance.

And they had slower learning. Technically, this can be modelled using the power law, which indicated that for the dyslexic group $t = 53.9n^{-0.07}$ where t is the time taken and n is the number of trials). The corresponding formula for the control group is $t = 39.4n^{-0.14}$. The constants reflect the initial performance (that is 53.9 vs 39.4 cs for the first trial). The exponents (0.07 vs 0.14) reflect the learning rate, with the dyslexic group having a learning rate only half that of the controls.

A key point is that the amount of deficit increases as a power function of task difficulty (that is, a small increase in task difficulty will lead to a larger deficit for the dyslexic children). So it should be no surprise that even with exemplary support, dyslexic children have difficulty mastering reading, because in common with most 'world class' skills, a skilled reader will probably have spent 1,000 hours reading. So on this analysis, if only these procedural learning skills are used, it is frankly impossible for a dyslexic child to become a fluent reader. There is some intrinsic problem with the learning process(es) involved.

Study 4: Extended training on a keyboard game

A further study reported in the same paper investigated extended learning on a keyboard-based computer game, where use of the keys moved the player around a maze, pursued by Pacman ghosts. The general results were similar to those reported above, slower initially, slower learning, slower asymptote. However, we also investigated the effects of changing the key mappings, thereby forcing the participants to 'unlearn' their previous key-finger mappings. Furthermore, we established that (after relearning the new mapping to automaticity) and then retesting six months later, the dyslexic participants were if anything less affected by interference while doing the task. We found that the dyslexic participants were actually more impaired by the change.

We concluded that the dyslexic participants had equivalent 'quantity' of automatic performance (as indexed by difficulty of unlearning and resistance to interference) but reduced quality of automatic performance (as indicated by speed and accuracy).

We believe that this study provides a window on the development of neural networks. Prior habits are harder to unlearn, and the resulting networks work less efficiently than normal, even when given ideal conditions of consistent mapping.

Nicolson and Fawcett Phase 2: Cerebellar deficit theory

We had actually completed the above research by the mid-1990s, and we realized that to further investigate the learning processes we needed to look at the underlying neuroscience. From my perspective, the major change in neuroscientific knowledge was the transformation of the role of the cerebellum from motor skill co-ordinator to 'all skills co-ordinator and learner', and in particular the emerging evidence that the cerebellum was centrally involved in language fluency. This formed the basis for our cerebellar deficit framework.

Theory: The cerebellum

The cerebellum is one of the major organs in the brain, with direct neural connections to almost all brain regions and all the body, with more than half the brain's neurons. It has long been known to be centrally involved in fluency of skill execution. Unlike the neocortex it does its job efficiently, reliably, without fuss, and without our knowing anything about it at all!

It is only with the advent of brain imaging that its ubiquitous role in all sorts of processing, from taste to speech to reading to automaticity, has been revealed. The first claim of cerebellar involvement in cognition was made in 1989:

> the 2-way connections linking the cerebellum to Broca's area [a pre-frontal region known to be centrally involved in speech production] make it possible for it to improve language dexterity, which combines motor and mental skills. (Leiner et al. 1989)

Their hypothesis, in terms of connectivity and function, has been completely vindicated (in normally achieving individuals) by subsequent cognitive neuroscience research. An influential summary by Desmond and Fiez (1998) confirmed the multiple skills involving cerebellar activation, from classical conditioning and pursuit learning to the core 'cognitive' skills of explicit memory retrieval, language/verbal working memory, verbal working memory, and sequence learning. Furthermore, the nature of the activation was distributed, with different regions involved in different tasks, but with also overlapping distributions of some skills.

In view of the phonological deficit account, and its extension to include both verbal working memory and speed of processing, the cerebellar link to the working memory, language and reading and both declarative and procedural knowledge is particularly suggestive.

Dyslexia: An ontogenetic causal chain

In a range of innovative studies we established clear, direct and indirect evidence of cerebellar deficits associated with dyslexia: functional imaging (Nicolson et al. 1999); anatomy (Finch et al. 2002); prism adaptation (Brookes et al. 2007); eye blink conditioning (Nicolson et al. 2002), and cerebellar signs (Fawcett and Nicolson 1999).

This led to a major achievement, the creation of an 'ontogenetic' (developmental) model of how the reading, writing and spelling deficits arise (Nicolson et al. 2001).

In Figure 1.3 development moves from birth through five years to eight years from left to right. The life journey starts with a cerebellar impairment, possibly attributable to abnormal brain neural migration processes, from birth (or pre-birth). We also note that it is possible that the other parts of the brain, the cortico-cerebellar loops, are involved.

So, what effects would this have by three years? Cerebellar impairment will frequently lead to balance impairment (depending upon the specific regions of the cerebellum and its neural connections that are affected) and also to motor skill impairment, articulatory

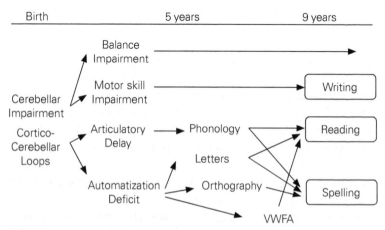

FIGURE 1.3 *Dyslexia: an ontogenetic causal chain*

delay (articulation is a motor skill) and also automatization deficit. What implications would this have over the years?

Balance impairment will have relatively little impact on school academic performance, although sporting skills might well be impaired. More general motor skill impairment would not be too problematic, though it might lead to impaired eye movement control (which would have a clear but unexplained effect on reading), and would have a direct effect on handwriting skill.

Articulatory delay is an interesting one, because it is now estabished that expressive speech and receptive speech, phonology, are directly linked (Gervain and Mehler 2010; Price 2012), and so articulatory delay would be hypothesized to lead to phonological differences.

And automatization deficit would lead to problems with identifying the individual letters, the spellings and, indeed, later on the development of the neural circuits for the Visual Word Form Area.

What effects would these have on reading? The impairments in phonology, the letters and the Visual Word Form Area would directly impact on the development of the reading circuitry. And the impairments in phonology, the letters and the orthography would directly impact upon the spelling performance. So this combination of impairments will lead to significant difficulties in learning to read. There is a 'triple whammy' here, both for reading and for spelling, but actually a different set of problems. This is consistent with the findings of different genetic underpinnings to phonological and orthographic (that is, the spelling) problems (Olson 2002).

Angela and I are particularly proud of this chart. It provides a principled explanation of the three criterial difficulties for dyslexic children (reading, writing and spelling). And it explains why there are phonological deficits and orthographic deficits. And it explains why there are various secondary symptoms not related to literacy. It provides a principled method for screening for dyslexia *before* a child fails to learn to read.

For the first time in any discipline, it provided a link between development, the brain and school achievement, explaining our highest-level cognitive skills of literacy in terms of the underlying developmental processes.

Subsequent research

An early meta-analysis of imaging studies (Eckert et al. 2003) concluded 'The cerebellum is one of the most consistent locations for structural differences between dyslexic and control participants in imaging studies. This study may be the first to show that anomalies in a cerebellar-frontal circuit are associated with rapid automatic naming and the double-deficit subtype of dyslexia.'

More recently Pernet et al. (2009) concluded:

> The right cerebellar declive and the right lentiform nucleus were the two areas that significantly differed the most between groups with 100 per cent of the dyslexic subjects (N = 38) falling outside of the control group (N = 39) 95 per cent confidence interval boundaries ... . Conclusion: These results provide evidence for the existence of various subtypes of dyslexia characterized by different brain phenotypes. In addition, behavioural analyses suggest that these brain phenotypes relate to different deficits of automatization of language-based processes such as grapheme/phoneme correspondence and/or rapid access to lexicon entries.

This is strong indeed. There seems little doubt that the cerebellum is somehow involved in the automatization deficits suffered by many dyslexic children.

Nicolson and Fawcett Phase 3: Procedural learning deficit

It will be clear from the previous discussion that we had incontro-vertible evidence that there were difficulties in skill procedurization, and that these were consistent with impaired cerebellar function. Furthermore, cerebellar abnormality is one of the most consistent features of brain imaging studies of dyslexia.

Nonetheless, there is a legitimate question over cause versus correlate. One intriguing possibility is the 'innocent bystander' hypothesis put forward by Zeffiro and Eden (2001), namely that the cerebellum was functioning fine; it was just that it was being given impaired data from other sources (such as the magnocellular sensory system). While the imaging data do strongly implicate cerebellar abnormality, there is certainly a possibility that for a subset of dyslexic children the problems might arise elsewhere in the learning circuits involving the cerebellum.

A further topic which has emerged more recently is the acceptance that many brain regions are involved in the acquisition and the execution of cognitive and motor skills, and that therefore it is important to consider the system as a whole, not just parts of it (Doyon and Benali 2005). This neural systems approach formed the basis for our integrative recent procedural learning difficulties framework.

I have already introduced the core distinction between procedural learning and declarative learning, with declarative learning directly related to language and thought, with conscious accessibility, but not to motor skills, which are procedural. However, Ullman (2004) radically enhanced this view by demonstrating that in fact the language system splits into two branches, declarative memory and procedural memory.

This integrated a range of findings in the literature, in particular the fact that there are different types of language skill, some of them explicit, available to conscious introspection, and some procedural and not consciously penetrable.

The declarative memory system involves the 'mental encyclo-paedia', through the temporal lobe and hippocampus, storage and use of knowledge of facts and events. It is a part of the 'ventral route' anatomically, and has direct conscious access.

In contrast, the Procedural Memory system handles the mental grammar, the rules of grammar. It is a network involving the basal ganglia, and specific frontal, parietal and cerebellar structures. It underlies procedural memory, which supports the learning and execution of habit-based language skills, especially those involving sequences. Anatomically it is known as the 'dorsal route'. And we have no conscious access.

For example, we just 'know' how to string our words together into a coherent sentence, one at a time, and it 'trips off the tongue' just like that. But we have no conscious access to the process (which remains a complete mystery to me!). That is the procedural language system. Furthermore, we can state whether a statement is grammatically correct or not without knowing why. That is again our implicit rule-based procedural language skill.

The procedural learning deficit (PLD) hypothesis

This insight led directly to our third framework for dyslexia, which is the procedural learning deficit hypothesis. Following Ullman, we speculated that most developmental disorders might be attributable to problems in some form of the Procedural Memory system.

Many developmental disorders are attributable to abnormal function of the procedural memory (brain-based) system – I label it the procedural learning system, to highlight its role in plasticity as well as memory.

And there are two different procedural learning systems, the motor procedural learning system and the language procedural learning system.

For dyslexia, we argued that we have Specific Procedural Learning Difficulty, specific to the language-cerebellum, but involving other procedural learning components to a greater or lesser degree.

This is in fact a refinement of the classic four-levels analysis from behaviour, cognition, brain, genetics. Our automatization deficit hypothesis was at the cognitive level, and our cerebellar deficit hypothesis was at the brain level, with the cerebellar deficit hypothesis providing a deeper explanation of the automatization deficit findings presented earlier.

The procedural learning deficit hypothesis lies in between the brain and cognition levels, at what we called the neural systems level. Placing the deficit at the level of the circuit rather than the structure directly addresses the 'innocent bystander' issue. And we believe that this neural systems level of explanation is a particularly fruitful one that provides the framework for explaining a range of different developmental disorders as I show in the next section.

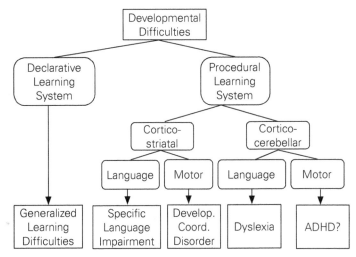

FIGURE 1.4 *Classification of developmental disorders in terms of declarative and procedural skills*

Declarative and procedural circuits in developmental disorders

This is an article taken again from Trends in Neuroscience, a 2007 paper. Developmental difficulties can be distinguished between the declarative learning system and the procedural learning system (Nicolson and Fawcett 2007).

Taking the declarative circuit, if there is a problem in declarative learning, this will lead to generalized learning problems, and hence poor reading but with no discrepancy, because there will be poor performance across the board intellectually. So, for us, we would call those generalized learning difficulties.

The procedural learning circuits can be divided into cortico-striatal ones and the cortico-cerebellar circuit. Striatal means basal ganglia. We can divide the cortico-striatal system into language and motor. Following Ullman's approach we allocate Specific Language Impairment to abnormal function in the language aspects of the cortico-striatal system. Developmental Coordination Disorder (clumsiness) to the motor component of that system. If we turn now to the cortico-cerebellar system, again we can distinguish between language and motor. The motor is probably attention deficit disorder, whereas the language component, the Specific Procedural Learning Difficulty, is dyslexia.

Recent evidence for the SpLD framework

There is strong, recent evidence for the framework. Reviews of the literature on the other learning disabilities are beyond the scope of this volume. Ullman and Pierpont (2005) had previously provided evidence of procedural learning problems in SLI, and subsequent research established difficulties in implicit learning (Lum et al. 2014).

Evidence relating to the DCD route is surprisingly sparse, given the expected role of the cerebellum in physical co-ordination. A study investigating prism adaptation in dyslexia established that children with DCD and dyslexia did have difficulties with prism adaptation, a cerebellar task (Brookes et al. 2007), whereas a small study of prism adaptation found differences in some but not all children with DCD (Cantin et al. 2007).

There is good evidence for motor skill deficits in ADHD. A recent meta-analysis (Kaiser et al. 2015) concluded that 'More than half of the children with ADHD have difficulties with gross and fine motor skills. The children with ADHD inattentive subtype seem to present more impairment of fine motor skills, slow reaction time, and online motor control during complex tasks.'

In terms of dyslexia, serial reaction time studies, that is implicit memory, which is procedural memory, show a consistent deficit for dyslexia, coupled with consistent problems in procedural learning (Lum et al. 2013).

Deficit in consolidation of procedural skill automatization in dyslexic children has been found by ourselves (Nicolson et al. 2010). Interestingly, there is also greater impact on the procedural learning of letters than motor sequences (Gabay et al. 2012).

Most intriguingly, a recent study has demonstrated better performance for dyslexic children than age-matched controls for learning and retention of declarative memory (Hedenius et al. 2013).

Overall, therefore, there is good evidence for the framework, and again it has been welcomed by researchers in the other developmental disorders. It does provide a principled explanation of the various disorders in terms of established neural networks.

It highlights the interplay between the different disorders. It is consistent with extensive evidence of difficulties in procedural learning, implicit learning and statistical learning in dyslexia.

Delayed neural commitment

The cerebellar deficit hypothesis is formulated at the brain level and provides a clear and principled explanation fully supported by extensive evidence of cerebellar involvement in the learning and execution both of sensory and motor skills and actions and also of cognitive language-based skills.

The procedural learning deficit account ties these two frameworks together by providing an explanation of how the procedural language circuit involving the cerebellum is specifically affected, which leaves the declarative learning circuits unaffected and maybe over-performing. This therefore explains strengths as well as weaknesses. It also has the major advantage of providing a principled link to the other learning disabilities thereby offering the opportunity to reunite the learning disabilities after a thirty-year divorce.

The most recent development of the framework derives from our attempt to link the latest findings on the neuroscience of the development of speech and language to this framework. Delayed Neural Commitment explains not only the delay in the development of specific skills and of automaticity, but also delays both in constructing new neural circuits (as required for executive function and for internalized speech) and in bypassing or eliminating the previous, less efficient neural circuits.

Learning to speak

One of the core reasons for the 'enigma' of dyslexia is that dyslexic children appear to learn to speak without any obvious difficulties, but then hit the wall when reading comes up. This indicates strongly that analysis of the differences between the two aspects of skill acquisition needs to be undertaken.

There is now a growing consensus as to the processes involved in learning to speak, knowledge that was not available when the phonological deficit hypothesis was first proposed. This analysis (Kuhl 2004) and the follow-up theoretical analysis (Meltzoff et al. 2009) represents the current understanding on how speech and language develop over the first year of life.

Kuhl and her colleagues consider two dimensions: receptive (speech perception) and expressive (speech production). In terms of perception, in its first six months, in principle any normally developing infant can discriminate any of the sounds in any of the human languages. However, in months six to twelve, the infant becomes a specialist in its mother tongue, essentially using statistical learning to identify the regularities of its heard environment.

This leads to good discrimination of the phonemes in its own language, but at the expense of phonemes in other languages. The classic example is the fact that Japanese infants can discriminate /l/ from /r/ at six months but lose this ability by twelve months, because the distinction is of no significance in the Japanese language. So we have language-specific speech perception by twelve months.

An equivalent set of processes occurs for speech production, with general processes occurring in the first six months (gurgling, banging, gaining control over the vocal system and limbs), but gradually in months six to twelve trial-and-error learning processes allow the infant to produce the language-specific speech sounds, providing a synergy between hearing and speaking.

So by twelve months the language-specific speech production and the language-specific speech perception capabilities have developed in synchrony, each scaffolding the other, a process I shall refer to as synergistic scaffolding.

The innate learning abilities of statistical learning, reinforcement learning, and trial-and-error learning are sufficient to bootstrap the language system, as long as there is an engaging language experience.

Statistical (self-organizing) learning 'tunes' the hearing of the infant to their own mother tongue phonology and prosody. Mere exposure to speech in its many forms and speakers allows the infant's auditory processing to 'neurally commit' to the phonemes that it encounters, and to classify the different sounds into the appropriate phoneme categories.

In terms of production, the nascent ability to create a sound (a vocal output) leads to an immediate auditory input. Analysis of the muscular actions taken and the ensuing sound is undertaken automatically. Following an extended series of babbling efforts, the infant gradually gets control over the actions involved, so that he or she knows how to make particular sounds. This, added to the innate imitation abilities, provides the opportunity to attempt to mimic the mother's speech, and the turn-taking opportunities allow the skills to develop further through trial and error. In short, the motor system and the auditory system are working together in natural unison.

In addition, and central to Kuhl's analysis, social learning occurs via interaction with the mother. The mother's infant-adapted prosody (motherese) is designed to emphasize the key components (nouns, verbs) in her speech, which in turn helps the child 'parse' the incoming speech, associate the speech sounds with the corresponding objects and actions, and helps the automatic statistical learning capabilities in the development of receptive speech.

Furthermore, turn-taking, in which the mother says something or asks a question, provides the opportunity for imitation and trial-and-error learning. This is all tied together, of course, by that potent reward-based system, the mother's attention, smile and approval.

All these factors, all general purpose learning capabilities, but scaffolded by personalized interaction with the mother, provide significant advantages for speech production and perception (Meltzoff et al. 2009).

Finally, as the language-specific hearing and speaking skills develop, the underlying neural circuits commit to that processing method. There is no going back. As we shall see, neural commitment is in my view a major explanatory concept.

The Delayed Neural Commitment hypothesis

This analysis of neural commitment in first-language learning motivates the Delayed Neural Commitment (DNC) hypothesis. At one level, DNC may be seen as a re-description of the three frameworks that I have already outlined: automatization deficit, cerebellar deficit and procedural learning deficit. All the evidence that has accrued for these frameworks is therefore directly applicable to DNC.

DNC also is directly consistent with studies that have revealed that some neonates (who were diagnosed as dyslexic eight years later) have no sensitivity to speech sounds at birth, and hence no learning in the womb (Molfese 2000).

And again, the influential Finnish studies on the development of dyslexia from pre-birth to ten years old run by Heikki Lyytinen and his colleagues suggest that there is delay in speech milestones and in some cases motor milestones (Guttorm et al. 2010).

DNC in general means that habits are less strong, and the mind is used to supervising with conscious attention even relatively simple actions so that neural commitment takes longer and might not ever occur. This leads to slower and more effortful processing, and difficulties with multi-tasking.

Furthermore, DNC highlights the difficulties of unlearning habits that have been acquired. This is consistent with the findings of Study 3 on the change of key mapping, and yet the resistance of the skill to perturbations. Furthermore, for some children the primitive reflexes that characterize newborn behaviour, in particular the tonic neck reflex in which movement of the neck to the left leads to movement of the right arm in synchrony, do not get fully unlearned (McPhillips et al. 2000).

However, though superficially relatively modest, the reformulation brings major changes in perspective:

First, it opens a direct link to current theories of the cognitive neuroscience of language and language development, a major issue for the understanding of phonological development.

Second, unlike all other formulations, it extends the discussion to consider the entire information-processing architecture, the Piagetian levels, the executive functions, the working memory, the ability to inhibit natural impulses, the ability to learn by being told. It encourages the consideration of the 'big picture' for human development rather than a series of independent skills.

Third, as I shall discuss in the section on reading disability, DNC has a very clear link to teaching methods, highlighting the need for adapting teaching method to the child's state of development, and in particular it leads to the need to focus clearly on how to optimize the neural commitments to the desired 'big picture' developments in information-processing architecture.

Fourth, unlike our other frameworks, which were all framed in terms of deficit, DNC is value-free with regard to advantage and disadvantage. It leads to drawbacks in some areas but can lead to advantages in others, especially in circumstances where it is useful to maintain earlier skills, or valuable to combine two different skills which do not normally occur within the same 'time window'. It also has the characteristic of making dyslexic people specialize in using their declarative processing systems rather than their habit-based procedural system. Extensive use of the declarative system will lead to increasing expertise in its use, which can lead to a range of benefits in the chosen area of specialization.

In my book *Positive Dyslexia* (Nicolson 2015) I develop this theme strongly, presenting and synthesizing evidence and theory to claim that DNC leads to the strengths of the 'Dyslexia Decathlon' found by my Sheffield research group (Agahi et al. 2015, forthcoming) and the MIND strengths discovered by Brock and Fernette Eide (Eide and Eide 2011). But those analyses are beyond the scope of this volume.

Fifth, and an aspect that may appeal to Elliott, DNC is not a dyslexia-exclusive description. It could well apply to a whole range of developmental disabilities, and will also apply to so-called normally developing children for specific aspects of their development.

That concludes my discussion of dyslexia as a specific learning difficulty. I turn now to dyslexia as a reading disability.

Dyslexia as a reading disability

As noted earlier, I am using reading disability to refer to the applied problems of dyslexic children in learning to read fluently. In fact many children actually fail to read fluently, and in common with US RD researchers and also in common with Elliott, it is appropriate to cast the net as widely as possible in an attempt to characterize the problems that might lead to reading failure.

In this section, as usual I preface the abstract analyses by means of concrete anecdotes personalizing the issues, and then move on to the theory, then the evidence, then relate it to the applied issue of learning to read. I will motivate the discussion with an attempt to engage the reader's empathy by giving some observations and quotations that I found memorable in the past, and I have felt needed to be integrated into any such analysis.

This personal anecdote goes back to when I was five-and-a-half years old. We had moved from Leeds to Sheffield. It was my first day at the new school. The teacher said, 'Why don't you write a story about what you did in your summer holiday?' I looked round. My classmates were all writing away. My school in Leeds had not started instruction in reading and writing. I drew a boat to show willing and I was immediately placed in the remedial reading group. Every Friday we had a class with the headmistress, Miss Needham. She went through what would now be called the synthetic phonics programme. '/c/ /a/ /t/ makes /cat/' she would say. I would think to myself, 'No it doesn't, it make cuh-ah-tuh'. I was just baffled. Every Friday, in Shakespeare's words I went 'creeping, as a snail, unwillingly to school'! Fortunately, I cracked it. I remember a Wednesday reading class the following summer. I realized that I was reading silently, whereas all the other children were sounding out the words. Furthermore, by knowing the spelling of words I was able to 'hear' the sounds in them. For me, the spelling scaffolded the phonics rather than vice versa! I never looked back.

The second anecdote relates to the powerful book by John Holt on seeing children as individuals (Holt 1964) *Why Children Fail*. His work is now less influential than it was owing to changing fashions, and is basically a series of anecdotes. It made a great impression on me when I read it in the 1970s.

> Most children in school fail. They fail because they are afraid, bored and confused. They're bored with the meaningless work, they're scared of being punished or humiliated, and confused by the fact that most teaching progresses from abstract concepts to concrete examples instead of – as would be more sensible – the other way around. In essence I'd realized, from observing and teaching, that school is a place where children learn to be stupid!

He also gives this great quote from his colleague, Bill Hull, which is highly relevant to reading: 'If we taught children to speak they'd never learn!'

My third anecdote is my memory of a talk by my friend John Rack, the education director of the (then) Dyslexia Institute (now Dyslexia Action) in 2002. The DI had just completed an ambitious evaluation of a reading intervention, including close observation of dyslexic children working in class on reading instruction. I recall a startling statistic that some of these children were spending no more than 20 per cent of their time 'on task'. It was surely not surprising that the remediation method was not working as planned! Why would that be, I wondered. What was stopping them working?

Learning to read

Reading instruction is a modern phenomenon. In earlier centuries only a few scholars were able to read, and they had the benefit of personal tuition, complete commitment, and complete immersion in reading (religious or scientific manuscripts, histories, military tactics) as a key part of their job and passion.

Learning to read: history

Modern reading research starts with the major contribution of Huey (1908). His analysis, added to by theoretical concepts such as practice and reinforcement, formed the cornerstone of reading teaching for half a century and more. He was the first reading researcher to realize the importance and form of eye movements during reading.

During the behaviourist era (roughly till the end of the 1950s), most countries used reading methods based on the tried-and-tested methods of the instructional approach: break a skill down into its components; identify how best to teach each component; develop a method of getting performance on the components automatic (often using rote learning, overlearning, distributed learning and repeated presentation every day) then once the components are learned, blend in the complete skill, while making sure that transfer to the whole skill is facilitated by practising it during the component-learning period.

In the USA, in the mid-twentieth century different states used different approaches, with some using the whole word 'look and say' method, and others using a systematic phonics method, and others using an 'intrinsic phonics' approach that combined elements of both. The 'reading wars' were started by Flesch's best-selling book on *Why Johnny Can't Read* (Flesch 1955), in which he attacked the whole word approach and strongly advocated phonics. An early meta-analysis (Chall 1967) of the effectiveness of the different approaches favoured phonics and intrinsic phonics over whole word methods, but whole word approaches were bolstered by the psycho-linguistic revolution emphasizing the importance of meaning and comprehension (Smith 1971).

Continuing controversy regarding the relative merits of the whole word methods versus the phonics methods led to a major initiative in the USA in the late 1990s and subsequently to establish the evidence needed to develop optimally effective reading instruction. This was the US National Reading Panel (NICHD 2000) which recruited all the US reading researchers and undertook a major investigation over those periods.

The NRP investigated the effectiveness of different reading programmes at different ages on word decoding, fluency and comprehension. Their main findings were that at the early reading levels, phonological interventions were consistently effective, but they were best augmented by further aspects of reading aimed to develop fluency and comprehension. For older children the value of phonics-based approaches was minimal.

In order to read a text fluently, it is necessary not just to read it, but to read it and comprehend it. It is therefore necessary to read a phrase within a couple of seconds, because that is the limit of our working memory. We therefore need to build vocabulary, fluency and comprehension, all in a relatively co-ordinated fashion. This was basically the NRP consensus, as described at length in the chapters of McCardle and Chhabra (2004), which has been interpreted as the 'five pillars of reading instruction', namely phonological awareness, the alphabetic principle (phonics), vocabulary, comprehension and fluency.

Interestingly, following subsequent discussions as to whether phonics-based instruction really was any more effective than other approaches (Camilli et al. 2006) the current view is that a systematic, well-supported method will out-perform an unsystematic method.

Regardless of whether it is a phonics-based method or indeed a whole word-based method, a key requirement is that it is systematic, and covers decoding, vocabulary, comprehension and fluency (Stuebing et al. 2008). This is a major revision of the NRP position but has been very little publicized.

In my view the most puzzling aspects of the NRP approach were that they were completely atheoretical – that is, they involved no theory of how children learn to read, and that they were largely based on mean class performance, rather than (in particular in the context of this book), the optimal methods for helping dyslexic children learn to read.

Consequently, as ever, when confronted by a brick wall of confusing and contradictory findings, I argue that we need to take a step back, to consider the underlying theory.

Theories of learning to read

It was not until relatively recently that 'cognitive' accounts started to appear. A range of information-processing models was developed in the 1970s. A highly influential model (LaBerge and Samuels 1974) stressed the concept of automaticity in fluent reading, and the model was substantially enhanced by research in the 1970s that led to Stanovich's 'interactive compensatory processing model' (Stanovich 1980), with automaticity and also fluent comprehension as the two keys.

There is no space here to provide a detailed account of the various theories of learning to read. An early, and justly influential, model (Frith 1986) involves three main stages:

a)   In the initial 'logographic' stage children learn to read a few words as icons (i.e., as a single unit, a sight word). This is a precursor of true reading, in that the child merely decodes the word as a whole, in much the same way as they decode the logo for well-known companies and the like.

b)   The next stage is the alphabetic stage, in which they learn the skills for decoding a word into single letters, which can then be combined into the appropriate sound using grapheme-phoneme conversion rules.

c) Next there is the orthographic stage, in which the child need not break down the word into single letters but need only break it down into a few orthographically standard chunks (letter sequences) which may be spoken via letter-sequence to syllable-sound rules. Orthography refers to the rules of written English, including the use of prefixes, suffixes and morphemes. In other words, children move from a letter-by-letter approach to a more efficient letter-string-by-letter-string approach.

Finally (although not discussed by Frith) a highly skilled reader might well develop essentially a logographic approach, in which their sight vocabulary might well expand to include almost all their reading vocabulary.

The subsequent approach of Goswami and Bryant (1990) suggests that it is easier for the child to concentrate on the 'onset' and 'rime' of words. The onset of a syllable is the set of consonants before the first vowel (the onset of 'cat' is 'c'; the onset of 'train' is 'tr'), and the rime is the rest of the syllable ('at' and 'ain' respectively). The advantage of using onsets and rimes is that one can learn rimes separately (e.g. by focusing on the word family 'at' – bat, cat, fat, hat, mat, etc.), and for simple words it is then easier to blend the resulting phonemes /c/ and /at/ go to /cat/, and so on. These simple alphabetic principles do not scale up well to longer words, for which the principles of orthography are needed.

The stage models provide an overwhelming rationale for abandoning the adversarial 'reading wars' approach to reading instruction, in that they make it absolutely clear that different approaches are needed at different stages, and that an effective method must be able to identify, for a particular child, what their stage of development is, and what is actually needed to help them move to the next stage.

The stage approach has been strongly supported by brain imaging studies of normal readers and dyslexic readers over the past decade. Functional reading networks 'migrate' during the acquisition of reading fluency (Schlaggar and McCandliss 2007).

For beginning readers there is an activity increase in the left temporal-parietal cortex (attributed to phonological processing) and then as fluency increases a gradual reduction in activity in the left temporal-parietal cortex and increasing activity in the left ventral occipital-temporal cortex, the 'visual word form area' (VWFA). The VWFA lies between the visual cortex and the earlier neural reading circuitry, and provides the opportunity for automatic sight word reading, akin to developments in other areas of visual expertise such as bird recognition and is arguably the most exciting brain imaging discovery relating to skilled reading (Dehaene and Cohen 2011; Hills et al. 2005). It appears that, even if dyslexic children do develop VWFA circuitry, it does not provide automatic access to sub-lexical word features such as syllable-level orthographic information (Van der Mark et al. 2009).

Learning to read: The bigger picture

The National Reading Panel focused on the language networks. Phonological and articulatory skills develop pre-school (though for dyslexic children their phonological skills tend to show considerable delay). Explicit teaching then allows the skills of grapheme-phoneme translation (saying the names of letters) to develop by five years, and then after extensive reading for four years or so, an automatic, visual word recognition module is created in the VWFA which allows the efficient reading of words by sight without the need for laborious phonological decoding. It is also important to develop an efficient verbal working memory, so that the words just read can be stored for combination with the new ones.

But, equally important, in parallel with these language skills, there are also sensory-motor skills and networks that need to be developed. There is the hand-eye co-ordination needed to be able to write the letters (while leaving some spare capacity to think what to write), and (less often considered) there is the binocular gaze control needed to be able to fixate on a single letter in a word for long enough without drifting or jumping. Absolute fixation accuracy and stability is rarely needed except for reading, and therefore normally improves only through reading.

Equally important is the creation of the necessary brain structures.

There is a combination of new circuits, executive function, sensory-motor-cognitive integration, VWFA development, and an increase in automaticity and in circuit efficiency, leading to greater processing speed. Also, and remarkably little researched, there is the need to internalize speech so that words can be read silently and efficiently. Furthermore, and almost always overlooked, the executive function skills need to be created during that period between four and seven years.

Consequently, any comprehensive theory of reading support, and any comprehensive approach to reading remediation, really needs to take into account this bigger picture of the skills and circuits underlying reading. If one ignores the extra-linguistic features of reading, one cannot give any accurate assessment of the real problems underlying failure in the early stages.

Accelerating reading readiness

Orton-Gillingham method

The first systematic method for teaching dyslexic children was the Orton-Gillingham multi-sensory method (Gillingham and Stillman 1960), which stresses the need for simultaneous use of all three 'learning channels', that is the visual channel, the auditory channel and the kinaesthetic-tactile channel. The two basic principles are:

> Training for simultaneous association of visual, auditory and kinesthetic language stimuli – in reading cases, tracing and sounding the visually presented word and maintaining consistent direction by following the letter with the fingers during the sound synthesis of syllables and words. Second, finding such units as the child can use without difficulty in the field of his particular difficulty and directing the training toward developing the process of fusing these smaller units into larger and more complex wholes. (Orton 1966)

There is also a comprehensive and flexible manual, highlighting the need to suit the intervention to the particular pattern of difficulties shown by the individual learner, which has been substantially updated over the years.

Reading recovery

Reading recovery, an intervention system designed to reduce the incidence of reading failure in a community, was developed in New Zealand by Marie Clay (1985). In reading recovery, at the beginning of the year teachers are asked to identify the children who are experiencing the greatest difficulty, for whatever reasons, in learning to read and write using the Observation Survey (Clay 1993). This has six components: letter identification; whole word reading; concepts about print (whether the child understands about books); writing vocabulary; dictation and running records (by the teacher) of text reading, and allows the teachers to devise an individually-crafted remediation programme, and to monitor the progress made.

Lindamood Phoneme Sequencing

The Lindamood Phoneme Sequencing (LiPS) programme (Lindamood and Lindamood 2011) is designed to help children develop the sensory-cognitive function of phonemic awareness. Unlike most reading, spelling, and phonics programmes, LiPS instruction directly applies phonemic awareness to the identification and sequencing of sounds in words. Students in the LiPS programme move through a series of steps to learn how their mouths produce the sounds of language. This kinaesthetic feedback enables them to verify the identity and sequence of sounds within words, and to become self-correcting in reading, spelling and speech.

Torgesen's interventions for reading

An elegant and comprehensive series of interventions by Joe Torgesen and his colleagues summarized in Torgesen (2001) provides revealing evidence on the importance of timing in intervention. One set of studies (Torgesen et al. 2001) was aimed at remediating struggling readers aged 8–10 years. Two remediation approaches were used, the LiPS programme and an embedded phonics programme which had a less explicit phonemic component. All children received 67.5 hours of one-to-one instruction in two 50-minute sessions per day for eight weeks. Both instructional programmes produced very large improvements in generalized reading skills that were stable over a two-year follow-up period. Children's average scores on reading accuracy and comprehension were in the average range at the end of the follow-up period, By contrast, the measures of reading rate showed continued severe impairment for most of the children.

A prevention programme (Torgesen et al. 1999) followed a similar design, with individual support for 88 hours with four 20-minute sessions per week continuing over two years, for children identified as the 12 per cent most at risk of reading failure in kindergarten, comparing different interventions. The PASP (prequel to LiPS) intervention, combining multi-sensory and articulatory learning, was the most effective, leading to substantial improvements not only in word reading accuracy but also in fluency.

Reading readiness, classroom readiness and executive function

The concept of 'reading readiness' (Petty 1939) was a major explanatory construct throughout the mid-twentieth century, but was downplayed in mainstream reading instruction (despite its emphasis in Reading Recovery) until re-emerging in the twenty-first century (Duncan et al. 2007). A major reason for this re-emergence was that theorists began to consider the bigger picture of classroom readiness (of which reading readiness is only one component) in terms of 'executive functions', a concept derived directly from the influential information processing approach to psychology. I consider that executive function development provides the key to understanding why limiting pre-school support to reading-related skills fails to address the major cause of reading disability, a theme I develop below.

In her recent review, Diamond (2013) identifies three core EFs – inhibition (inhibitory control, including self-control (behavioural inhibition) and interference control (selective attention and cognitive inhibition)), working memory (WM), and cognitive flexibility (mental flexibility, or mental set shifting and closely linked to creativity). These may be considered as the top-down processes that operate in more affectively neutral contexts ('cool EF'). It is also important to distinguish 'hot EF', the top-down processes needed for control of anger, aggression, impulsivity and anxiety that occur in motivationally and emotionally significant situations (Zelazo and Carlson 2012).

It may be seen that cool EF is the way of maintaining conscious control, and in many ways it is the controller of the declarative memory system. Clearly executive function develops with experience and maturity, and recent analyses (Bauer and Zelazo 2014) reveal a consistent overall improvement throughout childhood and adolescence.

The development of executive function

The development of EF is an area of extensive current research, so any generalizations at this stage are risky. However, current views suggest that at three years of age, EFs are relatively uniform, but they differentiate into the three cool EFs and the hot EFs over the next few years.

The role of executive function problems in ADHD is long established (Barkley 1997; Willcutt et al. 2005) with the key issue being inhibitory control, though Barkley also highlights the issue of speech internalization. There has also been considerable recent advocacy for executive function differences in dyslexia (van Daal et al. 2013; Varvara et al. 2014; Wang and Gathercole 2013), with particular emphasis on working memory, but here the issue is clouded by the fact that the participants are inevitably at least 8 years old, and the earlier development of executive function is therefore unclear.

Fortunately, common sense allows us to make considerable progress for the key changes associated with classroom instruction.

Consider the classroom situation. This represents a completely different learning challenge than the natural, small group, active learning activities undertaken previously. The teacher addresses a whole class explaining what to do. Each child must maintain in memory the required objectives without speaking, while still taking in the further observations made by the teacher. This is a dual task with a high working memory load. Once the teacher stops talking, the child must then switch from listening to doing, a case of set-switching, and try and prepare to do the task while maintaining all the goals in memory (working memory, dual tasking, attentional control). The child also needs to be able to inhibit the tendency to turn-taking, shouting out, asking questions, talking to peers and so on, a high requirement on inhibitory control. Finally, the child must do the task, using the procedural neural circuitry, while maintaining goals, and so on, in working memory (declarative circuitry), and ideally monitoring errors (declarative and procedural) and adjusting the plans (declarative) or actions (procedural). This is an extraordinarily demanding situation for an immature executive system.

Consequently, of particular significance here is the recent literature on the development of executive function from three to six years, and in particular the role of executive functions in 'school readiness' (Fitzpatrick et al. 2014). An early review (Blair 2002) highlighted the importance not only of the 'cool EF' capabilities described above but also the emotional and social EF requirements for school readiness.

The challenges and opportunities are well summarized by Zelazo and Carlson (2012). The preschool years may be a particularly valuable window for intervention:

> ... and a boost in EF just prior to the onset of school may initiate a cascade of beneficial events for children. ... Research on hot EF and how best to foster its healthy development may be of particular practical importance during this transition, helping children to face what can be a daunting set of new emotional and interpersonal challenges. (p. 357)

Intervention for executive function

There has been considerable, and successful recent research on interventions designed to improve executive function pre-school (Diamond 2013; Fitzpatrick et al. 2014). These are mostly on children from disadvantaged backgrounds, but I consider that the findings are of general applicability.

A clear review, Diamond (2012), concludes that EF can indeed be successfully enhanced, with the key principles being that the training must be related to children's ongoing interests and passions, it should be joyful, involve repeated practice, and it should be challenging (but achievable). There is strong evidence that some programmes satisfying these criteria led to significant and lasting gains. The really exciting findings are that these interventions prove to be most valuable for those who have the most to gain, that is disadvantaged children (and, I hypothesize, dyslexic children).

Summary of reading readiness and dyslexia

Both reading readiness and classroom readiness are needed to benefit from classroom teaching of reading. Reading readiness includes established skills such as phonological awareness and letter knowledge, together with appropriate eye fixation control and knowledge about print. Classroom readiness includes both the cool EFs of working memory, response inhibition and task maintenance and the hot EFs of emotional control, anger control and aggression control.

Children with delay in any aspect of these underlying capabilities will not be ready for classroom reading instruction. Research has demonstrated that children from disadvantaged backgrounds are at risk of not acquiring the readiness capabilities in time.

Dyslexia is associated with 'delayed neural commitment' which will lead to delays not only in phonological processing but also in various other of the readiness capabilities. They are therefore (of course!) likely to suffer difficulties in learning to read.

This account therefore provides a principled and novel analysis of why dyslexic children are not ready to learn to read, drawing on the new literature on the development of executive function. It also provides a principled explanation for why interventions designed to improve just one of the necessary reading readiness and classroom readiness skills are highly unlikely to prove effective. In consequence, a dyslexic child will suffer extended reading failure in a classroom situation.

Fortunately, there are interventions that can be undertaken for pre-school children to improve both reading readiness and social/emotional/sensory-motor readiness, as discussed in the previous section.

Stress, anxiety and learning

I motivate the section with a discussion of 'maths anxiety', a highly prevalent mathematics learning disorder.

Mathematics anxiety

Early arithmetic learning involves automatization of tables and number bonds and it is no surprise, therefore, that dyslexic children often have difficulties with arithmetic. But many normally achieving readers are poor at mathematics. Indeed, many more boys than girls have dyslexia, but the opposite is true for dyscalculia (Goetz et al. 2013). So why might children suffer from dyscalculia but not dyslexia?

It appears that the root cause may be maths anxiety. Recent research has shown that maths anxiety is present even at the beginning of formal schooling (Maloney 2012). Furthermore, it appears that maths anxiety is more about fear than mathematics.

> When anticipating an upcoming math-task, the higher one's math anxiety, the more one increases activity in regions associated with visceral threat detection, and often the experience of pain itself (which is the bilateral dorso-posterior insula). Interestingly, this relation was not seen during math performance, suggesting that it is not that math itself hurts; rather, the anticipation of math is painful. (Lyons and Beilock 2012)

This analysis is supported by brain imaging studies that indicate that the cognitive information-processing deficits arising from maths anxiety can be traced to brain regions and circuits that have been consistently implicated in specific phobias and generalized anxiety disorders in adults (Young et al. 2012). So it is the maths anxiety that causes the problems. It is rather like the anticipation of pain, or even a phobia.

Learned helplessness and fear conditioning

The term 'learned helplessness' was introduced by Maier and Seligman (1976) following a conditioning study on dogs. The dogs were trained to avoid a foot shock by jumping across a barrier on hearing a tine. Most dogs learn this very quickly. But some dogs just lay down and did not escape. Seligman discovered that those dogs had been inescapably shocked earlier and had just 'learned to be helpless'. This is probably associated with a 'freezing' response to threat.

More recently, the genetic mechanisms for learned helplessness have been revealed following a study of fear conditioning (Zovkic and Sweatt 2013), in which rats were subjected to inescapable foot shock and the gene expression monitored. The authors concluded that inescapable, repeated, fear-inducing experiences led to long-term changes in subsequent behaviour, and, presumably, learning.

It is also important to highlight the effects of chronic stress on human behaviour and well-being. The 'General Adaptation Syndrome' to stress (Selye 1946) remains a major explanatory model for the long-term effects of stress. There are three distinctive stages in the syndrome's evolution, namely the alarm reaction, the initial 'fight or flight' response. Next, following prolonged exposure is the 'stage of resistance' (or adaptation), in which the body adapts at many levels in order to reduce the effects of the stressor. Finally the stage of exhaustion is reached, in which the body's resistance to the stress becomes exhausted (typically via immune system depletion) leading to major collapse.

More recent frameworks (McEwen 2012) maintain that after prolonged chronic stress, changes in plasticity take place, primarily in the neural circuits involving the hippocampus and amygdala. This impairs hippocampal function, which can have two effects: to impair hippocampal involvement in episodic, declarative, contextual, and spatial memory; and to impair hippocampal regulation of hormonal regulation via Hypothalamic-Pituitary-Adrenal (HPA) activity, particularly the termination of the stress response, leading to elevated HPA activity and further exacerbating the actions of adrenal steroids in the long-term effects of repeated and chronic stress exposure.

The stressing effect of verbal abuse should not be underestimated. A study by Teicher et al. (2006) concluded that although research has focused primarily on the effects of physical abuse, sexual abuse, or witnessing domestic violence, parental verbal aggression leads to equivalent and sometimes more extreme effects on symptoms of 'limbic irritability', depression, anxiety, and anger-hostility.

In short, high levels of fear, anxiety or stress cause highly aversive reactions, leading to behavioural responses of learned helplessness, which are underpinned at the brain level by long-lasting and probably irreversible epigenetic modifications. These can lead to significant impairment in hippocampal function, both for declarative processing and for recovery from stress.

Stress and learning

There is now clear evidence that even mild versions of these situations actually affect the brain circuits involved in learning. Basically, stress shifts processing from the declarative system to the action-based procedural system, the fight or flight, as one might expect in order to escape from that situation.

An elegant series of studies by Schwabe and his colleagues (Schwabe and Wolf 2013) concluded that 'After stress, hippocampal activity was reduced and even negatively correlated with learning performance. ... Stress impaired the hippocampus-dependent system and allowed the striatum to control behavior. The shift toward "procedural" learning after stress appears to rescue task performance, whereas attempts to engage the "declarative" system disrupt performance.'

This 'procedural shift' could lead to particularly adverse consequences for dyslexic people because it shifts them from their stronger, declarative neural system, to their weaker, procedural, learning system.

Learning to fail: An integrated account

This analysis of the 'acute' and 'chronic' effects of stress provides the final pieces of the jigsaw for why some dyslexic children fail. A visual representation is given in Figure 1.5, with the lower curves representing the incremental failures that may be suffered by dyslexic children, building to what I have called toxic failure.

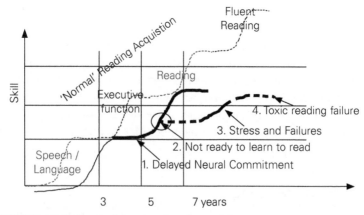

FIGURE 1.5 *Failing to learn then learning to fail*

Stage 1: Failing to learn – dyslexia as a procedural learning difficulty

Classroom instruction involves a change of emphasis from natural, turn-taking, action-based learning to a 'learning by being told' declarative learning process that places heavy emphasis on a range of executive function skills.

Delayed Neural Commitment associated with procedural learning difficulties means that dyslexic children (and indeed some children from disadvantaged backgrounds) are not 'classroom ready' or 'reading ready' at the age at which reading instruction starts (stages 1 and 2 in Figure 5).

Delayed Neural Commitment also hinders the 'unlearning' of skills. Dyslexic children therefore have particular problems in two-stage learning, where first one learns a bridging skill then replaces it by a more complete skill. This leads to problems with phonics-based instruction.

Dyslexic children therefore do not succeed at their learning tasks in the classroom.

Stage 2: Learning to fail – dyslexia as a reading disability

The learning failures lead to acute, context-dependent stress, triggered by the reading context, which causes a procedural shift, which makes them even less likely to learn in the classroom situation (stage 3 in Figure 1.5).

The continuing failures and confusion lead to chronic stress, which leads to two adverse effects:

First a 'General Adaptation Syndrome' of compromised immune system function in response to the chronic stress may lead in turn to a range of adverse consequences in terms of hippocampal and immune system function extending into adult life.

Second, the acute stress response to the reading situation will become entrenched, acquiring the status of a phobia, a 'mental abscess' that prevents learning and has highly damaging consequences. In particular, the stressors are associated with the context of learning, the reading situation specifically, and perhaps the classroom situation more generally. The 'fight, flight or freeze' habit-based responses to stress may lead to disruptive behaviour, truancy or complete disengagement (stage 4 in Figure 1.5).

It is important to emphasize that this analysis therefore suggests that dyslexia as a reading disability is actually an acquired disorder, acquired as a tragic mismatch between classroom readiness, learning abilities and teaching methods.

The analysis paints a grim picture. However, it does have some surprising and positive implications.

Succeeding with reading

The above account gives a coherent and comprehensive account of why dyslexic children fail to learn to read. In this final section, I provide an outline of what we can do about it.

Closing the loop

This has been a lengthy journey, both for writer and reader! I felt I needed to present strong academic evidence relating to each of the components of my explanation, since this evidence has not previously been collected in the same place. It is now time to try to close the loop by illustrating how the newly developed framework meshes with the anecdotes, evidence and theories I presented earlier. I will start with the anecdotes.

The anecdotes

I return to the concrete examples I gave to motivate the discussion in sections 1 and 3, explaining how these anecdotes are consistent with the framework I have developed.

First, the Child A versus Child B responses from the introduction. Why did Child A refuse to engage? The answer that emerges from my analysis is that Child A had essentially learned to be helpless, and the reading context triggered a 'freeze' response that led to a range of adverse effects, both internally and also externally in that teachers do not tolerate children who appear not to be trying.

Second, Elliott's four questions. I will answer these at the end of this section.

Third, my early phonics experiences. Clearly I was not 'ready' to learn phonics. The stress and anxiety are as expected. Fortunately, I got past this stage quickly and was able to use my abilities in terms of internalized speech to minimize my need for phonics, moving rapidly on to the fluency building process. By this stage the reading and spelling did indeed synergistically scaffold each other, as Frith suggested.

Fourth, John Holt, *Why Children Fail* (section 4). I have now built this anecdotal evidence into the explanation in terms of confusion leading to failure to learn, leading to stress, learned helplessness and mental abscesses.

Fifth, the Dyslexia Institute study – why do dyslexic children spend so little 'time on task' for reading? This is of course exactly the same explanation in terms of learned helplessness, freezing and avoidance.

The four Sheffield studies

How well does the framework account for the evidence created by our studies?

In Study 1, balance and dyslexia, we established that our adolescent control participants were able to balance automatically whereas the dyslexic participants were not. We interpreted this in terms of an automaticity deficit. Interestingly, though, our findings were actually that the dyslexic children wobbled a lot more in a dual task situation. That is, they were unable to multi-task. While the findings are consistent with the automatization deficit framework (and directly consistent with the 'conscious compensation' explanation for adequate single task performance), they are also consistent with a 'delayed executive function' explanation, and in particular the possibility that dyslexic children have more difficulties in task switching, goal-maintenance and response inhibition.

In Study 2, primitive skills and dyslexia, we established that, if one prevents conscious compensation by using 'primitive' procedural tasks, most dyslexic children show deficits compared with same age controls on most tasks, but their skills do improve with age, so that their performance is generally at the same level as (younger) controls with the same reading age. However, as tasks get more complex, their degree of relative impairment increases, suggesting an interaction with task complexity (and hence executive control). These findings strongly support the inference I have made that dyslexic children will show a delay in the development of executive function pre-school (though there is little directly relevant empirical evidence), since it is likely that executive function circuitry is one of the most complex learning tasks, and therefore likely to be particularly delayed.

In Studies 3 and 4 (longitudinal studies of the learning process) we found clear evidence of delay in the proceduralization process and also delay in the 'unlearning' process. These studies also strongly support the likelihood that executive function neural circuitry will show clear delays.

In short, the empirical evidence I presented earlier is strongly supportive of the 'proceduralization deficit' framework, as one would expect as this formed the basis for the Delayed Neural Commitment framework. More impressively, it strongly supports the 'Executive Function Delay' framework that is central to the reading disability explanation.

Changes to diagnostic methods

We are at last in position to resolve the Diagnostic Dilemma raised by Elliott (section 1), the pointlessness of undertaking a dyslexia diagnosis given that the same recommendations are made regardless.

We have already seen that the specific recommendations to be made for a particular child should in fact take into account not just the levels of skill and the skill gaps, but also the maturity of executive function development, the history of learning failure (and thus the contexts and approaches to be avoided), and the interests, skills and aspirations of the child (which allow an individual education plan to be aligned with internal motivators).

The availability of a range of approaches to scaffolding the five 'pillars of reading' allows the approach taken to take account of each child's developmental state when determining the appropriate sequence, intensity and mode of learning. The availability of computer-based methods within school provides a further opportunity for avoiding learning failure and for engineering success (and enjoyment). Furthermore, the availability of computer support and apps outside the classroom allows, for the first time, support systems to be constructed that allow the child's family to be engaged in the support network, thereby creating a very much more powerful and integrated learning environment.

In short, rather than de-skilling the assessment process, there is the opportunity to improve the quality of the assessment very substantially, looking at the whole child, the whole environment and the whole panoply of support opportunities. These should be exciting times for educational psychologists.

Summary and conclusions

Summary

Confusion lies at the heart of dyslexia research and practice. I cut through some of the confusion by distinguishing between dyslexia as a specific learning difficulty (SpLD), which is the intrinsic brain difference characteristic of dyslexia, and reading disability (RD), which is its behavioural manifestation in the reading domain.

I demonstrated that SpLD is well described as a difficulty in proce-dural, habit-forming learning, which leads to developmental delay in a range of sensory-motor, language and internalization skills that are the pre-requisites of 'reading readiness'. There is also delay in the construction of the neural circuitry involved in the executive function skills of attention, working memory, goal maintenance and response inhibition that are the 'classroom readiness' abilities needed for tradi-tional school-based instruction.

Reading disability arises when the problems of SpLD are compounded by the introduction of formal teaching before the reading readiness and classroom readiness skills and executive function circuits are mature. The ensuing repeated, inescapable failures lead initially to a continual state of confusion, followed by the rapid conditioning of reading anxiety that disables the declarative learning capabilities required for school instruction. This anxiety may generalize to the complete school environment, leading to what is in effect an anxiety disorder that may manifest as delinquency, depression or General Adaptation Syndrome. Reading disability may therefore be seen as an acquired learning disability arising from a mismatch between teaching method and SpLD.

Assessment for reading success therefore needs to involve three dimensions. First, assessment of reading disability, which needs to include traditional reading measures but also the extended measures of executive function and reading anxiety, with different assessments needed for different ages. Second, assessment of specific learning difficulties, with a view to identifying which skills and neural circuits are strengths and which are weaknesses. Third, assessment for success should determine the individualized intervention programme needed to boost executive skills, reading readiness, sensorimotor integration and self-esteem, while eliminating anxiety and aiming for success.

Answers to the four key questions

I set myself four key questions to answer. What is dyslexia? What and why is reading disability? What is the most effective solution to reading support for all, and what should be the role of an educational psychologist in reading support? I am finally in position to answer them.

What is dyslexia?

I distinguish between the underlying neural differences, which I term dyslexia, and the behavioural manifestations, which may be termed phonological delay, reading disability, balance problems, slow processing speeds, and so on, as appropriate.

Dyslexia is best described in the traditional UK fashion as specific developmental learning difficulties. The specificity of the learning difficulties reflects the fact that they are specific to the 'primitive' brain-based learning processes rather than the consciously accessible, mind-based, declarative learning processes.

These difficulties result in developmental delay for a range of skills, including language and phonology, and also lead to delay in the building of new brain circuits for efficient processing of phonological information, for co-ordination of visual, auditory and mental information, for the internalization of speech, and for the development of executive functions such as goal maintenance, response inhibition, focused attention, verbal working memory maintenance, and 'learning by being told'. 'Unlearning' of previous habits and brain circuits will also be delayed.

Effective methods to further enhance efficient development of these skills and circuits involve three key components: a supportive, immersive learning environment; efficient learning processes and sub-processes; and a natural, 'organic' cumulative development of more complex skills on top of simpler skills. Any deviation from these requirements will increase the risk of developmental delay.

There is a wide range of sub-processes involved in these skill-building and circuit building processes, and delay can be caused by difficulties in any or all. It is likely that the 'risk factors' are cumulative, and so a child with inefficient statistical learning, inefficient error-based learning, and an unsupportive environment is likely to be severely at risk of subsequent reading failure. At the pre-school stage, there will be considerable commonalities between most of the developmental disorders. Children with marked difficulties in spoken language that are diagnosed pre-school, such as Developmental Coordination Disorder and Specific Language Impairment will not be diagnosed with dyslexia because of the prior diagnosis, but may nonetheless suffer reading problems.

What (and why) is reading disability?

Reading disability is a disorder in the acquisition of reading, such that fluent reading is not merely delayed but will in fact not develop at all without extensive additional support. It is the behavioural manifestation of dyslexia in the reading domain.

There are three major reasons for the development of reading disability. First, Delayed Neural Commitment for dyslexic children means that many of the pre-requisites for reading readiness and classroom readiness, letter knowledge, phonological awareness, executive function, internal speech, are not in place when formal reading instruction starts.

Second, failure, and especially repeated, inescapable failure, in the reading domain leads to anxiety, stress, and confusion that tips the brain into its 'fight, flight or freeze' primitive procedural response system that is essentially incapable of learning the nuanced skills needed. Further repeated failure leads to the development of learned helplessness, a reading phobia, and an aversion to the reading situation and maybe school itself.

Third, perseverance with teaching methods that are ill-suited to the child's state of development, or teaching methods that force the learning of one sub-skill (such as phonics) in isolation, exacerbate and even create the problems of confusion and aversion, and may interrupt the natural development of executive control.

These three factors can therefore combine to cause what is, in effect, an acquired learning disability, acquired through a mismatch between the learning and teaching environment and the reading readiness skills.

What is the most cost-effective solution to reading support for all?

The current emphasis on reading support in the UK is that of early intervention. This certainly beats late intervention, which is why Angela Fawcett and I developed the first normed screening test for dyslexia (Nicolson and Fawcett 1996) which could be administered before reading failure (at 4.5 years upwards).

Unfortunately, over-prescriptive formal teaching at an early age is likely to do much more harm than good, preventing the synergistic scaffolding of different skills that develops through natural learning. This can create isolated 'skill silos' that cannot be easily integrated with other skills, thereby over-stressing the immature executive function capabilities. This can potentially lead to catastrophic stress-based problems and also steals the time needed for natural development of executive function.

As will be clear from Figure 1.5, my view is that the major pre-school intervention to undertake is that of support for the development of executive function in its many forms. Executive functions tend to develop organically, in spurts, with some children developing one first, others another, but with each scaffolding the development of the others, a process Piaget referred to as décalage.

What is the role of an educational psychologist in dyslexia support?

An educational psychologist has three advantages compared with the classroom teacher: greater knowledge of child development; skill in the use of sophisticated individual assessment methods; lack of association with the specific school context; and the opportunity to consider an individual child in depth. He or she has the major difficulty of attempting to make assessments for support on the basis of only limited interaction with the child (and teachers).

In my view, there are four key opportunities at the assessment stage. The key requirements are: to identify the barriers to learning, the learning profile (in terms of the various learning abilities), the state of executive development, the state of reading development, and the general likes, dislikes and preferred activities or strengths.

This analysis should lead to a feel for the barriers to progress (in terms of affect, knowledge and skill), together with the potential motivators. This can then lead to the development (in conjunction with the teacher and parents) of a truly individual education plan that considers the whole individual and his or her environment rather than just the reading plan for example.

A much broader role for the educational psychology profession as a whole is to wrest back the agenda for the development of educational theory from economists and managers who have no understanding of child development.

Conclusions

The tragedy for dyslexic children is that dyslexia is defined in terms of reading problems, yet by the time that they fail to learn to read considerable damage has already been done.

Dyslexia is associated with delay in reading, and in many other skills, including the development of the neural circuitry needed to benefit from classroom instruction. Trying to accelerate the learning pre-school or in early school by means of formal instruction is ineffective and even perilous.

The most valuable pre-school activities will be those designed to match the natural learning capabilities of the child while building the skills and neural circuitry needed to underpin classroom readiness and reading readiness. This is now readily achieved by means of computer-based and individual support for executive function development.

The difficulties faced by dyslexic children in later life are a consequence not only of dyslexia, but also the school experiences they have suffered. In my final contribution to this book, in addition to responding to Elliott's initial section, I will argue that delaying the start of formal instruction to seven years, and extending the pre-school experience to include greater reliance on playful and natural development of reading readiness skills and executive function will transform the effectiveness of early schooling, and substantially increase the overall happiness of schoolchildren while allowing substantial financial savings.

2

Dyslexia: Beyond the debate

Julian Elliott

Introduction

In homes and schools across the world, children will be struggling to develop age appropriate reading skills. Often these young people will seem to have a particular difficulty in acquiring basic decoding and spelling skills. In the infant classes, as the nature of the books that the child brings home each week is noted, it will become noticeable to the parents that their youngster is beginning to lag behind their peers. As the child moves into the junior school classes, and social comparison processes become stronger, the child will also become increasingly aware that 'they have a problem'. They will begin to be teased at school by their classmates and, at home, they will become cognisant of rising parental concern. Reading will have failed to become the pleasurable activity that other children seem to enjoy. Indeed, it has become an aversive experience that is best avoided, particularly when frustration boils over and the child is accused of not trying or caring sufficiently. For some family members, the child's progress can result in a growing sense of embarrassment that is best kept hidden from other parents (Carey 2014). By secondary school, the child's sense of agency in respect of reading may be low and their main goal may be to protect their sense of self-worth and, in particular, to guard against accusations of low intelligence.

Observing a child's hurt and humiliation is a painful experience for all those who care for their wellbeing. There is often a sense that there must be something else that can be done, that if only the experts could identify the exact nature of the problem, it would be possible to put into place appropriate interventions. It is unsurprising, therefore, that when the suggestion is made to the parents that perhaps the child 'has dyslexia' and that it would be a good idea to get this checked out, the response is usually enthusiastic.

Eventually the child is assessed by a suitably qualified professional and, in such cases, it is common that a diagnosis of dyslexia (sometimes qualified by additional descriptors as 'severe' or 'mild') results. The parents typically react with a mixture of emotions. They are usually delighted that, at last, the true nature of their child's problem has been identified and are optimistic that this will now lead to more appropriate forms of intervention suitable for dyslexic children, and the freeing of additional resources ring-fenced for those with demonstrable forms of special educational need. For older children in particular, parental pleasure is sometimes tempered by anger that no one thought to check for this condition earlier. Some believe that because of the seeming ignorance or indolence of the child's teachers, identification of the condition was delayed with resultant disadvantage to their child. However, it is often argued that teachers are not specialists in the field of dyslexia and their failure to spot the condition is a consequence of inadequate training.

Given these perceived benefits, it is unsurprising that challenges to the scientific integrity of the label are often met by incomprehension and, on occasions, hostility (Elliott 2014b). To those close to the child the label seems to describe very real phenomena that have often caused great distress. The notion that dyslexia 'does not exist' seems to undermine everything that has been fought for.

The primary challenge to the notion of dyslexia should not concern the spurious question as to whether such a condition exists. Clearly, the problems of severe reading difficulty are all too real. Rather, the dyslexia debate (Elliott and Grigorenko 2014) concerns whether this term adds anything to our current understandings or, alternatively, whether it further confuses an already controversial field. Furthermore, while there may be benefits for those so diagnosed, we should ask whether the use of the term as a diagnostic label results in many others with reading difficulties being more poorly served as a consequence. Thus we need to consider firstly, whether this family's response to the diagnosis reflects a misunderstanding about its scientific validity and, secondly, irrespective of this, whether any advantages accrued are at the expense of others.

From the outset, it needs to be made clear that there is a long and detailed history of accounts of people who have struggled with literacy. The first recorded account of word blindness was provided by a German physician in 1676, although it was in the Victorian period that significant interest became apparent. The early pioneers in the field were largely physicians who described the effects of brain trauma upon their patients' ability to read and spell. Around this time, in 1887, a German ophthalmologist first recorded the term dyslexia to describe the effect of brain lesions upon decoding ability.

These early studies focused primarily upon situations where their patients had lost an already developed ability to read (sometimes known as acquired dyslexia). These often dramatic cases are more salient than the kinds of problems encountered by young children. However, gradually, the notion took hold that such problems could be developmental as well as acquired. Thus, at the end of the nineteenth century, Pringle Morgan (1896) noted in a case study of 'congenital word blindness' the problems of a 14-year-old boy with a puzzling difficulty in learning to read. He reported that the boy's schoolmaster had commented upon his advanced oral skills that were indicative of high intellectual ability. Pringle Morgan also commented that such problems seemed to run in families, and concluded that these were likely to be a congenital problem in which the ability to store the visual impression of words was defective.

A few years later, an ophthalmologist, James Hinshelwood, came to a similar conclusion. In highlighting the need for understanding and early intervention, Hinshelwood (1902) pointed out that common misconceptions could have a powerful effect upon the child's wellbeing:

It is a matter of the highest importance to recognise as early as possible the true nature of this defect, when it is met with in a child. It may prevent much waste of valuable time and may save the child from suffering and cruel treatment. When a child manifests great difficulty in learning to read and is unable to keep up in progress with its fellows, the cause is generally assigned to stupidity or laziness, and no systematised method is directed to the training of such a child ... The sooner the true nature of the defect is realised, the better are the chances of the child's improvement. (Hinshelwood 1902, cited in Shaywitz 2005: 21–2)

Hinshelwood's words will strike a chord with many contemporary observers, as such concerns persist to this day. However, as will be discussed below in some detail, it is easy to confuse a) the imperative that we should separate decoding skill and its development from issues of intelligence and motivation, with b) the suggestion that this concern should apply only to a dyslexic subset of a wider pool of poor decoders.

Given that there seems to be little doubt that some children (and adults) struggle from infancy to develop sound reading skills, even when tuition is appropriate, the next consideration is how we should best understand and help such people. In particular, we need to be clear as to whether all those with such difficulties share the same underlying problem or, alternatively, whether we need to differentiate between them. We also need to be clear as to whether there are others who share the same condition (dyslexia?) but who have nevertheless managed to develop sound reading skills (sometimes known as 'compensated dyslexics'). As Rice and Brooks (2004) point out: 'The critical question in dyslexia research is not whether dyslexic people in particular differ from "normal" readers. It is *whether dyslexic people differ from other poor readers'* (p. 33) (emphasis as in original).

Dyslexia: Multiple understandings

One of the greatest difficulties in gaining a grasp of the term, dyslexia, is that it is used in so many different ways. Yet, despite this, there is a widespread assumption that the term is consistently employed and understood. In reality, this is far from the truth. Table 2.1 outlines some of the many different understandings that pertain.

TABLE 2.1 Differing understandings of who may be considered to have dyslexia (Source: Elliott and Grigorenko 2014)

a) Anyone who struggles with accurate single word decoding.
b) Anyone who struggles with accurate and/or fluent decoding.
c) Those who score at the lowest end of the normal distribution on an appropriate reading test.
d) Those for whom decoding is merely one element of a more pervasive dyslexic condition marked by a range of comorbid features. This can include compensated dyslexics who no longer present with a severe reading difficulty.
e) Those whose decoding difficulties cannot be explained in alternative ways (e.g. because of severe intellectual or sensory impairment, socioeconomic disadvantage, poor schooling, or emotional/behavioural difficulty).
f) Those for whom there is a significant discrepancy between reading performance and IQ.
g) Those whose reading difficulty is unexpected.
h) Those whose poor reading contrasts with strengths in other intellectual and academic domains.
i) Those whose reading problems are biologically determined.
j) Those whose reading problems are marked by certain associated cognitive difficulties (in particular, phonological, rapid naming, and verbal memory deficits).
k) Those poor readers who also present with a range of symptoms commonly found in dyslexics (e.g. poor motor, arithmetical, or language skills, visual difficulties, and low self-esteem).
l) Those who fail to make meaningful progress in reading even when provided with high-quality, evidence-based forms of intervention.

Anyone who struggles with accurate single word decoding

For many reading disability researchers, dyslexia is best understood as a difficulty in single word decoding (Fletcher 2009). The primary reason for the focus upon the single word, rather than continuous text, is because in typical reading, one can draw upon semantic and syntactic cues to help decode unfamiliar words. Isolated words, in contrast, can only be decoded on the basis of the arrangement of a particular configuration of letters (Vellutino et al. 2004). Fletcher (2009) argues that dyslexia should not be employed as a term to describe problems concerning fluent reading or comprehension of text, although, some will encounter difficulties in all these domains. Some comprehension problems will be a product of poor decoding while others will reflect more general language comprehension problems (Spencer, Quinn and Wagner 2014). Many poor decoders gradually improve their ability to read words during their school career, yet fluency can often remain a problem throughout their lives (Biancarosa and Snow 2006).

Anyone who struggles with accurate and/or fluent decoding

Although recognized as one of the foremost researchers in the field of reading disability, Fletcher's position is not shared by the majority of professional and dyslexia lobby groups. In most definitions and descriptions employed, there is typically a reference to problems involving both reading accuracy and fluency. Thus, the UK government-sponsored Rose Report (Rose 2009) highlighted dyslexia as a problem that affects the skills involved in accurate and fluent word-reading and spelling. A similar conceptualization had been provided by the British Psychological Society's Division of Educational Child Psychology (British Psychological Society 1999).

An increasing focus upon fluency in the research literature partly reflects greater interest in reading disability in other languages where the orthographies often tend to be more transparent. Indeed, there has been criticism of the fact that, hitherto, most research has focused upon English, for some, an outlier language that may be of limited value for furthering a universal science of reading (Share 2008). It is generally the case that in contexts where a highly transparent orthography is employed, most children's decoding problems will involve slow, laborious reading, rather than the specific word-reading problems that are common with more opaque languages such as English.

Those who score at the lowest end of the normal distribution on an appropriate reading test dyslexia represents the lower end of a normal distribution of word-reading ability. (Peterson and Pennington 2012: 1997)

For many researchers in the fields of genetics, neuroscience, psychology and education, terms such as dyslexia, reading disability, reading disorder, specific learning difficulties, and specific reading disabilities are used interchangeably. In each of these cases, of course, it is important to differentiate between decoding (the primary topic of investigation here) and comprehension of text.

The great majority of studies of dyslexia concern all those who struggle to decode, not a particular subset of poor decoders who present with a particular set of cognitive strengths and weaknesses deemed to be indicative of dyslexia. If one were to examine the participant recruitment practices in scientific studies of dyslexia, it would be immediately apparent that the selection of the dyslexic sample is typically made on the basis of performance in one or more standardized reading tests. In many cases, there are some additional exclusionary factors (for example, where reading is not impaired because of complex sensory impairments which might render the study problematic). Similarly, in most of the major intervention studies for struggling readers that are reported in the scientific literature (for example, Vaughn et al. 2009, 2010, 2011, 2012; Wanzek et al. 2013), participants are typically selected on the basis of their performance on standardized reading tests.

Of course, if one identifies dyslexia on this basis, identification would be relatively simple. It would still be necessary to ascertain that a poor performance on a standardized measure offered a fair reflection of the individual's typical performance, that is, that any significant difficulties noted were persistent rather than merely anomalies resulting from test-taking behaviour on one particular occasion. The capacity to administer an appropriate reading test should be available in school, and the child's teachers should be able to confirm that any problems identified are meaningful and persistent.

There are many who do not accept that dyslexia can be identified in this way as, in their opinion, this does not permit differentiation between 'true' dyslexics and other struggling readers (Herrington and Hunter-Carsch 2001; Thomson 2002, 2003; Ramus 2014b). As will be illustrated subsequently, those holding such views tend to argue that only those with particular cognitive profiles should be considered to be dyslexic.

Another difficulty with an approach that is based upon an individual's position on a normal distribution is that it is difficult to determine where the cut-off for a diagnosis of dyslexia should be. It is now widely accepted that reading ability (and disability) is dimensional and therefore there can be no clearcut dyslexic/non-dyslexic distinction. It is hardly surprising, therefore, that estimates of dyslexic individuals can be as high as 20 per cent (Shaywitz, 1996), although in her writings, Shaywitz often uses the term dyslexia and reading disability interchangeably. Similarly, the US National Institutes of Health state that reading disabilities, seen to be 'synonymous with dyslexia' (Coles, 1998: 190) affect approximately 20 per cent of American children. Subsequently, the National Institute of Child Health and Development, has claimed that language disability is a problem for between 15 and 20 per cent of the United States population, with most of these involving dyslexia. Many lobby groups, such as the British Dyslexia Association suggest figures of around 10 per cent. The International Dyslexia Association, however, refers to those who have some symptoms of dyslexia, and suggests that this may apply to 15–20 per cent of the population (http://www.interdys.org/ewebeditpro5/upload/DyslexiaBasicsREVMay2012.pdf [retrieved 15 November 2014]).

Those using the normal distribution curve will variously utilize cut-off points of one, one and a half, or two standard deviations below the mean. Snowling (2013) suggests cut-off points of one and a half and two standard deviations below the mean to represent moderate and severe reading difficulty respectively. In many cases, test performance one standard deviation below the mean is used in research studies, resulting in about 16 per cent of the population being eligible to comprise the dyslexic/reading disabled sample.

It is interesting to note that such figures represent a significant increase in the proportion of children who were originally considered to suffer from such difficulties. Thus Hinshelwood (1917) commented that educationists were identifying word blindness in as many as one in 1,000 children. He contended that this was excessive as estimates were sometimes based upon cases where there were only 'slight degrees of defect in the visual word center, while the early writers had reserved it for only those grave cases which could be regarded as pathological' (p. 82). One wonders how Hinshelwood would react to current estimates of dyslexia involving up to 20 per cent of the population.

Those for whom decoding is merely one element of a more pervasive dyslexic condition marked by a range of comorbid features. This can include compensated dyslexics who no longer present with a severe reading difficulty

It is important to note that there are some who consider that current definitions of dyslexia often inappropriately exclude others with this condition. For those who hold such a view, a requirement that there should currently be a significant reading difficulty is inappropriate as, where an earlier reading problem no longer exists, this would rule out from a diagnosis those who struggle with a variety of other associated difficulties such as filling in forms correctly or coping with mathematical or musical notation (Cooke 2001).

The tendency to diagnose dyslexia on the basis of the presence of certain cognitive difficulties appears to be a significant issue for the British university sector (Elliott 2014a). Here a diagnosis can be made for those who do not present with significant decoding problems. Instead, it can be used as a label for students exhibiting one or more of a wide range of cognitive difficulties involving areas such as memory, speed of processing, attention, concentration, analysis and synthesis, organization and self-regulation. Such elements, most of which are more likely to be (but not necessarily) found in poor readers, have somehow become exemplars of dyslexia even where there is an absence of severe literacy difficulty. Diagnosis can then lead to the provision of additional resources (although more recently, the British government has sought to reduce funding for various forms of disability). As Elliott (2014a) points out, there are major conceptual problems here that result in serious concerns about equity for all students.

Those whose decoding difficulties cannot be explained in alternative ways (e.g. because of severe intellectual or sensory impairment, socioeconomic disadvantage, poor schooling, or emotional/behavioural difficulty

The US Office of Education's (1977) regulatory definition of a learning disability (a broader conception involving a range of difficulties which included poor reading) identified a number of exclusionary factors: visual, hearing or motor handicap, mental retardation, emotional disturbance, or environmental, cultural, or economic disadvantage. Similar thinking shines through in many accounts of dyslexia, although more recently, there has been reduced emphasis upon exclusion as a basis for identification (Lyon and Weiser 2013). This trend is certainly to be welcomed, as arriving at a diagnosis of dyslexia on the basis of the absence of factors such as those indicated above is highly problematic.

In relation to intellectual impairment, it is surely indisputable that the reading difficulties of those with severe or profound intellectual difficulties (i.e. those whose cognitive problems are of a level of severity that they are unlikely to be able to cater for themselves independently as adults) are likely to reflect more general language and perceptual problems. Interestingly, however, with the exception of greater emphasis upon the acquisition of sight word vocabulary, approaches to the teaching of basic reading skills are typically similar to that for other struggling readers (Elliott and Grigorenko, 2014). For the purposes of psychiatric diagnosis, however, the fifth edition of the Diagnostic and Statistical Manual (American Psychiatric Association 2013) uses a cut-off point of two standard deviations to differentiate learning disabilities from an intellectual disability (see the American Association on Intellectual and Developmental Disabilities (2010) for a similar position.

Of course, difficulties in learning to read can be a consequence of poor vision or hearing and it is essential that any child experiencing learning difficulties is screened for sensory impairments from the outset. Clearly, a child who has very little residual vision or hearing will have obvious problems in acquiring the ability to decode written formats. As regards using the presence of these as exclusionary factors for a diagnosis of dyslexia, however, the issue becomes more complex for those with less severe impairments. Conductive hearing loss can be easy to miss, particularly as the severity of the problem can fluctuate depending upon the child's health. Such problems will often impede the child's language development which will usually have deleterious consequences for literacy acquisition. Visual difficulties can also be missed, a factor not aided by the reluctance of some young people to wear glasses.

While it would be a grave error to identify a child as reading disabled or dyslexic when their real problem is largely an inability to see the words on the page, there are conceptual difficulties, notwithstanding. Thus, there is a long tradition whereby dyslexia has been held to be a consequence of various visual processing deficits (Stein and Kapoula 2012; Washburn, Joshi and Cantrell 2011). Some of these will be considered in the relevant section below. The substantive point here, however, is that deficient visual processes that some would argue rule out a diagnosis of dyslexia are also key factors that others employ in their explanatory accounts of this condition. Similarly, there are various explanations for dyslexia that involve auditory processing difficulties (Farmer and Klein 1995; Tallal and Gaab 2006; Corriveau et al. 2010; Goswami et al. 2013).

It is unsurprising that socioeconomic disadvantage will often be put forward as a reason why a given child is encountering difficulties in learning to read (Heaton and Winterton (1996). It is clear that several components of socioeconomic status, such as family income, level of parent education, and parent employment are predictors of how well children will progress with literacy (Hartas 2011; Herbers et al. 2012). As regards schooling, Buckingham Wheldall and Beaman-Wheldall (2013) note that a child's academic performance is not only predicted by their own socioeconomic status but also, and significantly, by the average socioeconomic status of their school (Holmes-Smith 2006; Thomson and De Bortoli 2010). However, socioeconomic status serves 'primarily (as) a proxy for more directly salient factors' (Buckingham, Wheldall and Beaman-Wheldall 2013: 190) that operate at home and at school. These authors consider the following to be important: early literacy ability, gene-environment interactions, home learning environment, time spent reading, sleep, school attendance, school mobility, school practices, and teacher quality (which may be lower in more challenging communities. These authors note that the combined effect of such factors is interactive, with socioeconomically disadvantaged children not only more likely to experience adverse conditions, but also more likely to be disproportionately affected by them than their peers.

Given this, one might be tempted to differentiate between the struggling reader whose problems are primarily a consequence of the cumulative effects of an unstimulating environment (Hartas 2011) and the dyslexic child whose reading problems seem to be largely unrelated to upbringing and experience. However, this could result in a situation in which struggling readers from socially disadvantaged environments would rarely be identified as dyslexic (Rutter 1978) with all the negative implications this can have for professional responses to the difficulties observed, and the level of additional resourcing that is deemed appropriate. However, even if we were to set aside the moral and ethical issues involved, as will be demonstrated in the discussion about the influence of schooling, below, this simple bifurcation into nature and nurture explanations provides an overly simplistic picture of what is a far more complex reality in which heritability estimates may vary between those who have experienced more or less favourable childhood experiences. Indeed, it is now understood that environmental experience in infancy can differentially affect subsequent brain structure and functioning (Jednoróg et al. 2012; Hackman, Farah and Meaney 2010). Despite the temptation for some clinicians to make a nature vs. nurture judgement, it is currently inappropriate to seek to distinguish between a neurobiological versus environmental aetiology in respect of an individual who has performed poorly on a measure of reading (Fletcher et al. 2007; Rutter, Kim-Cohen and Maughan 2006).

Where exclusionary factors for a diagnosis of dyslexia are listed, poor schooling is commonly cited. On first consideration, this would seem to make a lot of sense as the crucial impact of teachers upon children's reading development is widely understood (Taylor et al. 2010). One can hypothesize that there are some students whose reading difficulties would persist whatever the quality of the teaching they receive, while other poor readers might be casualties of poor quality education. In such a scenario, it is only the former group that would typically be adjudged to be dyslexic.

However, once one tries to make a diagnostic judgement about a specific individual, problems soon arise. First, one would need to determine what set of accumulated factors would constitute poor schooling. Would extensive absence from school be sufficient, or would there need to be evidence that the teachers in the school were failing in some way? Perhaps the most obvious element would concern the approach utilized by the school to teach reading. As Elliott and Grigorenko (2014) discuss in some detail (pp. 124–8), fierce debate between the proponents of structured phonics teaching and those who have advocated whole language approaches (sometimes referred to as the 'Reading Wars') has raged since the nineteenth century (Chall 1996; Snow and Juel 2005). In the former camp were held to be those often seen as 'traditionalists' who advocated, 'an approach to, or type of, reading instruction that is intended to promote the discovery of the alphabetic principle, the correspondences between phonemes and graphemes, and phonological decoding' (Scarborough and Brady 2002: 236). In the other camp were the 'progressives' who, arguing that children learn to read naturally even when there is no explicit or systematic instruction (Goodman 1967, 1986), espoused approaches that eschewed structured skills-based approaches in favour of those that emphasized reading for meaning. Goodman, a leading proponent of this approach, famously described the reading process as a psycholinguistic guessing game in which the skilled reader drew upon semantic and syntactic information to help in their identification of words.

Although the Reading Wars continue to rage in professional circles, accumulated research has clearly demonstrated that, unlike speech, reading is not naturally acquired (Liberman 1999; Tunmer and Nicholson 2011) and that: 'teaching children to decode by giving primacy to semantic-contextual and syntactic-contextual cues over graphemic-phonemic cues is teaching them to read the way weak readers read!' (Pressley 2006: 164).

While it is possible that highly structured approaches to the teaching of reading may not be necessary for all children (Juel and Minden-Cupp 2000; Arrow and Tunmer 2012), it is now widely accepted by researchers these are essential for those who encounter reading difficulties. Irrespective of the supposed aetiology of their difficulty, poor readers are less able to discover letter-sound patterns as a result of their reading, and, for such individuals, explicit teaching of essential phonic skills and knowledge is essential (Calfee and Drum 1986; Torgesen 2004), albeit within a broad-based literacy curriculum that includes reading for meaning (Torgerson, Brooks and Hall 2006).

Given this imperative, one might argue that some children will have struggled to acquire sound reading skills because they have experienced an inappropriate approach to teaching and learning. However, it would surely be unwise to use this as an exclusionary factor for dyslexia. The importance of placing significant emphasis upon the explicit teaching of decoding skills typically applies to those who already have an underlying difficulty. Thus, a failure to provide appropriate learning opportunities cannot, in itself, be taken to be the cause for the difficulties encountered. Put another way, the more one has an underlying reading disability (whether one wishes to call this dyslexia or not), the more important it is that the educational environment is optimal.

It is understandable why one might wish to suggest that there are cases where reading difficulty is a consequence of the individual's emotional distress or poor behaviour, factors that may result in a failure to engage sufficiently in the learning process. However, utilizing emotional or behavioural difficulties as exclusionary factors for a possible dyslexia diagnosis is difficult to achieve in practice. Children who struggle with reading difficulties are, indeed, more likely to contend with a variety of emotional and behavioural problems. These can include poor attention and concentration (Chhabildas et al. 2001; Willcutt et al. 2007, 2010; Prochnow, Chapman and Tunmer 2013), internalizing disorders, for example, anxiety and depression (Mugnaini et al. 2009), and externalizing disorders such as juvenile delinquency (Grigorenko 2006; Kirk and Reid 2001). However, the problem of disentangling cause and effect can be a significant challenge as persistent academic struggle and frequent experience of failure are likely to place strain upon the child's ability and willingness to engage and persevere in an enterprise that may often be unrewarding. In such circumstances, it is unsurprising that learning difficulties are often associated with emotional problems in childhood (Eissa 2010; Goldston et al. 2007). Morgan et al. (2008), for example, found that problem behaviours in third grade were more likely if reading difficulties had been evident for these children two years earlier, even when prior behaviour and potential environmental confounds had been controlled for. Similarly, McIntosh, Sadler, and Brown (2012) showed poor phonological awareness at the beginning of kindergarten predicted chronic behaviour problems five years later. Interestingly, behaviour proved to be less of a problem for those who made progress during their kindergarten year. Morgan et al. (2008) argued for a bidirectional causal model in which early learning problems result in negative feedback which serves to reduce academic engagement and increase subsequent problematic behaviour. Other work (Grills-Taquechel et al. 2012) has shown how the experience of early reading difficulties can result in reduced academic conscientiousness. If a clinician or a teacher were to come across a poor reader presenting with various emotional and behavioural problems, it would surely be invidious to use this profile to conclude that the child should not be considered to suffer from dyslexia.

Given the difficulties outlined above, it is unsurprising that the use of exclusionary factors has been questioned (Rutter and Maughan 2005; Fletcher 2009). However, these may have more validity for selecting participants for research studies than for making diagnostic judgements. For some research purposes, it may be helpful to exclude those with certain problems in order to isolate a particular factor for consideration. In such cases, however, one must be careful about the nature of any subsequent generalizations from the findings that are made to a wider population.

Those for whom there is a significant discrepancy between reading performance and IQ

There is a longstanding belief that IQ tests offer an indication of one's potential. Sir Cyril Burt, the UK's first educational psychologist argued that: 'Capacity must obviously limit content. It is impossible for a pint jug to hold more than a pint of milk and it is equally impossible for a child's educational attainment to rise higher than his educable capacity' (1937: 477). Thus, one might anticipate that it would be those with high IQ whose poor reading has most scope for improvement. Similarly, it is conceivable that those with a low IQ and limited reading skill are achieving at an expected level. One can understand why many researchers and clinicians have differentiated between those weak readers whose performance appeared to be commensurate with their general level of intellectual functioning and others (dyslexics) where there appeared to be a significant discrepancy. This distinction was given extra weight by Rutter and Yule's (1975) famous Isle of Wight studies in which their results led them to identify two groups of poor readers, those identified as having specific reading retardation, and others who were considered to be more general backward readers. Ultimately, however, the methodology used for the study was seen as problematic, as those in the backward readers group included children with very low intellectual functioning and a variety of neurological disorders. Once these individuals were excluded, the difference between the two groups was no longer apparent.

Since this time, there have been many studies examining various aspects of the discrepancy model and several meta-analyses (Stuebing et al. 2002, 2009; Fletcher et al. 2007). Fletcher (forthcoming) has described the 'incredulous responses' of reviewers when his team (Stuebing et al. 2002) reported no significant differences between high and low IQ groups on a range of reading-related cognitive variables such as phonological awareness, rapid naming, verbal short-term memory and vocabulary.

Of particular importance here is whether the identification of particular subgroups of poor readers can serve to inform tailored interventions or resourcing decisions. In this respect, studies have consistently failed to demonstrate any practical value resulting from the differentiation of IQ-discrepant and non-discrepant poor readers. IQ scores cannot help us predict who will be most responsive, or resistant, to intervention (Gresham and Vellutino 2010; Flowers et al. 2001), nor help us select the most appropriate forms of intervention. Stuebing et al. (2009) found that IQ predicted only 1–3 per cent of the variance of children's response to intervention, a figure that could not justify the use of a relatively expensive and time-consuming form of assessment particularly given that a simple baseline assessment of word-reading skills is a much stronger predictor (Vellutino et al. 2008).

Some have contended that while the use of a full IQ score has failed to provide an acceptable means of diagnostic differentiation, particular groupings of subtests from these measures may be of value. Indeed, one US study undertaken at a time when profiling of this kind was more popular (Pfeiffer et al. 2000) reported that 89 per cent of school psychologists used this approach and almost 70 per cent stated it as one of the most beneficial aspects of the IQ test concerned.

For those who supported profiling in this way, the ACID profile from the Wechsler Intelligence Sales for Children has arguably achieved most popularity (Vargo et al. 1995). The ACID acronym refers to Arithmetic (largely involving mental arithmetic problems), Coding (a test of processing speed), Information (represented by general knowledge questions), and Digit Span (a measure of working memory). Having completed the full IQ test, the task is to ascertain whether the individual's scores on these for the four subtests are lower than for the remainder. If this is the case, it has been argued, one can conclude that the individual is showing the hallmarks of dyslexia.Other popular approaches of this kind include Kaufman's (1975) Freedom from Distractibility Index (ACID without the Information subtest) and the SCAD profile (in which a Symbol Search task replaced Information).

Profiling from IQ subtests has now largely fallen into disuse because, ultimately, this approach has not been found to be helpful for diagnostic purposes (British Psychological Society 1999; Frederickson, 1999) although there remain some researchers who argue that profiles can provide supplementary information (Tamboer, Vorst and Oort, forthcoming). One problem is the rarity of this phenomenon, with the prevalence of the ACID profile in children with learning disabilities having been found to be between 3–5 per cent of this population (Ward et al. 1995; Watkins, Kush and Glutting 1997). In a study of Portuguese children, Moura, Simões and Pereira (2014) found that it was difficult to identify any subtest profile that could discriminate poor from normal readers. Perhaps the major weakness of subtest profiling, however, is that there is little logic to support its use. As is noted in subsequent sections of this chapter, there is a greater incidence of arithmetical, working memory, and processing speed problems in children who struggle with reading, but it is difficult to argue that this is indicative of a dyslexic subcategory of poor readers (see De Clerq-Quaegebeur et al. 2010). General knowledge is, of course, likely to be depressed in cases where children read less (Ritchie, Bates and Plomin, 2015), and in socially disadvantaged homes where one might anticipate that there is less cultural capital or discussion about the wider world. Finally, despite the claims of Thomson (2009), there is little evidence to indicate that use of the ACID profile (or, indeed, any IQ subtest profile has any value for informing intervention (Canivez 2013).

In their wide-ranging review of the scientific literature of reading disability/dyslexia, Vellutino et al. (2004) conclude that intelligence tests are of little value for diagnosing reading disability. In what is perhaps one of the key recommendations for this field, these authors recommend that practitioners should: 'shift the focus of their clinical activities away from emphasis on psychometric assessment to detect cognitive and biological causes of a child's reading difficulties for purposes of categorical labelling in favour of assessment that would eventuate in educational and remedial activities tailored to the child's individual needs' (p. 31).

As will be discussed later, we typically gain much more information from an analysis of an individual's academic skills for the purposes of reading intervention than we can from an IQ score (Connor 2010). This is not to say, however, that assessing intellectual functioning is not important in deriving a broad picture of an individual's strengths and weaknesses. Clearly, teachers should have a sound understanding of a child's cognitive ability in order that they can provide a broad educational experience with appropriate intellectual challenge, and sometimes IQ tests can correct any misunderstandings in this respect.

The use of a discrepancy model is no longer supported by major dyslexia support/lobby groups such as the International Dyslexia Association and the British Dyslexia Association. Interestingly, the Australian Dyslexia Association states that: 'Dyslexia is best understood as a *persistent difficulty* with reading and spelling', but then goes on to add: 'Individuals with dyslexia have average to superior intelligence and can learn they just learn differently (sic) and therefore need to be taught differently' (http://dyslexiaassociation. org.au/index.php?page=what-is-dyslexia [retrieved 13.12.14])

Despite the overwhelming scientific evidence, the use of the discrepancy model continues to be widely employed by clinicians and other practitioners in schools (Machek and Nelson 2007; O'Donnell and Miller, 2011) and in the British university sector (Elliott 2014a). Elliott and Grigorenko (2014) discuss a number of reasons for this puzzling (Stanovich 2005) phenomenon. These include the longevity of the discrepancy model (Catts and Kamhi 1999), confusion as to the boundary between low IQ and intellectual disability, the use of IQ in selecting participants for studies of reading disability/dyslexia in order that underlying cognitive mechanisms are more easily revealed (Snowling 2008), concerns about the viability of alternative approaches (Elbeheri and Everatt 2009), the requirement in some countries for IQ to be used when ascertaining eligibility for additional resources, the more meaningful role for IQ when examining higher order reading comprehension difficulties involving such processes as inference, reasoning and logical deduction (Christopher et al. 2012), and the professional kudos, influence and status derived from the restrictions placed upon which professionals are permitted to use IQ tests.

Perhaps the most powerful reason for the resilience of the discrepancy model lies in its attractiveness to those who encounter reading difficulties, and their family members. As the accounts of those with difficulties frequently attest (Riddick 2010), those who struggle with reading disability have often been treated as if they are lacking in intelligence. The humiliations and hurt engendered by the teasing of peers and the misunderstandings of teachers are often severe and threaten the individual's sense of wellbeing. Parents of children with reading disability often worry that teachers will attribute their child's difficulties to stupidity or laziness and thus fail to offer the sympathetic challenge that is necessary. Already coping with the stress of reading failure, unhelpful comments from teachers or peers may lead to a form of self-worth protection (Covington 1992) by which the child deliberately and visibly reduces effort in order that future difficulty is attributed to a lack of endeavour, rather than to low ability. Problems may also emerge in the university sector where academic staff may also find it difficult to accept that reading disabilities are not an indicator of lower intellectual ability (Callens Tops and Brysbaert, 2012).

Given such scenarios, it is unsurprising that a diagnosis that manages to decouple reading skill from intellectual ability is one that will be highly desired. Indeed, the notion that dyslexic individuals often have high levels of ability (and, indeed, gifts in other cognitive realms (Davis 1997)) renders the diagnosis even more attractive. Thus, gaining the dyslexic label, irrespective of the individual's actual cognitive functioning, may be perceived as a means of strengthening their position within their social circles. It also has the capacity to help the individual gain a more positive self-perception: Those so diagnosed will often comment that they had long thought that they were stupid and are now relieved to discover that this is not the case.

While the discrepancy model is scientifically untenable, the fallacy of treating poor decoding as indicative of low intelligence needs to be vigorously challenged. The reality is that because there is little or no relationship between IQ and decoding skill, it is wholly inappropriate to make ability predictions of one on the basis of the other. Unfortunately, this error is still being made too frequently with potentially serious ramifications for poor readers who do not show this discrepancy. However, there continues to be confusion between a) the challenge to the scientific credibility of a dyslexia diagnosis and b) the belief that such a line of argument implies that poor readers lack intelligence (Elliott 2014b).

Those whose reading difficulty is unexpected/ those whose poor reading contrasts with strengths in other intellectual and academic domains

For many, a hallmark of dyslexia is its unexpected quality when considering the individual's other abilities and educational experiences. However, once one tries to ascertain specifically what factors one would draw upon to make such a determination, problems soon emerge. 'Developmental dyslexia or reading disability refers to unexpected poor performance in reading. Poor performance in reading typically is defined as performance markedly below that of one's peers or expectations based on some form of standards. What constitutes an unexpected level of poor performance in reading has been more difficult to define' (Wagner 2008: 174).

For most observers, the most likely factor that might make poor reading appear to be unexpected, would be a seeming discrepancy with general intelligence (Thomson 2003). However, as discussed above, this cannot serve as a basis for such a judgement. Others might prefer the position advocated by Shaywitz (2005) that the person with dyslexia often has a 'sea of strengths' in a variety of other domains. Perhaps these include higher performance in curricular areas or in respect of particular cognitive processes such as problem solving, vocabulary, critical thinking, comprehension and general knowledge.

There are a number of difficulties with such a conception. The functioning of a child struggling to learn to read will, in domains such as vocabulary and general knowledge, surely be more dependent upon the sort of environment in which they develop than would typically be the case for their peers. Hart and Risley (2003), for example, describe an impoverished community in the United States where disadvantaged children were found to have 32 million fewer words spoken to them than was the experience of the average middle-class child. However, it is likely that the quality of language encountered is as important as its quantity (Pan et al. 2005). As has been shown elsewhere (Hoff 2003), the reduced exposure to high-quality parental verbal interchanges experienced by socio-economically disadvantaged children accounts for much of the disparity in their productive vocabularies. Although issues concerning comparison between language and reading skills are considered in a later section, it is relevant here to note that using high linguistic ability as a basis for determining 'unexpectedness' is highly problematic.

Reading ability appears to influence the development of the child's vocabulary and general knowledge (Ritchie, Bates, and Plomin, 2015). However, irrespective of decoding ability, the vocabulary and general knowledge of a socioeconomically disadvantaged child are likely to be more restricted in those cases where the written word is a less powerful medium for learning about the world. Where the written information is less accessible, the child will become more reliant upon other aspects of their day-to-day experience for learning about the wider world. It is not difficult to see how a child enjoying an intellectually rich home background will be more likely to perform better on measures of general knowledge (and vocabulary) than someone with very similar reading ability but whose home circumstances are less favourable.

The unexpected nature of a child's reading may, alternatively, be based upon their performance in other curricular areas. Of course, performance in these subjects will be strongly affected by a child's intellectual functioning. As stated above, the use of general intelligence (as is often measured by IQ) to indicate dyslexia is now discredited.

An obvious academic discipline with which to compare reading performance would seem to be mathematical performance. However, scrutiny of Table 2.1 demonstrates that the presence of mathematical difficulties is considered by some to be an indicator of dyslexia. This leads to something of a conundrum, however. Although weakness in mathematical ability is perceived as a common feature of the dyslexic individual, somewhat paradoxically, high mathematical ability can also be seen as pointing to the unexpected nature of the reading problem. Thus, in relation to mathematics performance, both strength and weakness can be seen as an indicator of dyslexia.

The reality is that mathematical difficulties are commonly experienced by those who struggle with decoding, with estimates of co-occurrence ranging between 30–70 per cent (Willcutt et al. 2013), although this is less true for the problem of reading comprehension (Vukovic, Lesaux and Siegel 2010). Studies of maths and reading difficulties have provided somewhat inconsistent comorbidity figures, often because of different measures, constructs and cut-off points (Landerl and Moll 2010). It appears that as cut-off points become more stringent the overlap becomes lower (Dirks et al. 2008) probably because adverse environmental factors tend to depress performance across most areas of cognitive functioning (Bishop 2001). While there is shared genetic variance between deficits involved in reading and mathematics disorders, both neurological and psychological studies appear to suggest that these are distinct conditions (Ashkenazi et al. 2013; Moll et al. forthcoming).

Those whose reading problems are biologically determined

Definitions of dyslexia frequently make reference to the condition's biological origin. Thus, the International Dyslexia Association highlights the statement by the US National Institutes of Child Health and Human Development that, 'Dyslexia is a specific learning disability that is neurological in origin' (Lyon, Shaywitz and Shaywitz 2003: 2). Similarly, the British Dyslexia Association notes that dyslexia, 'is constitutional in origin, part of one's make-up and independent of socioeconomic or language background' (http://www.bdadyslexia. org.uk/dyslexic/definitions [retrieved 4 December 2014]).

It is possible at a theoretical level to differentiate between the poor reader whose problems are considered to stem largely from neuro-biological factors and the person whose reading problems are primarily a consequence of adverse environmental experiences. Findings from genetics and neuroscience are routinely cited in order to support the use of dyslexia as a diagnostic label. According to proponents, dyslexia has an important genetic component, and it is possible to point to certain structures and functions of the brain which seem to be associated with this condition.

Detailed consideration of the extant knowledge base of the genetics and neuroscience of reading disabilities is provided in Elliott and Grigorenko (2014: 88–122). Some of the key points in relation to the focus of the present chapter are now provided.

a) Genetics

In recent years, increasingly sophisticated genetic studies, drawing upon a variety of approaches, have demonstrated that across all abilities, the development of reading has a strong genetic component (Hart et al. 2013), with heritability estimates (about two-thirds of the differences among children's literacy being explained by genetic factors) proving to be higher than for general intelligence (Kovas et al. 2014). Additionally, many of the personality characteristics associated with educational achievement (in addition to general intelligence) have been found to have a strong genetic component (Krapohl et al. 2014).

It appears that genetic influences may be particularly influential in cases of reading disability with their role increasing in line with the severity of the condition. Recognition of the heritable basis of reading disability reaches back to the pioneering case studies of the Victorian physicians where it was commonly noted how such problems seemed to run in families (Hinshelwood 1907; Morgan 1896). Since this time we have learned much but, despite such gains, we continue to have only a rudimentary understanding of the multiple ways by which deficiencies in the genetic machinery of an individual adversely affect the development of the 'reading brain'.

Genetic influences can be found in almost all the major processes that underpin reading: phonological processing, orthographic processing, and semantic processing, with estimates tending to be lower for very young children (Byrne et al. 2009). The extent of genetic influence appears to vary across languages (Naples et al. 2009) and the particular characteristics of the samples involved (e.g. ethnicity, nature of schooling and socioeconomic status (Taylor et al. 2010)).

Despite the volume of research directed to understanding the role of genes and the genome in reading disability (see Elliott and Grigorenko 2014: 110–22), we need to be cautious of the value of the current knowledge base for practitioners. We know that reading and reading disability have a genetic basis but, beyond this, our understanding about the operation of specific mechanisms is rudimentary. While there is scope for optimism that future work in this discipline will be able to inform clinical and educational practice, we must be aware of the limitations of our current knowledge and expertise.

There is, however, another important point that is often misunderstood. Genetic studies typically employ participants who are primarily selected on the basis of observed reading difficulties (or those of their families). It is important to recognize, therefore, that such work concerns the genetics of poor readers, not a dyslexic subgroup that has been identified on a clear and consistent basis. Clearly, it is illogical to undertake a research programme working with a sample of poor readers, identify a genetic basis to their difficulties, and then seek to differentiate between dyslexic individuals and 'garden-variety' poor readers on these very same grounds. While we may hypothesize that there are some struggling readers whose problems lack a genetic basis, we are still wholly unable to make any such judgement for a specific individual.

b) Neuroscience

The promise of neuroscience for educational practice is exciting, beguiling and seductive. However, this can result in misunderstandings and overblown claims (so-called neuromyths) that are unhelpful to the field. Neuroscience has helped us gain greater understanding of the structure and operation of the brain in relation to reading and reading disability. The major techniques involved are listed in Table 2.2. Details of the particular contributions of each of these are provided in Elliott and Grigorenko (2014: 93–110).

Recognition that damage to the brain could be a cause of reading disability was reported in scientific journals at the end of the nineteenth century (Berlin 1887; Hinshelwood 1895; Morgan 1896). However, it was in the second half of the twentieth century that increasingly sophisticated post-mortem studies (e.g. Geschwind and Levitsky 1968; Galaburda et al. 1985) began to point more clearly to specific abnormalities in the brains of poor readers.

The early post-mortem studies were subsequently overtaken by a neuroscience of reading involving more sophisticated approaches to studying what structures in the brain are engaged in the task of reading, and their degree of engagement. Here, key techniques include magnetic resonance imaging, voxel-based morphometry

TABLE 2.2 Approaches to studying brain structure and function

- magnetic resonance imaging
- functional magnetic resonance imaging (fMRI)
- voxel-based morphometry
- diffusion tensor imaging
- magnetic resonance spectroscopy
- positron emission tomography
- magnetoencephalography
- electroencephalography

and diffusion tensor imaging. A variety of abnormalities in several regions of the brains of individuals with reading disabilities has been identified. It is considered that these may be related to early stages of brain maturation and development (Galaburda et al. 2006).

Another group of studies is concerned with examination of the brain's functioning. Functional imaging of the brain seeks to detect changes in metabolism, blood flow, or regional chemical composition. Unlike structural imaging techniques, functional imaging is able to identify *in vivo* changes in the brain when various tasks, such as reading, are undertaken. As is the case for structural imaging, there are many different approaches, the most important for the study of reading being: positron emission tomography, functional magnetic resonance imaging, magnetoencephalography, electroencephalography, and magnetic resonance spectroscopy. These techniques have led to the identification of processing difficulties in a variety of areas of the brain (see Elliott and Grigorenko (2014: 88–110) for detailed discussion of specific regions and processes identified by both structural and functional studies).

While neuroscience has provided valuable insights into the reading process, it is necessary to be circumspect about its role in guiding assessment and intervention for those with reading disabilities. This work has shown that the brain's involvement is systematic, consistently engaging specific pathways of information processing and automatizing processes as much as possible. We now understand that the brain enters the stage of reading acquisition functionally different from the time when the individual becomes a skilled reader. Thus, the brain changes as the skills of reading are developed. The brain basis of several key cognitive processes associated with reading and reading disability is now clearer (Norton, Beach and Gabrieli 2015).

Researchers have been able to observe the impact upon brain functioning, and behavioural correlates, of various interventions designed to improve reading skill (Aylward et al. 2003; Richards and Berninger 2008; Spironelli et al. 2010). Studies have demonstrated that subsequent improvements in reading accuracy and fluency can be coupled with cortical plastic reorganization (Penolazzi et al. 2010; Shaywitz and Shaywitz 2008) although it cannot be clearly determined whether this phenomenon reflects a causal or a correlational relationship. The direction of any possible causal relationship is also often unclear. Krafnick et al. (2014), for example, conclude that, unlike what is often believed, differences in grey matter volume (often found to differentiate normal and struggling readers) are most likely to be a consequence of reading experience, with only a fraction being the result of any pre-existing biological condition. Finally, there is some emerging evidence that neuroimaging measures can serve as predictors of subsequent reading abilities (Bach et al. 2013; Hoeft et al. 2011; Myers et al. 2014). However, this field is in its infancy, partly because such studies tend to be complex, expensive, and time consuming (Barquero, Davis and Cutting 2014).

Advances in the neuroscience of reading have led some to suggest that findings from this field have incontrovertibly demonstrated that dyslexia 'exists'. However, closer consideration reveals the folly of such statements. What this work actually demonstrates is that we can identify certain areas and functions of the brain that are associated with reading disability. The reading difficulties of participants involved in relevant research studies certainly exist, but, we hardly require neuroscience to demonstrate this. It is important to recognize that the colourful images of functioning brains frequently found in the neuroscience literature are typically composites reflecting the activity of many participants. To go from group average differences to a detailed image of an individual's functioning represents a major challenge to the field (Giedd and Rapoport 2010). Thus, at a clinical and educational level, neuroscience can currently offer little to inform work with a given individual. It is unable to help us identify a dyslexic subset of a wider poor reader population; neither can it provide guidance about appropriate forms of differential intervention. A further complication is that current costs would render its routine use with individual poor readers prohibitive. Of course, there is great promise that this work will one day inform intervention (Black and Hoeft 2012; Norton et al. 2015) yet it is essential that both researchers and practitioners remain realistic about the limitations of current knowledge.

As noted above, one may wish to differentiate at a theoretical level between those whose reading difficulties are biological in origin and those where environmental factors appear more influential. However, it is becoming increasingly clear that the complex biological and environmental interaction that underpins a child's development is such that a bifurcation of this kind is largely meaningless. Certainly, it would be inappropriate to conclude that because a poor reader is growing up in unfavourable circumstances, he or she does not also have a biologically based difficulty. Indeed, there is no test available that can identify a biologically based dyslexic condition as opposed to an environmentally determined disorder. Furthermore, such a distinction would currently offer no information of value for intervention above and beyond that which can be obtained from existing behavioural measures.

Those whose reading problems are marked by certain associated cognitive difficulties (in particular, phonological, rapid naming, and verbal memory deficits)

The belief that dyslexia can be diagnosed on the basis of certain cognitive deficits is prevalent in many countries. Indeed, it has even been suggested that dyslexia and non-dyslexia can be identified using cognitive assessments rather than measures of reading or spelling (Le Jan et al. 2013). However, there is widespread variation in the extent to which certain cognitive processes are embedded within definitions of dyslexia. In highlighting the reading and spelling difficulties of those with dyslexia, for example, the International Dyslexia Association argues that these typically result from a deficit in the phonological component of language. In contrast, the British Dyslexia Association avoids citing any underlying cognitive deficits as causal and, instead, states that characteristic features of dyslexia are difficulties in phonological awareness, verbal memory and verbal processing speed. The Scottish Government (2009) follows a similar line and lists as associated difficulties the following: auditory and/or visual processing of language-based information, phonological awareness, oral language skills and reading fluency, short-term and working memory, sequencing and directionality, number skills and organizational ability.

For the purposes of the present chapter, I shall focus upon the three cognitive processes where deficits that are most often associated with dyslexia occur. Together these can be subsumed within the phonological deficit hypothesis. Details about the evidence for each of a range of other, less commonly cited, processes are provided in Elliott and Grigorenko (2014: 42–87).

For some, the phonological deficit hypothesis relates to the three processes (phonological processing, short-term/working memory, and processing speed) that most seem to differ between normal and struggling readers (Johnson et al. 2010). In respect of these, there are particular features: phonological awareness, verbal short-term/working memory and the ability to speedily retrieve phonological information stored in long-term memory (typically assessed by measures of rapid naming of everyday items). [This term can be confusing, however, as some researchers (e.g. Nicolson and Fawcett 2008) prefer to treat phonology as separate from memory and rapid naming]. Certainly, the majority of research studies that examine underlying cognitive processes typically compare the relative influence of each of these three components. Thus, for the purposes of the present text, I shall deal with each in turn.

i) Phonological awareness

As is noted above, this term is understood in different ways. Thus, Duff, Hayiou-Thomas and Hulme (2012) include measures of memory and rapid naming within their understanding. Phonological awareness is typically understood, however, to refer to the ability to detect and manipulate the sounds of spoken language (Liberman and Shankweiler 1985). This operates at both the level of the phoneme (the most basic elements of speech) and the syllable (Bryant et al. 1990). Awareness of the larger segments, such as syllables and rimes, tends to precede that of phonemes (Carroll et al. 2003). Phonemic awareness, the ability to segment spoken words into their phonemic elements, appears to be particularly important for the development of reading ability. It appears that this skill is advanced through the process of being taught to read. Children who have poor phonemic awareness are likely to struggle to grasp letter-sound relationships and have poor alphabetic coding skills (Ehri et al. 2001; Shankweiler and Fowler 2004).

There are two major contrasting understandings in relation to the particular phonological weaknesses of those with reading difficulties.

An influential theory was that such children struggle because of faulty representation of speech sounds which become degraded (more fuzzy, noisier, less precise) and thus hinder the acquisition of phonological skills (Vellutino, Scanlon and Spearing 1995). Weak phonological coding is likely to impact negatively upon the child's ability to establish a strong connection between the visual and verbal counterparts of printed words.

A second explanation (Ramus and Szenkovits 2008) is that, for poor readers, the phonological representations are not degraded (except, perhaps for a very small minority) but, instead, are difficult to access. Thus, the key difficulty concerns the exercise of various cognitive skills that apply to these representations for the resolution of particular tasks. Such a perspective has echoes in the earlier work of Shankweiler and Crain (1986) and Hulme and Snowling (1992). The key problem in reconciling these two differing accounts is that it is difficult to design helpful experiments, as cognitive tasks that tap phonological representations necessarily require access to them. Ramus has reported findings from cognitive psychology and neuroscience to support his account (Ramus and Ahissar 2012; Berent et al. 2012; Ramus 2014a) although he accepts that these have not yet proved sufficient to resolve the debate. Recently, Boets (2014) has tried to resolve this debate by suggesting that the nature of this difficulty changes over time. Initially, degraded representations are more likely to be problematic for young poor readers but, as they mature, such difficulties are resolved (partly as a result of instruction). Subsequently, phonological problems for these individuals would increasingly concern their ability to gain access to largely intact representations.

A substantial number of studies have provided powerful evidence that phonological awareness is a key predictor of subsequent reading ability (National Early Literacy Panel 2008). In this respect, it appears that phonemic awareness is particularly powerful (Snowling 2000; Melby-Lervåg et al. 2012). In their meta-analytic review, Melby-Lervåg et al. (2012) concluded that the accumulated findings lent support to the 'pivotal role of phonemic awareness as a predictor of individual differences in reading development' (p. 322). It is important to note, however, that its influence appears to be greater for reading in the early years when sequential letter-to-sound decoding takes precedence over more automatic word-reading processes (Caravolas et al. 2012; Vaessen and Blomert 2010). It also appears more influential for opaque languages (such as English) than transparent orthographies (such as German or Russian), particularly during the later stages of reading development (Arnoutse, van Leeuwe and Verhoeven 2005; Furnes and Samuelsson 2010; Landerl and Wimmer 2000; Ziegler, Bertrand et al. 2010).

The pioneering work of Bradley and Bryant (1983) led to many subsequent studies all suggesting that phonological problems appear to be a direct cause of reading impairment for most children who encounter significant reading disability (Vellutino 1979; Snowling 2000). However, these have typically been correlational or cross-sectional and thus causal claims are rather more tenuous (Castles and Coulthart 2004). To render matters even more complex, any causal relationship appears to be bidirectional, as increasing proficiency in reading appears to lead to improved phonological skills (Castles and Coulthart 2004; Bishop 2006). Evidence that phonemic awareness may be as much a cause as a consequence of reading development has arisen from longitudinal studies where phonological deficits have been found prior to the onset of formal reading instruction (Boets et al. 2010; Lyytinen et al. 2006; Richardson et al. 2003). Nevertheless, these studies have largely been unable to rule out all other confounding variables (Byrne 2011; Olson 2011) that might represent the true underlying cause of the observed associations.

One of the problems with the cognitive variables identified as underpinning dyslexia is that particular deficits are not always present in struggling readers. In the case of phonological awareness deficits, not all poor readers demonstrate such a difficulty (White et al. 2006), and some who experience phonological problems can develop sound reading skills (Catts and Adlof 2011). Some theorists emphasize other factors (for example, auditory or visual processing difficulties) yet consider a phonological deficit to be an important mediator between these and reading impairment (Tallal 1980; Nicolson et al. 2012; Stein 2001). In contrast, others (e.g. Ahissar 2007; Vidyasagar and Pammer 2010) do not consider a phonological deficit to be necessary for all forms of reading disability.

Despite the strong evidence from both behavioral and neuro-imaging studies (Diehl et al., 2011) pointing to the importance of phonological awareness in reading, theoretical understanding of this construct continues to be unclear. While it is almost universally agreed that a phonological deficit is a key factor for most children with reading disability, there continues to be significant debate as to its precise nature and role. Despite more than thirty years of research into the phonological deficit, '... we still don't know what it is' (Ramus and Szenkovits, 2008, p. 165).

It would be a serious error to seek to differentiate between so-called dyslexic and other struggling readers (sometimes known as 'garden-variety' poor readers) on the basis of performance on one or more phonological awareness tasks. Not only do factors such as the individual's age and orthography affect the predictive power of phonological awareness, such a distinction would have minimal relevance for clinical intervention or broader educational practice.

ii) Rapid naming

It has been regularly found that poor readers struggle to rapidly name images of everyday items placed before them. This process, sometimes known as 'rapid automatized naming' (RAN) has been frequently studied in relation to reading difficulty. In general, a relationship between RAN and general reading ability has been found although its predictive power appears to vary (Savage 2004) depending on whether the task involves letters, numbers, pictures or colours (Christopher et al. 2012; Mazzocco and Grimm 2013; Poulsen, Juul and Elbro 2015; Schatschneider et al. 2004), whether the tasks require serial or discrete processing (i.e. items are presented together in a row or singly in turn), whether the participant is required to give a written or an oral response (Georgiou et al. 2013), and whether the outcome of interest is reading accuracy or fluency (Savage and Frederickson 2005).

Although naming speed has limited predictive power for the progress of normal readers (National Early Literacy Panel 2008), it appears more influential for those encountering reading difficulties (Lervåg, Bråten and Hulme 2009; Scarborough 1998), although see Koponen et al. (2013). While a universal phenomenon (Wolf et al. 2009), it also is a more powerful predictor for transparent languages, where an emphasis upon reading fluency, rather than reading accuracy, contrasts with that for more opaque languages such as English.

The relative predictive power of phonemic/phonological awareness and rapid naming for reading accuracy and fluency has been extensively studied with, in the main, consistent findings. In general, rapid naming tends to be a stronger predictor for fluency (or speed reading) measures than for accuracy, with the opposite relationship pertaining for phonemic awareness (Landerl and Wimmer 2008; Juul, Poulsen and Elbro 2014).

According to Wolf's double deficit model (Wolf and Bowers 1999), those who have both phonological and rapid naming difficulties are likely to experience particular difficulties with reading. This suggestion has been supported by findings from several research studies (Wolf, Bowers and Biddle 2000; Steacy et al. 2014) although several researchers have queried the suggestion that there is a meaningful subgroup of poor readers with naming speed deficits but no phonological deficits (Vaessen, Gerretsen and Blomert 2009; Vukovic and Siegel 2006).

As is the case for the phonological deficit, it has proven difficult to arrive at a widely agreed theoretical understanding of the nature and role of rapid naming in respect of reading (Georgiou and Parrila 2013; Lervåg et al. 2009). The issue is complicated by recognition that rapid naming essentially serves as an indicator of an underlying problem that impacts upon reading speed (Wolf 2007). As noted above, there is disagreement as to whether naming speed should be included within a more overarching phonological account (Snowling and Hulme 1994; Nicolson and Fawcett 2006). There is also a divergence of opinion as to whether rapid naming should be considered as a subcomponent of general processing speed. It appears that, on the basis that rapid naming can be a problem for struggling readers, some clinicians are using slow processing as an indicator of dyslexia. However, several researchers have demonstrated that using speed of processing may not be an adequate explanation for the relationship between RAN and reading (Cutting and Denckla 2001; Poulsen, Juul and Ebro, 2015; Stainthorp et al. 2010).

Of course, even if such a link could be demonstrated, it would still be inappropriate to use a rapid naming deficit as a means to diagnose dyslexia. What we know is that rapid naming difficulties in young children can help identify those who will later develop reading difficulties. However, as has repeatedly been pointed out in this chapter, it is one thing to note a weakness or deficit that is commonly found in poor readers, but it is quite another to then use it to diagnose dyslexia in a given individual. Such a step might have some value if any such differentiation were able to highlight a particular form of intervention suitable for these individuals. Unfortunately, this is not currently the case and those with naming speed problems have not been shown to respond to particular interventions in ways that differ to other poor readers. There appears to be no evidence that differentiating between double deficit and single deficit (i.e. with solely a phonological or a rapid naming difficulty) groups has any implications for differential intervention, and it would appear that all benefit from traditional multicomponent reading instruction (2009; Steacy et al. 2014). Finally, there is no evidence to show that increasing naming speed, if this were possible, would produce a concomitant improvement in reading performance (Norton and Wolf 2012; van der Leij et al. 2013).

iii) Short-term/working-memory deficits

Studies have repeatedly shown that children with short-term memory (STM) or working-memory (WM) deficits are likely to experience a range of difficulties with learning (Alloway et al. 2009). Both concern the ability to retain information for brief periods of time. Where they differ is that short-term memory is concerned solely with the passive storage of information, whereas working memory involves both storage and processing, the latter appearing to draw upon executive functioning. Short-term memory is often assessed in experimental studies with simple digit span or non-word repetition (Snowling 2000) whereas working-memory tasks may vary from backwards digit span to relatively complex activities.

Both short-term and working memory have been shown to be associated with reading difficulties involving both reading accuracy/fluency and reading comprehension (Alloway et al. 2009; Gathercole et al. 2004; Kibby et al. 2004; Swanson, Ashbaker and Lee 1996), although see Van Dyke, Johns and Kukona (2014). Some further support for this relationship has been provided by findings from fMRI studies of brain functioning (Beneventi et al. 2010; Berninger et al. 2008).

However, there is considerable debate as to which particular aspects (or systems) comprising different models of STM/WM (Baddeley, 2012) and the many various measures of these (see, for example, Savage, Lavers and Pillay 2007; Cowan and Alloway 2008) are most important for different reading-related (and spelling) tasks. There is also disagreement as to the extent to which these two forms of memory should be seen as distinct operations (Hutton and Towse 2001; Swanson 2006). Such issues are further complicated by the need to examine the role of memory processes across differing orthographies (see, for example, Brandenburg et al. 2015 Landerl et al. 2013). It is also important to separate out the role of memory for reading accuracy/fluency (the domain that is pertinent to debates over dyslexia) as opposed to reading comprehension.

It is usually helpful to differentiate between verbal and visuo-spatial forms of STM and WM. In general, studies have indicated that verbal measures are more powerful predictors for decoding skills (Pham and Hasson 2014). In contrast, studies of visuo-spatial WM have yielded rather more inconsistent results, perhaps because of greater diversity in the methods and tasks utilised (Menghini et al. 2011). In particular, performance may partly depend upon the extent to which there is a verbal element in terms of coding/processing the visual stimuli.

While STM and WM difficulties are more prevalent in struggling readers, they are by no means consistently found in all cases (De Clercq-Quaegebeur et al. 2010). Furthermore, they tend to have less predictive power than phonological processing and rapid naming, and there is some debate as to how much memory deficits make a unique contribution. Various studies and meta-analyses (e.g. Wagner et al. 1997; Savage et al. 2007; Melby-Lervåg et al. 2012) have suggested that, when multivariate studies are undertaken, memory appears not to add greatly to prediction for word reading. Indeed, much of the variance can be explained by phonological/phonemic awareness although, for younger children in particular, these processes are closely related (Wagner and Muse 2006). A further difficulty is that, despite a plethora of intervention studies there is little evidence that experimental attempts to boost WM can result in improved performance for these with reading difficulties (Elliott et al. 2010; Chacko et al. 2013; Dunning, Holmes and Gathercole 2013).

Understandings about the presence and role of various cognitive processes in reading disability have become confused and are often widely misunderstood. For some, dyslexia is only evidenced when difficulties in certain cognitive processes (primarily those subsumed within the phonological deficit theory) are apparent. Others believe that those with dyslexia tend to have weaknesses in such processes but their presence is not a pre-condition for diagnosis. In higher education in the UK, some will diagnose dyslexia when these processes are problematic even when there no longer exists any obvious reading problem. Currently, there are no secure grounds for using phonological, rapid naming or memory deficits as means to differentiate between dyslexic and garden-variety poor readers. While we know that there is a greater incidence of such problems in struggling readers, such information cannot be used to make a diagnostic judgement. Certainly, with the exception of phonological awareness in young children, there is no evidence that targeting these processes for intervention can have benefits for poor readers. Indeed, concern has been raised that the benefits of phonological interventions may not persist over time (Olson 2011).

Those poor readers who also present with a range of symptoms commonly found in dyslexics (e.g. poor motor, arithmetical, or language skills, visual difficulties, and low self-esteem)

Although it is possible to construct a long list of symptoms more commonly found in those with reading difficulties than normal readers, we must be cautious about ascribing causal relationships or, indeed, seeing these as indicative of an underlying dyslexic condition.

It has been estimated that between one-third and two-thirds of those with reading difficulties demonstrate motor impairments of one kind or another (Chaix et al. 2007; Kaplan et al. 1998). Many such difficulties are also held to be indicative of dyspraxia (or developmental co-ordination disorder), although one would anticipate that most clinicians would consider the extent of any literacy difficulties as a key criterion for differentiating between these conditions (Elliott and Place 2012). As Rod Nicolson shows (this volume, Ch. 1), there are a number of theories which seek to explain this phenomenon. However, the evidence for a causal relationship between motor impairment and reading skills is generally considered to be weak (Rochelle and Talcott 2006; Savage 2004). Furthermore, there is little empirical support for the notion that improving motor functioning can help to resolve severe reading difficulties.

As noted above, there is strong evidence of co-occurrence of mathematical and reading difficulties. However, it would be inappropriate to seek to diagnose dyslexia on the basis of the presence, or the absence, of mathematical problems. Similarly, there is a detailed literature showing that language difficulties (an area that is also highly problematic in respect of clinical diagnosis (Bishop 2014)) are often associated with reading disability. However, research has consistently demonstrated that these are best considered as two distinct sets of disorders that are often comorbid (Ramus et al. 2013).

The case for a visual basis for reading difficulty is rather stronger although, here too, there is much disagreement. It is possible that the presence of visual difficulties could be seen to both indicate, and to rule out, a diagnosis of dyslexia. In considering the nature of an individual's reading problems, a clinician should always seek examination of hearing and vision. Clearly, if one of these senses is significantly impaired, and not adequately addressed by suitable aids, one might conclude that any significant reading difficulty was most likely a consequence of this sensory impairment.

However, visual problems of various kinds are sometimes seen as a marker of dyslexia. The Victorian physicians who first produced case studies of poor readers generally assumed that their problems had a visual basis and the term, 'word blindness', was widely employed at this time. The perceived importance of visual factors was central throughout much of the twentieth century and still persists in the everyday understandings of the general public. Thus, when asked about the nature of dyslexia, descriptive accounts will often involve written words being perceived as upside down, reversed, blurry, or moving around the page. For some, such visual distortions are the product of visual discomfort (also known as scotopic sensitivity or Meares-Irlen syndrome) (Singleton 2009) although these should not be seen as synonymous with reading disability/dyslexia. Rather, it may be that visual sensitivity of this kind is particularly problematic for those who struggle to decode, as such individuals often need to pore over the written word and any visual discomfort would render fluent reading even more difficult (Wilkins 1995).

The work of Vellutino (Vellutino 1979, 1987; Vellutino et al. 2004) challenged predominant understandings by showing that earlier studies of visual processing were flawed and visual perception and visual sequencing were not responsible for reading disability. At about this time the phonological deficit hypothesis became the dominant account and reading disability/dyslexia became widely understood as primarily a problem of language rather than vision.

In its *Joint Statement – Learning Disabilities, Dyslexia, and Vision*, the American Academy of Pediatrics states that:

> there is inadequate scientific evidence to support the view that subtle eye or visual problems, including abnormal focusing, jerky eye movements, misaligned or crossed eyes, binocular dysfunction, visual-motor dysfunction, visual perceptual difficulties, or hypothetical difficulties with laterality ... cause learning disabilities. Statistically, children with dyslexia or related learning disabilities have the same visual function and ocular health as children without such conditions. (American Academy of Pediatrics 2009: 842)

This statement was subsequently updated in a joint technical report which considered issues of intervention (Handler et al. 2011). Taking a similar stance to the earlier document, the report endorsed the view that various forms of vision therapy for those with learning difficulties had not been scientifically validated:

> Scientific evidence does not support the claims that visual training, muscle exercises, ocular pursuit-and tracking exercises, behavioral/perceptual vision therapy, training glasses, prisms, and colored lenses and filters are effective direct or indirect treatments for learning disabilities. There is no evidence that children who participate in vision therapy are more responsive to educational instruction than those who do not participate.

While it is difficult to disagree with the conclusions concerning some of the processes listed in the 2009 statement, it does appear that there may be a greater role for visual factors in reading disability than was formerly appreciated (Bellocchi et al. 2013; Dehaene 2009; Szwed et al. 2012). Of particular interest are recent research findings in relation to visual attention. In contrast to visual perception, this concerns the ability to select rapidly the most relevant information from an array of letters and words on a page. There is a variety of different accounts of visual attention which include sluggish attentional shifting (Hari and Renvall 2001; Lallier et al. 2010) the visual attention span deficit (Bosse, Tainturier and Valdois 2007), and abnormal crowding (Aleci et al. 2012; Collis et al. 2013). Despite some research support for each of these in relation to the strug-gling reader, it should be noted that there is currently little scientific research in respect of any associated interventions.

Lists of symptoms of dyslexia often include items such as low self-esteem and an unwillingness to read aloud. Of course, it is patently obvious that these are unfortunate consequences of the hurt and humiliation that result from a struggle to learn to read. There is no logic to the argument that such features are markers of a dyslexic condition that contrasts with the problems of other poor readers.

Those who fail to make meaningful progress in reading even when provided with high-quality, evidence-based forms of intervention

It has been argued that one potentially valuable use of the term dyslexia, would be to apply it to those individuals who have received systematic, substantial, evidence-based intervention over a lengthy period of time but whose reading skills continue to be highly problematic (Elliott and Gibbs 2008). It is clear that there is a significant proportion of poor readers for whom even the best available approaches appear relatively ineffective (Wanzek et al. 2013; Scammacca et al. 2015). At the present time, researchers are unsure how best to respond other than to recommend that educational interventions should be more intense (i.e. by increasing time and duration of specialized assistance or decreasing instructional group size). Such steps may not prove significantly more effective, given these students' struggles to benefit from the help they have already received (Fuchs et al. 2013).

The case for describing such individuals as dyslexic on such a basis is predicated on an assumption that such a label would reflect recognition that further significant gains are unlikely. While further specialist tuition may prove helpful, albeit leading to, at best, modest gains in many cases, significant effort should be put into training those labelled in this way to be able to utilize high-quality techno-logical provision (e.g. speech chips, voice recognition, scanners, voice recorders). Accordingly, dyslexia could be relatively easily diagnosed (on the basis of long-term response to specialized literacy intervention) and, in the light of this, there would be clear implica-tions for educational intervention and resourcing.

Using the label 'dyslexic' in this way overcomes the major criti-cisms of current understandings outlined in this chapter.

It clearly identifies a particular subgroup of poor readers on the basis of clear criteria, and such a classification would have important (and justifiable) implications for a differential form of intervention and specialist resourcing. However, it is questionable whether those who advocate the wider use of the label would find this a satisfactory resolution to the current debate.

The failure of the dyslexia label

When our hypothetical family set out to ascertain whether their child is or is not dyslexic (pp. 73–4), one might anticipate that their actions were underpinned by the following set of beliefs:

a) There is a clear, widely understood condition called dyslexia that can be reliably and validly identified.

b) Dyslexia is not merely a synonym for reading disability. Rather it provides additional diagnostic information that differentiates the dyslexic child from other 'garden-variety' poor readers (Share 1996).

c)   Identification that a child has dyslexia enables more effective forms of educational and clinical intervention to be put into place.

d)   Identification of this condition can justifiably result in the allocation of additional resources that would otherwise be unavailable to poor readers generally.

As this chapter has sought to demonstrate, current conceptualizations as to the nature of dyslexia are so varied, and often so muddled, that any claim that a diagnosis has a secure, scientific basis is highly questionable. It is largely because of such diverse understandings that the most recent version of the American Psychiatric Association's *Diagnostic and Statistical Manual* (5th Edition – DSM-V) dropped dyslexia as a diagnosis in favour of Specific Learning Disorder. This diagnosis is followed by specification of the particular domain (e.g. reading) and subskills (word-reading accuracy) (note that after fierce lobbying from dyslexia groups, the term dyslexia was subsequently permitted to be used as a specifier).

It is interesting to note that a number of eminent researchers are not easily persuaded that the problems of the dyslexia construct outweigh its usefulness (e.g. Ramus 2014b; Cutting 2014). This may be largely because researchers who seek to gain greater understanding of the nature of reading difficulty, and how to treat it, find the construct valuable for their purposes. Their focus and needs are, however, wholly different from those who seek a diagnostic label to describe the nature of an individual's difficulties. As noted above, participants in research studies are rarely differentiated into two groups, those considered to be dyslexics and others who are 'just' poor decoders. Ramus (2014b), for example, criticizes Elliott and Grigorenko (2014) for their challenge to the dyslexia construct and argues for a position in which, the terms dyslexia and specific reading disability or disorder (as cited in DSM-V) can be used interchangeably. However, Ramus's conception would offer little additional insight for our hypothetical family in their search for a diagnosis that advances what is already known about their child's difficulty.

One of the most pervasive misunderstandings of dyslexia is that a diagnosis will inform educational and clinical intervention. The reality is that, were our hypothetical family to receive such a diagnosis, it would not, in itself, offer any additional information about how the child might be best helped. Although there are many mooted special treatments for dyslexic children and adults (see Elliott and Grigorenko 2014: 123–65, for a detailed review), the only forms of intervention for poor decoders that are consistently supported by rigorous, scientific examination are those which involve systematic, educational instruction. This is not to suggest, however, that, 'all poor readers benefit from the same kind of evidence-based reading interventions', a misrepresentation of Elliott and Grigorenko's position that forms part of a critique by Ramus (2014b: 3373). Neither does it mean that these approaches can resolve all poor readers' difficulties. Certainly, as noted above, there is a small proportion of poor readers who continue to challenge the best efforts of all those who seek to construct more effective interventions. However, what is indisputable is that there is no evidence that current evidence-based approaches are differentially effective for so-called dyslexic and garden-variety poor reader groups. Thus, identifying a poor reader as dyslexic or not cannot, at present, help a teacher or clinician in preparing appropriate interventions. Rather, those charged to help the struggling reader should seek to look to identify and build upon their particular mix of academic strengths, weaknesses and needs (Vellutino et al. 2004).

According to Vellutino et al. (2004), the assessor is advised to focus upon the individual's response to the educational interventions offered. This: 'would provide guidance as to his or her long-term instructional needs, regardless of the origin of his or her reading difficulties' (p. 35).

Of course, it would be wholly wrong to suggest that there is a clear consensus on how best to operate response to intervention systems (Fuchs et al. 2010). However, it is surely possible to agree about which sorts of problems, to what degree, should trigger different levels of response. Response to intervention approaches permits regular screening, a process that should not be undertaken as a one-off event as the presence of reading disabilities can fluctuate through a child's lifespan (Etmanskie, Partanen and Siegel, 2016).

As is happening in several countries, particularly the US, response to intervention programmes largely operates on the basis of system-wide procedures and, unlike many assessments by privately funded specialists, are open to scrutiny and comparison. Such a system has the benefit of ensuring that special provision is made available on the basis of need, rather than the persistence and persuasive abilities of those who are better placed to seek and obtain a dyslexia diagnosis. There is no justifiable rationale for providing additional resourcing to dyslexic individuals at the expense of others whose literacy skills operate at a similar level. Our hypothetical family may indeed obtain additional help, having received a dyslexia diagnosis, and this is likely to justify their actions from their perspective. One of the main defences of the dyslexia construct is that, despite its flaws, it is a primary means to receive additional help. Here, there is confusion between the scientific validity of a construct/label and the pragmatics of operating within a confused system. Unless we are prepared to tackle the origins of the confusion we will continue to fail to develop intervention systems that are most economical and beneficial for all.

Some forty years ago, the UK's Department of Education and Science (1975) concluded that the term dyslexia served little purpose other than to draw attention to the problems encountered by those experiencing severe reading disability. It was argued that the term dyslexia: 'serves little useful purpose other than to draw attention to the fact that the problem of these children can be chronic and severe. It is not susceptible to precise operational definition; nor does it indicate any clearly defined course of treatment' (p. 268).

The following year, Yule (1976) stated that the dyslexia label: 'has served its function in drawing attention to children who have great difficulty in mastering the arts of reading, writing and spelling but its continued use invokes emotions which often prevent rational discussion and scientific investigation' (p. 166).

Four decades later, the dyslexia label is once again being challenged. Despite huge advances in genetics, neuroscience, cognitive science, psychology and educational evaluation, the charges against the label are still much the same. While attractive to lobby groups, policy-makers and those with learning difficulties of various kinds, the term is still employed in multiple ways. These render it more difficult to arrive at clear and consistent understandings that can operate across academic disciplines, professional specialisms and lay interests.

There continues to be no value in a diagnosis for the purposes of treatment or intervention, and no justification to favour resourcing for dyslexic over other poor readers.

The case for the construct is often made forcefully through appeals to the emotions. Without the dyslexia label, it is argued:

a) children would be written off by their teachers as stupid or lazy;

b) the public's (and, therefore, the politicians') interest in tackling reading difficulties would be reduced;

c) we need this term in order to develop different interventions for different sorts of problems;

d) such labels are the only means to obtain extra resources; and

e) the label makes those with learning difficulties feel better about themselves.

Such problems are all too real and do need to be addressed. However, we should tackle these at their source rather than persisting with this nebulous construct. Certainly, even if the term dyslexia continues to be used loosely by researchers for studying reading difficulties, it should not be employed as a label or diagnosis for individuals with learning difficulties, at least until such time that we are able to resolve the conceptual and scientific issues raised in this chapter.

3

Response to Julian Elliott

Rod Nicolson

Introduction

In this response to Elliott's introductory chapter, my aim is indeed to move 'Beyond the Dyslexia Debate', to identify areas of common ground and areas of disagreement, with the intention of developing a convincing and coherent programme that will allow us to move forward. For such an initiative to succeed, it is necessary to demonstrate that it will be valuable for all the stakeholders in education, the children, the parents, the teachers and the funders of education. Whereas Elliott presents a pessimistic view, I take the opposite approach, that it is now timely to make major changes that will indeed benefit all the stakeholders, transforming the value and the effectiveness of education, equipping the new generation for the uncertainties and change of the twenty-first century.

The outline of my response is as follows. First I will summarize Elliott's and my initial contributions in order to identify the areas of agreement and of disagreement. I conclude that we are in substantial agreement over the problems but in complete disagreement over the solutions!

Following two further anecdotes I put forward my analysis of why the educational system appears to be 'broken'. It is not the fault of the teachers, the funders, the parents, society, the children or even the government. It is the fault of the implicit 'deficit' model that permeates the educational system, and, indeed, society in general.

I take particular issue with the current orthodoxy that if children are not ready to learn to read at five years, then reading instruction should start earlier. I argue that in fact reading instruction should start later, with the early school years focusing on the development of the executive function capabilities and the positive attitude to learning needed to succeed. Such an approach will allow almost all children to thrive at school, save significant resources, which can be effectively applied elsewhere, and will lead to happier schools and better performance. This analysis underpins my conclusions.

Elliott's initial chapter

Elliott starts with the scenario of a hypothetical family whose child has been diagnosed with dyslexia, and outlines the path from hope that the diagnosis will lead to positive change, to disillusion when the reality turns out differently. He presents ten different possible definitions of dyslexia, concluding that none of them is supportable theoretically, or of definite value for diagnostic purposes. He also considers the phonological deficit framework in some detail, highlighting the fact that recent theorists appear to have subsumed within in its framework three cognitive capabilities: phonological awareness, working memory and speed of processing. He considers other approaches, namely genetics and neuroscience, and other symptoms – motor difficulties and visual problems – very briefly. He concludes that the label 'dyslexia' is 'guilty as charged', that is:

> One of the most pervasive misunderstandings of dyslexia is that a diagnosis will inform educational and clinical intervention. The reality is that, were our hypothetical family to receive such a diagnosis, it would not, in itself, offer additional information about how the child might be best helped.
>
> There continues to be no value in a diagnosis for the purposes of treatment or intervention, and no justification to favour resourcing for dyslexic over other poor readers.

I do agree with these statements as a description of the 'situation on the ground', and as a clear statement of the problems of the current system. Overall, it is difficult not to be rather depressed on reading Elliott's long lament as to the lack of rigour, lack of clarity, and lack of usefulness of the thirty years of research based around dyslexia as a phonological difficulty.

I am relieved that I have not done Elliott an injustice in my initial anecdote. You may recall I reported Elliott's central concern that there is a three-step process to supporting dyslexia: Step 1, diagnosis; Step 2, educational plan; Step 3, implementation. Elliott raises fundamental concerns about all three: the theoretical basis of Step 1; the dissociation between Steps 1 and 2; and the likely outcome of Step 3. Consequently the three-step system is incoherent theoretically, unsustainable financially, and ineffective individually. No wonder he is concerned. It is difficult to disagree with his clear demonstration that the system is broken, not fit for purpose.

Unfortunately, that is where Elliott's analysis stops. In the remainder of my contribution, I consider how to move forward.

My initial chapter

I set myself the challenging target of addressing the four central issues for research and practice on dyslexia. What is dyslexia? Why does dyslexia lead to reading disability? What is the most cost-effective solution to reading support for all, and what is the role of an educational psychologist in dyslexia support? In addressing these issues I made the key distinction between the theoretical basis of dyslexia as a specific learning difficulty (SpLD) as against the applied basis of dyslexia as a reading disability (RD), and argued that one of the major reasons for confusion in the area was the failure even to recognize the difference.

I then developed the position that in terms of the underlying learning difference, dyslexia is well characterized as a slightly reduced speed of neural commitment, which delays automatization of skills, leads to difficulties in unlearning bad (and superseded) habits, and delays the development of the new neural circuitry needed for executive function and for reading.

These difficulties result in the dyslexic child not being classroom-ready or reading-ready at the time of initial reading instruction, and the attempts to accelerate the reading to deal with the reading disability go catastrophically wrong, leading to continual failure and chronic reading-related stress. This leads to toxic learned helplessness which substantially disables learning in the reading context. In short, the RD is at least partly an acquired disability, resulting from the mismatch between the child's learning readiness and the timing of the instructional approach taken.

These analyses are based around the developmental context of learning, are novel within the dyslexia context, and are not addressed by Elliott's review. The analyses allowed me to construct an initial answer to three of the four questions I raised, but I deferred my answer on the solution. Clearly, if I argue that the reading disability is acquired, it is incumbent on me to say how we can avoid this catastrophe, how we can help all children to learn to read effectively and successfully. This is my aim in the remainder of this contribution, but first I need to consider whether Elliott is likely to agree with me. What are our areas of agreement and disagreement?

Areas of agreement and disagreement

I will start by detailing areas of agreement and then differences between us. For the sake of clarity, I present these in tabular form. This does require some over-simplification, but allows me to present the full picture at a glance. I end up with ten agreements and five disagreements.

With the exception of the value of diagnosing dyslexia, Elliott's answers to these key questions are pretty much the same as any mainstream US dyslexia researcher. It is my answers that are actually exceptional, but not without justification, as I have argued earlier.

Issue	Julian Elliott	Rod Nicolson
1. Dyslexia is a highly prevalent and deeply distressing condition.	Yes	Yes
2. Is a diagnosis of dyslexia valuable to the child and family?	Useful for reducing trauma but not for treatment	Yes
3. Is it fair to provide additional support for dyslexic children as against other poor readers?	No	No
4. Should we attempt to support all poor readers?	Yes	Yes
5. Is there a single cause of dyslexia?	No	No
6. Are phonological difficulties and speed difficulties associated with dyslexia?	Yes	Yes
7. Are phonological difficulties and speed difficulties associated with other poor readers?	Yes	Yes
8. Is the current approach to supporting the reading of dyslexic children effective?	No	No
9. Is prevention better than cure?	Yes	Yes
10. Is the current system broken?	Yes	Yes
11. Is the 'diagnosis' of dyslexia a waste of resources?	Yes	No
12. Can we characterize differences between dyslexic and other poor readers?	No	Yes
13. Is learning the key theoretical construct?	No	Yes
14. Is teaching the key applied construct?	Yes	No
15. Is there a constructive answer to the diagnosis-to-teaching puzzle?	No	Yes

Toward a rapprochement

Let us consider, therefore, whether there is indeed any opportunity for a rapprochement between these approaches, an opportunity to move forward toward an effective agenda for change, so as to answer question 15 positively.

Anecdote 1 – ski evolutif

Seymour Papert (1980) caused something of a revolution in educational theory in his book *MindStorms* when he confronted the issue of how to help children learn mathematics. Consider skills in which we are all expert, skills like walking and speaking, seeing and listening. These in fact require a high degree of skill, and take a long time for children to learn. Children do get thousands of hours' practice at talking and walking, but they are mostly self-taught. The world provides the learning environment!

Papert advocated wholesale changes in education, putting forward the telling analogy of ski evolutif. In the 1960s, beginning skiers were issued with skis 10 per cent longer than their height. Because the skis were long and cumbersome, it was necessary to teach the beginners a method of controlling them, the snow-plough, and the snow-plough turn. Once the skiers became more expert, they were then able to learn the much smoother parallel turn method. To do this, they had to unlearn the snow-plough turn, and learning to ski well was therefore a slow, expensive and frustrating business.

The revolution occurred when it was noticed that children with short skis seemed to just learn the parallel turn naturally, without bothering with the snow-plough. Ski evolutif, in which beginners were issued with short skis and taught parallel turns from the start, was born. Learning to ski is now simple and natural.

'How do children learn to speak French?', he asked. The best way is to live in France, to be immersed in the culture and the language. Surely the same thing would be true for mathematics. What we need is a 'Mathland' where mathematical principles are all around us. He designed the computer language Logo for children to use, together with a programmable 'turtle' which could be programmed to travel forwards, backwards, left and right, so that they could experiment, and learn from their mistakes. He reasoned that this would give children the 'natural' learning environment, so that they would discover mathematical ideas for themselves.

While Papert's ideas were probably forty years ahead of their time (but are now feasible with the advent of pervasive mobile computing) his book made a great impression on me, not least because I had myself suffered the trauma of the traditional skiing instruction, wrestling with giant skis and not managing a decent turn in my whole first week. And learning the bad habit of snow-ploughing interfered with the parallel turn. I didn't enjoy it. I got stuck with snow-plough and couldn't progress. For snow-plough turn think 'phonological decoding', a good servant but a bad master.

Anecdote 2: The Southern Rail timetabling fiasco

On a lighter note, I report my memory of a doomed attempt to rationalize a railway timetable around 2009. Southern Rail had the franchise for passenger trains from the south coast to London. This is a heavily populated region with complex junctions and outdated rail infrastructure. Southern Rail suffered continual failure to meet the stipulated targets in terms of frequency and timekeeping, largely because a problem anywhere in the rail network led to knock-on effects throughout. After careful systems analysis they determined that a 10 per cent reduction in frequency would lead to very substantial benefits, and proposed to have higher capacity, less frequent trains with high reliability. This proposal led to an outcry (and was rejected) because it represented a breach of the initial contract to meet the targets. The service continues to suffer intrinsic reliability problems.

It is possible to view this issue from two perspectives. From the perspective of the taxpayer, equity between bidders for the franchise does clearly preclude the relaxation of constraints subsequent to securing the franchise. From the perspective of the smooth operation of the system (and therefore, ultimately, the commuter) the proposal appeared to me to make a lot of sense. A system that is run close to the limits of operational feasibility is a disaster waiting to happen. The outcry of the commuters appeared bafflingly irrational to me.

At an abstract, systems level, this appears to me to have clear resonance with the challenges of trying to get a child up to speed to learn to read at the target age.

If we have a system for teaching reading that proves beyond the abilities of 25 per cent of teachers to implement and beyond the abilities of 25 per cent of the children to achieve, then it is the system itself that must be changed, not the teachers nor the children!

Systems analysis: The education system

Let us consider briefly the political currents that have resulted from this broken teaching system. Elliott criticizes the emphasis of many researchers on searching for the underlying brain-based causes of dyslexia. US researchers have no alternative! The reason that US researchers have to do this is that in the USA in order to receive federal support it is a requirement that a developmental disorder is in some way intrinsic (that is, brain-based) rather than produced by the environment. Consequently, for political reasons, there just has to be a neural basis, politics first and science second.

Second, Elliott criticizes the emphasis on IQ-based diagnostic methods. There is (or at least was) no alternative! The reason for IQ-based diagnosis is that it is a statutory requirement that a formal diagnosis is made by a suitably qualified professional, and this is a diagnosis of dyslexia, rather than (as most educationalists would prefer) a diagnosis for dyslexia, taking into account each individual child's learning abilities, strengths, weaknesses, motives and passions, system first and science second.

The remainder of this commentary is aimed directly at the goal of outlining a new and better system that leads to less stress and more success for teachers, children and parents.

Toward the effective learning of reading

Supporting each child in learning to read

We are now finally in a position to consider how best to support dyslexic children (and other children) in learning to read. The methods depend, of course, on the age of the child. Indeed, I will argue that the requirements are quite different depending on the child's length of experience of reading failure. I will first consider support at junior school since that is the traditional age at which dyslexia is identified.

Junior school support (8 years plus)

It is important to recognize that by this age the child will have had extensive experience of reading instruction. Of necessity, therefore, for a child still to be in need of support, the phonics learning experiences will not have been happy ones. We are therefore attempting to build on a 'brownfield site', where there is already the detritus of a history of failed and aversive learning experiences. It is crucial to be aware of the sensitivities arising from such previous failure.

For children with extended experience of reading failure, the very presence of a reading context will lead to their being context-dependent, reminding them of previous failures, which will therefore increase the stressfulness of the situation. Recent neuroscience research (Schwabe and Wolf 2013) has shown that stress leads to a bias towards procedural (existing habits) rather than declarative processing, and therefore severely curtails the cognitive resources available for the learning task. If this negative experience is consistently repeated this exacerbates the effects of the previous failures to create a 'learned helplessness' situation (Abramson, Seligman and Teasdale 1978) which effectively prevents learning and creates a major aversion to any context associated with these traumas.

Consequently, if there is any danger of context-dependent learned helplessness, it is crucial to change the context of learning. Individual support may therefore lead initially to good progress, but once the failure context is reactivated, the individual support also triggers the toxic context. In my book *Positive Dyslexia* I outline a series of strategies for avoiding any such 'mental abscesses', from 'working to strengths' to use of positive apps, to a variety of methods of retraining the brain to associate reading with success. Unfortunately there is too little space available here to reiterate these suggestions.

Fortunately, it is evident that the most cost-effective, and most sensible approach is to avoid getting into this situation at all. This is of course the standard approach: to provide proactive support so as to get the infant up to speed by the time reading instruction starts. However, as I have made clear above, and re-emphasize below, I consider that this well-intentioned approach is actually counter-productive, and likely to exacerbate rather than eliminate the subsequent problems. My anecdote regarding Southern Trains provides the rationale. There is simply too much to develop before five years of age, especially if a child suffers disadvantage socially or environmentally, or has delayed neural commitment cognitively. Focusing on only one aspect of skill development will not only delay other natural skill developments, but may actively interfere, leading to major subsequent developmental problems.

First school support

It is important to realize that it is not just skills that are being developed from the age of three to six years. This is a period of extraordinary cognitive development for the child, in which he or she effectively builds a completely new language-based, cognitive operating system to replace the more primitive sensory-motor operating system.

Over this period, as Piaget, Vygotsky, Bruner and other major developmental psychologists have shown, the child learns to internalize speech, creating a basis for thought, to develop the ability to inhibit natural reaction, to sit still and listen, to start to reason, to develop the ability to store verbal information in working memory, to maintain goals in memory while doing other tasks, to develop the theory of mind about other people's needs, and in general to develop a whole, integrated set of executive function skills that build the foundation for all subsequent learning.

If these skills are not solidly developed, teaching methods that presuppose there is a solid foundation for this 'controlled processing' can lead to catastrophic failures of learning which interfere not only with the specific skills being taught, but with the much more important process of building the operating system.

The key reading requirements here are threefold: letter fluency, sight word fluency, and writing, together with what Marie Clay (1993) calls reading readiness. There is a further set of 'classroom readiness' executive function (EF) skills, both the cool EFs of cognitive control and the hot EFs of social/emotional control. These skills, more properly described as the executive control processing architecture, develop naturally, but can be accelerated by appropriate, natural interventions (Diamond 2012).

To avoid loading the immature cognitive system with non-natural learning requirements, at this age it is best therefore to rely on the natural learning capabilities of a young child. These comprise: imitating actions, playing, naming concrete objects, social interactions, and rote learning. More complex skills, such as reliance on working memory, inhibition of spontaneous actions, abstract learning, and ability to learn in groups silently by just listening, have not yet developed to the stage where they can form a solid foundation for traditional schooling.

Changes to the school system

It is now time to confront the implications of the framework I have derived. I have argued that dyslexic children, and children with other risk factors such as disadvantaged background, will have delays in the development of the executive function and reading-related skills that underpin classroom readiness and reading readiness. We have seen that attempts to improve any one of the necessary skills and circuits in isolation are likely to be ineffective (or, worse, counter-productive, leading to the need for unlearning). We have seen that Torgesen's studies showed that it was possible to intervene successfully at the early school stage, but that this was a very costly approach, with eighty-eight hours' individual support per child.

We are therefore left with the conundrum of how can we intervene earlier to help dyslexic children acquire the necessary reading readiness skills, when so doing may well adversely affect the classroom readiness skills. I advocate two approaches: using personalized apps, and delaying the start of reading instruction.

The transformative opportunities of mobile computing

In my book, *Positive Dyslexia* (Nicolson 2015), I make a strong case that we can transform education by applying the positive approach. Here, however, I limit my analysis to how we can succeed within the constraints of the current educational model.

The core difficulty for children learning to read is that they have to make the transition from the natural learning processes that permeate early development to the artificial learning of the instructional classroom: learning abstract concepts lacking real world meaning, learning without any intrinsic motivation, learning by being told, learning without any reciprocity. This is a major challenge for anyone, but especially for a young child whose underpinning executive function circuits are not yet sufficiently developed.

My 'ski evolutif' anecdote provides the key dimension to transforming the process. For ski evolutif, substitute mobile computing, the availability of personalized apps on tablets and smartphones. These make it possible to apply the principles of natural learning, one-to-one, personal, enjoyable, immersive learning, to the classroom.

The transformative power of individual apps is that they can be used to personalize children's learning experience within school (with resources created for each child) and also home-based (giving parents and carers the opportunity to provide appropriate, synchronized support and conditions of unstressed, individualized, quality time).

It is of course unrealistic to expect this educational revolution to take place immediately, and indeed a strong case can be made that this will further disadvantage the already disadvantaged. The default process in school and life is what Stanovich (1986) called the Matthew Effect, that is the rich get richer and the poor poorer. In other words those with more mental, social or financial resources tend to gain more from new opportunities. What would be ideal would be interventions that actually prove more effective for those in the greatest need. Interestingly, interventions for executive function satisfy exactly this criterion as highlighted by Diamond (2012), as discussed in the initial chapter.

Delaying reading instructional age

Rather than trying to hot-house the reading process, so that no child is left behind, why do we not just delay the start of reading instruction, so that almost all schoolchildren are both reading ready and classroom ready?

This is of course not a novel suggestion, even though it is counter to current educational practice. For example, a recent perspectives article in the *New Scientist* (Whitebread and Bingham 2013) summarized the concerns as to the 'schoolification' of childhood. What is novel is that I have produced overwhelming multi-disciplinary evidence to support a coherent, science-based explanation.

In Scandinavia, compulsory school starts when the child is seven years old, considerably later than in England or the USA. As noted earlier, the PISA review (OECD 2010), ranked the UK twenty-fifth for reading, a considerable fall from the 2006 rating, whereas the Scandinavian countries are traditionally among the top performers.

It is of course not appropriate to compare these outcome data directly. Advocates for the early phonics-based approach argue that the Scandinavian languages are more regular than English (this is true for Finnish, but Swedish is by no means regular) and therefore easier to learn. These advocates do not explain why it is that the Scandinavian countries do delay reading instruction, since the logical inference would be that the Scandinavians should start even earlier than in the USA! In fact, in Sweden and Norway almost all children attend kindergarten prior to compulsory attendance in Grade 1, but the kindergarten curriculum emphasizes social, emotional, and aesthetic development rather than early literacy acquisition. That is, the Scandinavian countries focus on the development of executive function skills before formal reading instruction.

However, comparison with reading in different languages is not sufficient in itself. What is needed is converging evidence from other studies. In particular it would be valuable to be able to compare the outcomes of reading instruction in the same country, with one approach having a reading instruction age (RIA) of seven years, and the other being the standard RIA of five years. This is precisely what was undertaken in a recently published New Zealand study (Suggate, Schaughency and Reese 2013). The study compared 283 children in Steiner schools (RIA seven years) with those in state schools (RIA five years). The authors were able to correct for many variables: receptive vocabulary, reported parental income and education, school-community affluence, classroom instruction, home literacy environment, reading self-concept, and age, and concluded in effect that the Steiner school children lagged behind in reading at 8 years (of course), but by 11 years had caught up in reading and were slightly ahead in comprehension. The authors correctly urge caution in the interpretation of results, but at the very least the study does indicate that delaying reading instruction does not lead to an enduring deficit (as might be expected from the Matthew Effect).

Unfortunately, the published paper did not give a breakdown of the effects in terms of initial reading ability scores. Consequently, I contacted Sebastian Suggate to enquire whether he had such information. In fact the authors had undertaken this analysis, but it was not included in the paper in order to save journal space. The results are shown in Figure 3.1. It may be seen that indeed, as hoped, the lowest quartile originally actually benefited the most from the delay in reading instruction (top panel), with reading developing slowly, but catching up with the control group of poor readers by age ten (who have plateaued out at around sixty), and actually get up to the average (100) mean by the age of twelve. The average readers also show an eventual benefit for the delayed reading instruction, leading to a score of around 120.

If we take the above studies as converging evidence supporting the view that delaying the start of formal instruction is at least not disastrous, we are left with the very clear pattern.

First, delaying RIA does not disadvantage the high achieving readers. They will learn to read on their own accord. Second, delaying RIA appears to have no adverse effects for normally developing children. They will certainly catch up by eleven years. Third, delaying RIA will be of considerable benefit to children with delayed neural commitment, or disadvantaged children. They will be able to keep up with the class instruction, and will therefore not suffer from the stress and failure that results in anxiety disorders and learned helplessness.

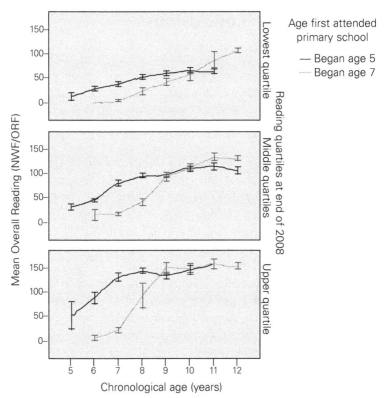

FIGURE 3.1 *Reading outcomes for different achievement levels*

Fourth, delaying reading instruction to seven years allows early school to focus on key skills including those underpinning reading readiness, school readiness and executive function. Fifth, the costs to educational attainment of delaying reading instruction are therefore negligible and probably negative (that is benefit). Sixth, there are clear financial benefits to the education system of delaying reading instruction, in that there is no need to undertake costly individual reading interventions. Seventh, the benefits to the individual children and their families of delaying reading instruction are immeasurable, transforming their life expectations.

Conclusions

In conclusion, I agree with Elliott that he has correctly laid out the many pieces of the puzzle relating to the need for an effective support system for dyslexic children and for other poor readers. The pieces do not fit within the simple linear, three-step 'assessment – individual education plan – support implementation' system currently in use.

Unlike Elliott, I believe that there is a simple and obvious solution, but it requires inclusion of the further (implicit) dimension, the 'elephant in the room' that Elliott has not discussed, namely the 'deficit model' that permeates education. In my view, a simple reconfiguration of the educational system will lead to immense benefits to children, parents, teachers, and attainment both for the cognitive and the affective (emotional) state of all concerned.

My explanatory framework is broad and brings in a range of constructs including learning differences, executive function, affective state, brownfield learning, and interactions between learning abilities and teaching methods. I make a strong case that by the time dyslexia is diagnosed, considerable damage has already been done, and that this damage interferes with the learning process, essentially disabling reading even with exceptional teaching.

My solution to this problem is twofold: first to develop positive teaching methods based around humans' natural learning capabilities, and second to delay the start of formal reading instruction for at least one year so as to allow the fuller development of the executive function neural networks and the pre-reading skills so that by the start of instruction all children are classroom-ready and reading-ready. This approach should be augmented by the development of individualized apps to make learning natural and stress-free.

This system is designed to reduce substantially the number of children who fall behind in the reading targets. One also needs to have a rescue system for children who do fall behind (and indeed the large numbers who have become reading disabled in the current system). Here, there is urgent need for a much more effective approach to the three-step cycle. In particular, the initial assessment step should surely attempt to establish why it is that a given child is struggling, and how best they can be supported in relearning how to succeed. For this a combination of at least four approaches is needed: reading (which skills and knowledge appear to be weak); executive function (how adequate are these capabilities); affect (whether there are school phobias, mental abscesses, and what triggers them); and strengths (what the child is good at, what they enjoy doing) should be undertaken. I consider that there is an increasing need for higher quality, expert 'assessment for dyslexia' rather than 'assessment of dyslexia'.

Development of the necessary tools and procedures for joined-up individual assessment and support for children with reading difficulties will lead to a transformation of the effectiveness of education and the quality of life of all children, dyslexic or not. The increase in effectiveness will in turn release further resources that will drive further progress. This is a worthy goal.

4

Response to Rod Nicolson

Julian Elliott

Different agendas?

Anyone reading the opening chapters produced by Nicolson and me will surely realize that we are pursuing somewhat different agendas. Nicolson seeks to produce an overarching theory that explains his own particular understanding of dyslexia. In contrast, I would wish to differentiate between the laudable scholarly pursuit of developing and testing a particular theoretical account of a condition that some would wish to call dyslexia, and the responsibility of researchers to guide and support practitioners and clinicians in the use of diagnostic labels that have clear and demonstrable scientific credibility and significant practical utility for action. One of my personal problems with regard to the dyslexia debate is that I have struggled to communicate this distinction sufficiently. Thus, scholars, confident of their own understandings of the term, have been genuinely puzzled by my criticisms, clearly not grasping the point that their particular perspectives are not necessarily shared by other, equally confident researchers and clinicians. It is principally because dyslexia is so variously understood and operationalized that Elena Grigorenko and I concluded in *The Dyslexia Debate* (2014) that this is not a helpful diagnostic term.

Areas of agreement

There are several aspects of Nicolson's account that I find very helpful. First, I agree that it appears that the currently dominant phonological theory is unlikely to be able to account for all reading difficulties. Certainly, it looks as if greater credence needs to be given to problems of visual attention (as opposed to visual processing), at least in a small proportion of cases. Second, the affective and conative barriers to learning experienced by those who struggle at school are all too real and must not be overlooked. Not only does continued struggle to make progress typically lead children to experience a sense of hopelessness and helplessness, but their need to protect their sense of worth in the eyes of others can lead to their public (and private) dismissal of the value of the activities themselves, with a concomitant reduction in engagement and persistence (Covington 1992).

Of course, negative reactions of this kind are not unique to decoding or, indeed, to other aspects of literacy such as reading comprehension and written expression. A significant proportion of children will struggle in various aspects of schooling because of general intellectual difficulties. Others will encounter unique problems in specific disciplines such as mathematics or science but be comparatively strong in other curricular areas. Some will experience attentional, organizational, and self-regulatory problems. Others will have poor fine or gross motor skills which, unfortunately, are sometimes associated with less productive peer relations (Leonard and Hill 2014). However, a difficulty in decoding ability, as Nicolson rightly indicates, is often particularly stressful for the child and we certainly need to work hard to maximize children's sense of agency in tackling such problems.

Areas of disagreement

I am a little confused by Nicolson's notion of dyslexia as a specific learning difficulty (p. 67). For many psychologists, this term is used to describe any one of a variety of particular difficulties which are perceived as inconsistent with the individual's overall functioning. Decoding difficulty can be identified as one of these, as may also be a specific problem with maths, motor, or other skills. In places, Nicolson seems to see dyslexia as one of several SpLDs, but, rather puzzlingly, he also states that, 'In the U.K., the "correct" description of dyslexia is "Specific Learning Difficulties"' and he contends that SpLD 'is the intrinsic brain difference characteristic of dyslexia'. So now we have dyslexia, SpLD, and reading difficulty. I would question whether we are clear enough about these distinctions to use them confidently and consensually, whether this clarifies our under-standings in ways that are scientifically supportable, and whether these differentiated terms are helpful as a guide to action.

In trying to grasp the tenets of Nicolson's theory, I became quite confused about how his account actually takes us forward in our understanding of developmental difficulties in general, and reading difficulties in particular. Nicolson argues that his notion of delayed neural commitment can apply to a whole range of developmental disabilities, and indeed, to normally developing children, so it seems that his explanation is not unique to dyslexia. There are clearly many differing types of developmental disorder with much overlap of symptoms. Inattention, physical clumsiness, poor organization, weak memory, impaired language skills, and difficulty in the automization of skills are common to many of these. Given this overlap, it is difficult, therefore, to draw upon the presence or absence of these to arrive at a differential diagnosis.

As a former teacher and clinician, I continually return to consid-eration as to how I might make sense of, and as a result help, a child who is struggling to make progress with reading. So where does Nicolson's theory take me in my attempts to make a difference? Well, it does offer one possible account, tapping rather briefly (perhaps a little too briefly?) into some of psychology's most powerful perspec-tives over the past fifty years. However, we should be mindful that there are many other scholars offering alternative theories who also readily cite such research findings to support their views.

As is noted throughout this book, of great importance in any account of learning difficulty is our understanding that early reading failure often results in an adverse emotional reaction that inhibits the drive and motivation required of the child to overcome, at least as far as possible, substantial challenges. Whatever one's views on the dyslexia debate, there is surely no disagreement about this. The key issue in respect of Nicolson's theory, seems to rests in his argument that formal schooling starts too early in the UK and that this leads many children to be hindered by their early negative experiences of literacy learning. When to commence formal instruction is an interesting question that requires an empirical answer but, notwithstanding the possible validity of Nicolson's position, we should not overlook the fact that problems that underpin reading disability are also encountered in societies in which children commence formal schooling at a later age.

To what extent do Nicolson's hypothetical and actual cases help to shed light on the issues under consideration? In his accounts, child A is described as the better reader. Here a diagnosis seems to have increased his sense of helplessness and reduced his willingness to seek to overcome his difficulties. Interestingly, although Child B is described as a poorer reader, the solution seems to have involved working in the area of number and computation. If this were true, one wonders about the extent to which Child A or Child B had severe reading problems. In my opinion, these cases serve to exemplify my point about the folly of using the dyslexia label to describe problems that range far beyond decoding.

Nicolson's personal anecdote about his early experiences of reading illustrates the difficulties that can be encountered where early reading experiences are not appropriate to the needs of the individual. However, as his account shows, the problem was merely temporary, and clearly, he did not have a serious reading disability. Inappropriate reading tuition will obviously affect the progress of some, if not all, children. However, this may prove to be a much greater problem for those children who would struggle whatever forms of instruction were provided. Thus, it has been repeatedly shown that approaches to the teaching of reading that emphasize whole language approaches are particularly ineffective for those who experience difficulty in the acquisition of literacy skills (Tunmer 2015). However, it should be noted that such teaching approaches appear to *exacerbate*, rather than *cause*, the child's difficulties.

So, where does Nicolson's account take us in our current endeavours to help those with reading difficulties? Well, I, like most researchers in this field, would certainly go along with his argument that complex reading disability is primarily a brain-based condition, although I would note that others offer alternative accounts of the particular mechanisms involved. My primary concern, however, is whether Nicolson would wish to contend that his use of the term dyslexia here applies to some or all of those with persistent and severe decoding problems. The latter reflects the position of most of the world's leading reading researchers. Of course, if we took this stance, when working with a child with significant decoding problems, we would not need to engage in detailed assessment procedures to determine whether or not the child is dyslexic. If, on the other hand, Nicolson is arguing that only some very poor decoders have this brain-based disorder while others (garden-variety poor readers?) are not dyslexic, we return to the thorny problem of a) how do we make this distinction? and b) what purpose would it serve to do this?

It is important to emphasize (and to continue emphasizing) that for almost all published studies in which the term 'dyslexia' is employed, it is the behavioural manifestation that is the primary determinant of the label. The confusion around this point renders it all too easy to confuse the use of dyslexia as a generic term with those many clinical/educational situations where it is used to differentiate a group located *within* a larger population of poor decoders. When Nicolson states, for example, that there is a 50 per cent chance of a child being dyslexic if a parent or sibling is dyslexic, he is drawing upon findings from studies that have typically selected participants on the basis of their poor decoding ability. The reality is that there is a 50 per cent chance of a child having a reading disability if the parent or sibling has a reading disability. This is a point that I make in my opening chapter, of course, but it is one worth restating here as it is crucial to understanding the dyslexia debate.

The role of motor skills in dyslexia

Nicolson is well known for his emphasis upon deficits in motor skills as indicators of dyslexia, and the use of special exercises to tackle what he describes as cerebellar problems (Nicolson 2005). However, the evidence here does not stack up.

It is widely accepted that motor skill deficits are more often found in those with various developmental disorders (Westerndorp et al. 2011), although prevalence figures vary widely across studies. Some have found group differences between those with/without reading difficulties (Fawcett, Nicolson and Maclagan 2001; Ramus, Pidgeon and Frith 2003; Wolff et al. 1995), while others have not (Kronbichler, Hutzler and Wimmer 2002; Savage et al. 2005; White et al. 2006). Furthermore, even when accepting evidence for comorbidity, one must be careful about concluding that there is a causal relationship of some kind. As noted in my earlier chapter, in the case of reading disability, there is little empirical support for this suggestion (Rochelle and Talcott 2006; Savage 2004; Chaix et al. 2007). Problems of balance have been found in comparative studies of poor and normal readers although the size of the difference varies greatly from one investigation to another. Interestingly, the differences in reading scores between the groups in these studies appear not to be related to the size of the difference in the balance scores (Rochelle and Talcott 2006). Loras et al. (2014) found no strong statistical relationship between postural control (balance) and measures of reading, cognitive functioning, or attention across a sample of normally developing 100 young adults. These authors concluded that the link between motor control and reading disability is: 'almost certainly accounted for by associations with processing domains other than reading, including those in which deficits are considered symptoms of other developmental disorders. Given the high diagnostic overlap between developmental disorders, symptoms of impairment in motor control may be better accounted for as non-specific symptoms that represent the overlapping dimensions of disability risk' (Loras et al. 2014: 7).

Since the days of Binet, educational psychologists have sought to predict future academic performance (Elliott 2003). In relation to reading, what is the value of doing this? Obviously, one would imagine that if we could identify who will later demonstrate reading difficulties we would be able to provide additional (and noting Nicolson's perceptive comment, appropriate) support at an early age (Al Otaiba and Fuchs 2006). There are two avenues here. First, we can consider who may be at risk of developing problems given normal educational experiences. Second, we can identify those who are not only at risk but also those who will struggle even if they were to be given additional help. Here, very intensive support is likely to be necessary. To what extent, therefore, does the consideration of a child's motor skill development help in this?

i) The role of motor skills in identifying children at risk

Many studies have examined the extent to which the presence of early motor difficulties can predict subsequent reading difficulty, with advocates such as Crombie and Reid (2009) arguing that early difficulties with crawling may be an indicator of later reading problems. Such a belief would appear to underpin the development of screening measures such as the Dyslexia Early Screening Test (DEST, 2nd edn) (Nicolson and Fawcett 2004). This measure, designed for children aged 4 and a half to 6 and a half, consists of twelve subtests, includes measures of rapid naming, memory, shape copying, postural stability, and bead threading. Interestingly, there is a parallel measure for use in the United States containing almost the same items. *Ready to Learn* (Fawcett et al. 2004) which is described as a tool for the identification of children at risk of reading difficulty, rather than dyslexia. Are these terms being treated synonymously, therefore? If so, how is this squared with the assertions Nicolson makes in his chapter?

While there tends to be some validity to the argument that motor difficulties may sometimes signal subsequent literacy problems, the evidence is weak. Barth et al. (2010), for example, found no meaningful relationship between motor items on the DEST and either reading ability or the children's response to subsequent instruction. Typically, there are many much stronger predictors of reading disability than motor functioning. Thus, in a study of the DEST, Simpson and Everatt (2005) found that subtests measuring auditory perception, rapid naming, and knowledge of lower-case letter names, proved to be better predictors of reading and spelling performance than the total test score which, of course, included the motor skills items. Examining the progress of a sample of young children from families with a history of reading disability, Thompson et al. (2015) examined a variety of different predictors over four annual time periods from the age of 3 and a half. Three measures of fine motor skill from the Movement Assessment Battery for Children 2 (Henderson, Sugden and Barnett 2007) were included alongside tests of language, non-verbal IQ, phonological awareness, rapid naming, executive skills (including spatial working memory), letter knowledge, word reading and spelling. The best predictors proved to be the same as those found in other studies: difficulties in respect of letter knowledge and phonological awareness. Motor skills appeared not to be important predictors, adding to the best-fit predictive model at only one time point when the children were aged six. In trying to explain this particular occurrence, Thompson et al. speculate that this may reflect the need for good pencil control at this age.

ii) Can motor skill performance help us identify those who will respond well when given extra assistance?

Difficulties with phonological awareness, rapid naming, vocabulary, and oral language skills have been identified as the most common cognitive attributes of poor responders (Fletcher et al. 2011; Al Otaiba and Fuchs 2002; Nelson, Benner and Gonzalez 2003; Torppa et al. 2013). There appears to be little evidence that measures of motor skill or executive functioning can add significantly to our ability to identify such children.

iii) Can perceptual-motor skill training help poor readers?

In relation to intervention, Nicolson is perhaps best known for his advocacy of perceptual-motor training interventions stemming from his theory of cerebellar impairment (Reynolds and Nicolson 2007; Reynolds, Nicolson and Hambly 2003). However, the general consensus is that the literature does not support their efficacy for those with reading difficulties (Kavale and Mattson 1983). Studies that appear to have produced supportive findings based upon various motor skill training initiatives have been widely criticized for their poor design (Bishop 2007; McArthur 2007; Rack 2003; Rack et al. 2007; Snowling and Hulme 2003; Hyatt, Stephenson and Carter 2009).

The role of executive functioning

In his opening chapter, Nicolson stresses how important it is that early educators should seek to support the development of the child's executive functioning. While I largely agree with this assertion, it should be noted that there is a big difference between identifying various components of learning that need to be recognized and fostered by teachers, and suggesting that working on the development of these with individual children will result in significant improvements for those exhibiting severe reading difficulties.

As noted in my earlier chapter, it would be an error, given current knowledge, to seek to ameliorate decoding problems by focusing primarily at the level of underlying cognitive processes (see also, Elliott and Resing 2015). Indeed, this prescription goes beyond decoding. A recent review of intervention studies designed to improve low-achieving students' academic performance by strengthening underlying cognitive processes concluded that there was insufficient evidence to support their use (Kearns and Fuchs 2013). Fundamentally, not only is there is any evidence to support the use of cognitive training for tackling reading difficulty generally, there is also no aptitude × treatment interaction whereby some poor readers (considered to be dyslexic) respond well to cognitive interventions, and other poor readers (considered to be non-dyslexic, garden-variety poor readers) are more effectively treated by means of an educationally based reading intervention (Fletcher 2009).

Others have suggested that assessment of cognitive processes has value in identifying which children will benefit from interventions. Recent studies (Miciak et al. 2014; Stuebing et al. 2015), however, have concluded that there is minimal value in assessing cognitive characteristics for the purpose of predicting how children will respond to intervention. Put simply, the additional information such assessments can provide, above and beyond that yielded by baseline reading assessment, is most likely not worth the investment of resources that is required.

In various ways, executive functions have become the new IQ, offering the promise of a new set of underlying processes that, if addressed, may result in academic gains (Elliott and Resing 2015). Executive functions are considered to be top-down cognitive processes that come into play when one must focus upon the completion of a task, rather than when one is providing an automatic, instinctive response. As Nicolson points out, core executive functions have been identified as a) the capacity to inhibit one's actions appropriately (to exercise self-control and to control one's selective attention); b) working memory; and c) cognitive flexibility (Diamond 2013). One problem, however, is that operational definitions of executive functions and approaches to their measurement, are far from consistent (Jacob and Parkinson 2015).

Findings from a number of studies have led to claims that executive functions play an important role in learning, and are related to performance in literacy (Bull and Scerif 2001; Borella, Carretti and Pelgrina 2010), mathematics (Duncan et al. 2010) and science (Nayfield, Fuccillo and Greenfield 2013). Unsurprisingly, there also appears to be a relationship between executive functioning and socioeconomic status in young children (Hackman et al. 2015).

However, as for other cognitive processes, it is questionable whether such functions should serve as the primary focus for predicting and tackling complex decoding difficulties. It appears that executive functioning in young children plays a greater role in maths performance than for basic decoding, most likely because the former makes greater demands upon more complex computational and problem-solving processes (Sasser, Bierman and Heinrichs 2015). In support of this suggestion, Thompson et al.'s (2015) study of predictors of reading disability in young children found that measures of executive functioning only contributed to the best-fitting model on one testing occasion, when the children were aged four-and-a-half. A year later, these items added nothing to the key predictors: a family history of reading difficulty, phonological awareness, and letter knowledge.

Furthermore, even where studies have shown an association with academic learning, we would still need to be cautious about causation and correlation. Thus, while a recent meta-analysis of school-based interventions indicated a moderate relationship (0.30) between executive function and academic achievement (note that this figure was approximately the same size for differing age groups) (Jacob and Parkinson, 2015), the evidence for any form of causal relationship was weak.

As I noted in my earlier chapter, those who struggle with severe reading difficulty are more likely than typical readers to demonstrate attentional, behavioural, and memory difficulties, factors that are seen to be components of executive functioning. Inattentiveness is highly likely to impact negatively upon the child's ability to profit from instruction and would appear to be a factor that inhibits the development of key literacy skills (Martinussen 2015; Miller et al. 2014). While it is quite possible that high-quality early years' education will help offset this risk and enable the child to develop their capacity for cognitive and behavioural self-regulation, not all would agree with confident assertions (Wass 2015; Diamond 2012, 2013) that cognitive training programmes are powerful means to improve executive functioning (Redick 2015). Even less rooted in evidence are claims that any such gains might subsequently boost the academic achievement of those with learning difficulties.

Interventions geared to improving working memory have been reported to lead to gains in performance in test situations (Holmes et al. 2009; Dunning, Holmes and Gathercole 2013) with some evidence that such training may impact upon neural connectivity (Astle et al. 2015). However, the design and statistical analyses of many intervention studies have been subjected to criticism (Kirk et al. 2015; Redick 2015) and there is limited evidence of transfer to memory tasks that differ substantially from the experimental format. For example, while Dunning, Holmes and Gathercole (2013) were able to demonstrate that working memory training improved performance on untrained tasks, the resultant gains appeared to have no impact upon classroom activities involving working memory. Thus, while we appear to be able to improve children's performance on experimental tasks (often computer-based activities), we have yet to obtain strong evidence that any such gains will improve 'real-world' working memory functioning. As Redick (2015) notes, there are neither adequate data, nor a sufficient theoretical explanation, to support arguments for transfer. Even more problematic for the issues examined in this book, there is no empirical support for the notion that working memory interventions can assist children with reading difficulties to become better decoders (Melby-Lervåg and Hulme 2013; Banales, Kohnen and McArthur, 2015). What this means in practice is that while it is useful to identify any difficulties with regards to a child's working memory, in order that this is not regularly overloaded, the belief that we can improve literacy difficulties by means of memory training programmes is not supported by the evidence available. Neither does working directly with teachers in 'real-world' situations seem to resolve this problem (Elliott et al. 2010). Of course, Nicolson may wish to argue that there is likely to be an effective procedure that has yet to be discovered. In response, my position continues to be that we must wait for such evidence to be provided before we dispense with those interventions that have currently proven to be the most effective.

In relation to inattention, of course it is very likely that helping the child to focus upon, and persist with, appropriate tasks will enable them to profit from structured literacy interventions. However, as is the case with working memory, there is insufficient evidence to support claims that attention-training programmes can result in academic gains for those with attention difficulties. Indeed, these may even serve as a distraction from more helpful academic interventions (Rabiner et al. 2010; Jacob and Parkinson, 2015).

Sasser, Bierman and Heinrichs (2015) differentiate between executive functions and learning-related behaviours. While these would seem to overlap to a significant degree, the latter are considered to represent adaptive responses to everyday classroom demands such as: following teacher instructions, engaging with interest, concentrating, and persisting even when struggling, or bored with, tasks. Such behaviours are associated with positive social behaviour and sound peer relations (Ladd and Dinella 2009). While it seems likely that maintaining a balanced focus upon fostering executive functioning and learning-related behaviours (however these are both understood) can prove beneficial for children's academic development (Sasser, Bierman and Heinrichs 2015), our current knowledge as to the specifics of systematic intervention is still rudimentary.

The key conclusion here is that whether we consider executive functioning, or various other cognitive processes, in those situations where children present with severe reading difficulties, current evidence continues to strongly support Vellutino et al.'s (2004) recommendation that we should focus upon educational, rather than cognitive, interventions.

The way forward

In presenting a hypothetical case of a child struggling to learn to read in my opening chapter, I have subsequently argued that seeking a diagnosis of dyslexia will not prove helpful, other than possibly offering some misguided relief to the child and their family. While acquiring the label is likely to please the recipient, we must remain cognisant of the deleterious implications of this Manichean dyslexic/non-dyslexic split for the many poor readers who are not so designated and who, as a result, may be perceived as less intellectually able, less motivated and less deserving of additional resources.

Helping struggling learners to feel more positive about themselves is a laudable and essential task, but arrival at any formal diagnosis should be predicated upon the operation of a rigorous, scientific procedure. While we must strive to ensure that those who struggle with literacy are not under-estimated, misattributed or ridiculed we should not require a diagnosis of dyslexia to achieve this outcome.

As noted above, even if we ignore conceptual irregularities we are left with another fundamental weakness. Such a diagnosis cannot directly assist us in determining a more effective intervention for the child concerned than would be offered for a 'non-dyslexic' poor reader. This does not mean that the child who struggles to acquire literacy cannot be helped. Thankfully, there is vast scientific literature indicating that significant gains can be made by many struggling readers. This is dealt with in detail in *The Dyslexia Debate* (Elliott and Grigorenko 2014) and the key steps are briefly summarized below:

1 Use a response to intervention approach that identifies any child who is struggling with literacy at as an early an age as possible. The particular difficulties that the child encounters

(accurate decoding, fluent decoding, reading comprehension, spelling, written expression, handwriting) should be clearly identified. The fundamental issue here is that assessment is undertaken for the purpose of guiding intervention, not for the purposes of classification or diagnosis.

2   Additional resourcing should be determined primarily by the child's response to the assistance that they have been given, rather than the outcomes of a labelling process. If the child continues to struggle after having received additional assistance, they should be provided with more frequent and intense help in smaller group and individualized settings.

3   The interventions used for any particular difficulty will only be those that have strong scientific support based upon rigorous and sustained trials. Given current knowledge about intervention for decoding difficulties, these will typically involve an emphasis upon the acquisition of basic reading skills using a structured approach involving small steps, reinforcement, and an emphasis upon automatization, although such instruction should be situated within a broad and balanced programme of literacy development.

Of course, in planning a broader educational programme, it is also important to consider the nature of the child's cognitive and linguistic skills and any affective or motivational factors that are likely to impair their learning and development. Often this function will be undertaken by skilled teachers although additional assessment by specialists, where resources permit, may also prove fruitful.

The role of intellectual assessment for poor readers is often misunderstood. Rather than being used to identify possible discrep-ancies between IQ and decoding ability for the purpose of diagnosis, its primary contribution is to help ensure that the general educational diet presented to the child (i.e. that operating across the curriculum) is well-matched to their cognitive abilities. On occasions, intellectually able children with reading difficulties are insufficiently challenged by the everyday classroom activities that are presented to them. This can often be the case when academic tracking, streaming, or setting decisions are based upon the child's performance in written tests or examinations. It is essential that teachers find a way to make high-level cognitive demands and avoid any tendency to water down academic challenge in order to accommodate a child's reading and writing difficulties.

In the case of children whose poor reading is matched by general cognitive difficulties, it is equally necessary to ensure that academic tasks are neither too demanding nor too easy. In particular, it is important to recognize that, unlike decoding, IQ is related to higher-order reading skills involving reasoning, inference and comprehension (Christopher et al. 2012; Vellutino et al. 2004). Clearly, the needs of students with specific difficulties such as decoding must be differentiated from those with more general cognitive difficulties, and the general educational diet provided should reflect this distinction (Hardy and Woodcock 2014).

Finally, we must recognize that current knowledge is such that there continues to be a proportion of poor readers (so-called 'treatment-resisters'), estimated to be between 2–5 per cent, who continue to struggle to decode despite receiving high-quality, evidence-based provision (see Elliott and Grigorenko 2014: 147–8, for discussion). Until we can identify more effective new forms of intervention, we shall need to ensure that such individuals are provided with a range of electronic devices that can help them access and produce the written word.

Clearly, we are a long way from knowing how to resolve the particular problems of children who encounter severe decoding difficulty. However, to make progress we need to be very clear that all who struggle in this way should receive appropriate support that utilizes those approaches that have been found to be effective by high-quality research. Current understandings of, and provision for, dyslexia continue to undermine this goal.

Afterword: Some philosophical reflections

Andrew Davis

Justice

I open with some observations on justice, fairness and equity in relation to the status of the dyslexia label. It soon becomes apparent that these issues are difficult to keep apart from debates about the 'reality' of this disorder. Accordingly, the middle section of this Afterword concentrates on 'reality' matters, before I return to fairness towards the end.

Elliott's focus on justice is explicit. He asks whether using the term 'dyslexia' means that some gain advantages 'unfairly'. Quoting from Elliott (2014a), he voices concerns about 'equity'. He takes a strong position, asserting (this volume p. 115) that there 'is no justifiable rationale for providing additional resourcing to dyslexic individuals at the expense of others whose literacy skills operate at a similar level'. Nicolson holds, unlike Elliott, that the dyslexia label *does* appropriately distinguish some students from other poor readers. Hence he will presumably contend that it is fair to afford these students special treatment in comparison with those other poor readers. However, he does not comment explicitly on the point in this book.

What justice considerations underlie the practice of allocating dyslexics resources over and above those offered to others? For it will be these resources that Elliott will argue should not apply exclusively to a subset of those with certain reading and language difficulties. Familiar examples include 'accommodations' for dyslexic students studying in higher education. Birmingham University (2015) tells prospective candidates that they are 'committed to offering full support for any of these conditions that could affect your ability to perform on an equal level with your fellow students'. Similarly, Southampton University (2015) say, 'Students with specific learning difficulties (SpLD) such as dyslexia and dyspraxia often need extra support at University to compensate for disadvantages resulting from such difficulties.'

Typical accommodations involve at least some of the following: extra time, a reader, oral language modifier, a scribe, using a computer instead of handwriting, using assistive software (screen reader/voice recognition), exam papers to be on a coloured paper in a dyslexia friendly font and supervised rest breaks (British Dyslexia Association 2015).

So why are these practices thought to be 'fair'? Perhaps we can answer this by appealing to the *validity* of the assessment. It may be held that the standard versions of tests and other assessment devices disadvantage certain groups of students because they fail to capture or measure the relevant knowledge and understanding of these subgroups. Dyslexia 'masks' true academic capabilities. So this 'fairness' narrative also relates to a version of equality of opportunity according to which people should obtain higher education places on the basis of their academic prowess. The conception of equality of opportunity deployed here has moved away from mere formal equality of opportunity, where the latter concentrates on what students can actually do. Fair equality of opportunity seeks to look beyond actual performance to 'potential'. The Rawlsian version discounts class, social background, gender, race and so on, 'assuming there is a distribution of natural assets, those who are at the same level of talent and ability, and have the same willingness to use them, should have the same prospects of success regardless of their initial place in the social system' (Rawls 1999: 63).

Let us consider this line of thought a little further. Accommodations seen as addressing validity problems in assessment would assume a distinction between observable performances on the one hand, and underlying knowledge, understanding and skills on the other.

(The Rawlsian term is 'natural assets', not a phrase I intend to use myself since it has some associations of fixed cognitive ability, an idea about which there are familiar disputes.) According to the 'validity' narrative, the actual performances of the dyslexic student cannot be identified with their 'true' academic quality. The special treatments would be designed to provide opportunities to display performances that represent true psychological states more accurately. Accommodations would not be offered to students (if any) displaying similar symptoms to those with the dyslexic label, but where the symptoms are not deemed to afford a misleading picture of their true knowledge, understanding and skills.

A key theoretical idea in this narrative is, of course, that of 'true' academic quality. This might be understood to mean some kind of generic cognitive ability. If there is such a thing (a contestable assumption), is that what is needed for success in higher education? Is the same thing needed whether the student is studying Maths, Fine Arts or Medicine? What about commitment, motivation, attitude or creativity? Might these not be relevant too?

The existence and 'reality' of dyslexia

Psychology sometimes invokes the idea of a construct. The latter seems to be understood as an identifiable and persisting state of an individual: a given test might fail to measure it, or it might succeed in measuring it to some degree. Such possibilities ground the idea of construct *validity*. An assessment has construct validity if it succeeds in measuring the relevant construct. One familiar narrative about individual differences draws on the idea of such constructs, and how they may be present at different levels from one individual to another. The obvious traditional example here is intelligence, or generic cognitive ability, with its controversial history of 'measurement' by IQ tests.

While the psychological states apparently invoked by construct discourse are thought of as existing over time, they need not be held to be unchanging. The distinction between fluid and crystallized intelligence would be one example; the clue being in the term 'fluid'.

A second instance may be found in one (contestable) interpretation of the so-called 'Flynn Effect', according to which we are looking at a worldwide increase in intelligence, detected by rising scores in intelligence tests. That interpretation flies in the face of earlier views of intelligence as basically fixed and largely rooted in the genetic properties of the individuals concerned.

Persisting states, whether linked to desirable traits such as intelligence, or to 'deficits' or 'dysfunctional' states that may be associated with dyslexia, are sometimes associated with aspects of brain functioning. For instance, Nicolson (this volume p. 67) talks of 'the intrinsic brain difference characteristic of dyslexia', of the 'neural circuits for declarative and procedural processing', and of explaining 'cognitive level deficits in terms of the brain structures that cause them'. Nicolson's position here is complex, given that he regards the 'behavioural manifestations' themselves that are associated with dyslexia as a 'reading disability'.

Difficult, interesting and important philosophical questions arise about what it means to say that a specific trait continues to exist over time. Dyslexia is just one rather special example. One source of persistence criteria for traits is the availability of directly observable features. Having blue eyes is a mundane example. The colour persists, though evidently it will seem to vary according to the lighting conditions at any one moment, and may gradually fade with age. Or again, having an illness over a period of time might be identified according to criteria linked to sustained observable symptoms. Evidently, however, cases of this kind may be much less straightforward than eye colour. Symptoms often change during the progress of the illness, one set being replaced by others in typical developmental sequences. To secure a robust meaning of a claim that the *same* condition has been present over time in these cases, we need to appeal to events within the body of the sufferer. For instance, characteristic internal physiological phenomena may be causally linked to a virus. Biologists will have to operate identity criteria for a virus over time, but it is beyond my scope in this book to discuss that issue.

Both Elliott and Nicolson refer to the familiar co-morbidity issue, that there is extensive overlap between the symptoms of dyslexia and many other developmental disorders such as ADHD. Note two distinct meanings of 'co-morbidity': first, symptoms may be co-morbid if they can be found to overlap when we look at particular individuals. In a second sense, if we research populations rather than particular individuals, we might say that two disorders are co-morbid if they correlate positively (Lovett and Hood 2014).

Consider then, the challenge posed by co-morbidity in the first of the above senses. Overlapping symptoms are less than helpful when we are trying to pin down what it might mean for a specific condition to persist. One way such persistence might be conceptualized could be by appealing to the idea of a *natural kind*. Paradigmatic cases of natural kinds are the chemical elements. The question whether a piece of material remains gold over time is settled by information about the persistence of certain essential properties. It has a specific stable atomic constitution, without which it would not be gold, and with which it 'must' be gold. Its observable physical properties depend causally on its constitution, yet are also a function of contextual factors such as temperature. For instance, if the temperature is over 1,064.18°C it will melt.

Suppose that a permanent state, echoing in some ways the essential properties of natural kinds, could be discovered in individuals, a state apparently responsible for symptoms associated with dyslexia. That discovery could form the basis of dyslexia's nature over time. It could not only trump the difficulties associated with the overlap between its symptoms and those of other disorders, but might actually be the focus of scientific research into how the symptoms could be mitigated. A condition modelling this possibility is Down's Syndrome. People with this condition have an extra copy of Chromosome 21. (I believe there may be another basis too, but for expository purposes I will keep things simple.)

Now, whether *psychiatric disorders* have essential properties has been widely debated by scholars from a variety of disciplines. Hacking (2013) in commenting on DSM V, refers to the history of classifying mental illness. He noted a 'botanical' emphasis. On the dubious grounds that organic illness classifications resemble plant classifications, it was thought that what was good enough for organic illnesses should be splendid for psychiatric disorders. Botanical classifications do not, in fact, precisely mirror natural kind categories but they certainly have something of that flavour.

Haslam has researched the lay tendency to essentialist thinking about a range of phenomena including traits, illnesses and psychiatric illnesses. Adriaens and De Block (2013) observe: 'some patients desperately want to be labelled with a particular diagnosis and are willing to act according to the relevant diagnostic criteria. By conforming to their diagnosis, they contribute to the perception of homogeneity in the population of psychiatric patients' (p. 120).

Both Nicolson and Elliott refer to accounts of dyslexia that are at first sight, related to natural kind ideas and essentialist perspectives (Elliott this volume p. 139, and Nicolson p. 67). For example, Nicolson distinguishes between dyslexia as a specific learning difficulty, and as a reading disability. He links the former to 'the intrinsic brain difference characteristic of dyslexia' (this volume p. 67) He devotes significant attention to cerebellar function, speaking at times of cerebellar abnormality.

Nevertheless, both authors also make points that count against natural kind thinking. They refer to the complexities involved in identifying the direction of causes here, whether, that is to say, symptoms associated with struggling readers *result* in any straightforward fashion from pre-existing biological conditions, or whether the biological conditions can, wholly or in part amount to *consequences* of certain learning experiences. Nicolson observes that 'there is a legitimate question over cause versus correlate' (p. 38). If causes can work in both directions, this challenges a purely essentialist account. The latter would run the causes *from* internal states of affairs to observable properties, as in the case of the chemical elements.

Zachar (2000), in his paper opposing essentialist understandings of mental disorders, claims that psychiatry employs a 'pragmatic' approach, in which labels are applied just in case a sufficiently substantial number of DSM criteria are satisfied. It looks as if Zachar would accept dyslexia as a reading disability in Nicolson's sense, but would not be interested in Nicolson's 'intrinsic brain difference characteristic of Dyslexia'. While Nicolson is certainly committed to the reality of dyslexia in some senses, I cannot find anything in his text that commits him to any kind of essentialist perspective.

Szasz (1960) explored the possibility that some psychiatric disorders were associated with brain lesions of certain kinds. For him, illness had to have a biological foundation. Were the right kinds of brain lesions to be discovered, they could constitute the 'essence' of a given disorder or illness (though Szasz famously did not believe in such lesions and concluded that mental illness is 'mythical').

The possibility of a 'lesion' or the equivalent seems to sit well with currently influential ways of seeing learning disorders. Along with many other commentators, Mehan (2014) notes of learning disorders that 'the dominant mode of representation is psychological/medical. Students are diagnosed as *having* a "learning disability", "an educational handicap," attention deficit disorder (ADD) or "special needs." These representations place the problem inside the child's mind or brain' (p. 59).

Papineau (1994), however, used an analogy with software to argue that there might be no type of brain damage or persisting abnormality grounding psychiatric disorders, but rather, brain events akin to 'malfunctioning software'. If my computer's software is failing to function properly, it would be a mistake to think of peering inside in the hope of uncovering the equivalent of a silicon chip 'lesion'. The malfunction could well be instantiated in perfectly functioning circuits. It is interesting to note a recent research paper where the 'reality' of dyslexia is explained in such a way that brain functioning is clearly implicated, yet where Papineau's software analogy possibility is left open: 'Dyslexia ... the disorder seems to be the result of a subtle yet significant snarl in the brain's ability to process information about words' (Underwood 2013).

On the one hand, the expression 'snarl' could refer to an organic lesion. It could, on the other hand, capture a problem with brain functioning that could be helpfully compared to a software issue, as Papineau suggests. It is possible that some of Nicolson's claims about neural concomitants of dyslexia could be likened to software malfunctions rather than to organic 'lesions'. At the same time, his use of expressions such as 'delay in the building of new brain circuits' (p. 43) and 'changes in the neural circuits involving the hippocampus and amygdala' (p. 61) may imply that with appropriate advanced brain-scanning devices, we should, after all, be able to detect organic culprits.

More needs to be said about Papineau and the possibility that psychiatric and learning disorders have 'essences'. First, let us focus on the term 'malfunctioning'. Kingma (2014) contrasts two approaches to health and disease. The approach dubbed 'Naturalism' views the terms 'health' and 'disease' as free of value, and the relevant classifications as 'representing the world as it is, rather than our evaluation of how things are' (p. 591). 'Normativists' deny such a value-free status and insist that decisions about treatments and resources are 'driven … by normative concerns' (p. 592) Kingma argues that the naturalism/normativist distinction is only really important in the 'theoretical' domain. This domain concerns the biological, whereas the realm of moral and social decision making relates to the applied domain. She holds that it is obvious that in the latter domain 'a completely value-free account of health and disease cannot directly determine moral and social decision-making' (p. 592).

Within the so-called theoretical domain, how should 'malfunctioning' be understood? When we speak of malfunctioning organs such as the heart, we refer to that which does, or does not contribute to the survival of the organism. A short-term version would relate quite literally to whether the malfunction was life threatening, while a broader interpretation would encompass biological 'fitness' and whether the malfunction restricted the organism's capacity to reproduce.

Now these biological interpretations are not obviously applicable to a 'snarl', the term attached by Underwood to dyslexia. For their appropriateness you would need to have grounds for thinking that dyslexia is linked to the survival of the people concerned or even to their capacity to reproduce. This seems less than plausible.

Accordingly, I would argue that, comprehensively to characterize the 'snarl' here, we have to appeal to social phenomena 'outside' the head of the person with the malfunctioning brain. One approach to naturalizing the notion of malfunction is to reference it to what is 'normal' in the social environment of our sufferer – this to be operationalized in statistical fashion. Since what is 'normal' varies from one place to another, and also will change over time, we are already moving further and further away from a purely biological account of disorder. Bingham and Banner (2014) note that on a statistical basis, and considering 'normal' functioning in this light, homosexuality would count as 'dysfunctional' in many societies (p. 539). Some would regard this point as constituting a *reductio ad absurdum* of any statistical construal of dysfunction, or even 'snarl'.

To investigate what is 'outside' the head in rather more depth, two key philosophical ideas are needed. Consider first the concept of the 'constitutive rule': In an early article, Rawls (1955) distinguished between two kinds of rules, the regulative and the constitutive. The former include everyday rules we regularly encounter, such as 'Drive on the left', 'Keep off the grass' and so forth. Examples of the latter are the rules of games such as chess. The rules governing how a castle-shaped piece may be moved horizontally or vertically mean that certain actions with the piece become 'moving the rook' acts. The rules 'constitute' the actions concerned. The actions are what they are in virtue of the rules.

The second notion is that of 'collective intentionality'. The American philosopher John Searle has had much to say about this (for instance, in Searle 1995). There are everyday individual intentions: I intend to shave this morning, and to walk to work later. In addition, group intentions feature at the heart of our social reality. For example, group intentions ground the meanings of road signs and the value of a £20 note. Group intentions underlie the existence of constitutive rules such as those of chess. 'We' intend that chess rules should apply worldwide. As long as we intend this, we sustain in existence those rules according to which, moving that castle-shaped piece in a certain way on the 8 × 8 squared board, just is a rook move. We intend that such and such a road sign means that you must not drive faster than 50 miles per hour, and that the £20 note has such and such a place in our economic and monetary system.

Both constitutive rules and collective intentionalities are central to the functioning of language in its broadest sense. When an English speaker uses the word 'dog', she succeeds in saying what she intends partly in virtue of the existence of collective intentions sustaining constitutive rules about the function of that word. If she uttered a very similar sound in a country where a language other than English was spoken, she may be credited with a different meaning.

It follows that the notion of a 'snarl' cannot be separated concep-tually and constitutively from these social phenomena in which individuals are embedded. A 'snarl' can only be fully characterized with reference to language. The term's definition links it explicitly to a capacity to deal with words. This in turn means that the very conception of a snarl incorporates aspects of social reality. An assertion that a snarl exists is about both something inside a person, and about their social and cultural environment. The said aspects of social reality are not fixed, of course, and will vary over time and from one social context to another. These points appear to distance conceptions of disorders such as dyslexia from anything exclusively inside individuals that would parallel the inner constitutions of natural kinds.

Davis (2008) questions the robustness of an essentialist perspective on some of the labels currently awarded to learners. His treatment draws on Ian Hacking's studies of kinds. Hacking defines 'indifferent kinds' as classifications indifferent to human activity, again the chemical elements would be paradigms. Of course, it is *people* who use language, concepts and labels to identify types of 'stuff' in the empirical world. Yet the chemical categories concerned would be as whether or not they had ever been so classified, or even if human beings had never existed. Gold is what it is, and is inherently different from iron, regardless of any human attitudes or activities. By way of contrast, Hacking offers ADHD as an example of an 'interactive kind'. The very existence of this way of categorizing people has effects on how they are treated, how they see themselves and how they behave. This in turn will further influence changes in the character of ADHD classifications themselves (Hacking 2006: 13). He notes that interactive kinds involve 'looping effects': 'We think of these kinds of people as given, as definite classes defined by definite properties ... But ... they are moving targets because our investigations interact with the targets themselves, and change them ...That is the looping effect. Sometimes our sciences create kinds of people that in a certain sense did not exist before. That is making up people' (Hacking 2006: 2).

Hacking explores the implications of making strong assertions about the 'reality' of psychiatric disorders and of some learning 'disorders'. For instance, he would like to say that there were no multiple personalities in 1955. Yet, by 1985, many were diagnosed with it. He appreciates that expressing claims in this fashion is 'contentious'. Such ontological assertions excite controversy partly because they seem permeated with scepticism about the relevant phenomena. It is as if the conditions concerned are 'merely' constructed by people, as opposed to 'really' existing in the light of some kind of biological substrate. Moreover, if conditions are constructed, could they be dispensed with? Nicolson is strongly opposed to any such move in relation to dyslexia, while Elliott in effect is arguing for just that.

A subtle and important variant of 'making up people' may include processes that encourage non-specialists to believe in essentialism for psychiatric conditions. Adriaens and De Block (2013) explore this possibility, referring to a 'folk biology' involving an 'essentializing mentality' that can extend its grip to ethnic groups and types of personality. Such folk thinking could also be brought to bear on learning disorders including dyslexia and ADHD. Nevertheless, it is important to note that however plausible these narratives may be, they do not actually settle the issue of whether, for instance, dyslexics really do share some kind of common essence. Even if conceptualizing dyslexia as a condition with essential properties is motivated by an essentializing mentality, it still might be *true* that the majority of those awarded a dyslexia label actually do share one or more objectively identifiable features. To suppose otherwise would be to commit the classic origin fallacy. To have suspicions about the irrational origins of a label does not by itself rule out the possibility that the label's status could be supported on better grounds.

If psychiatric and learning disorders could appropriately be conceptualized along the lines of natural kinds with essential properties, then we should be able to distinguish sharply between those with the disorders and those without. After all, either a substance is gold, or it is not, depending on its inner atomic constitution.

However, it is sometimes claimed in this connection, that we need to be clear about the difference between so-called 'dimensional disorders' and 'taxonic disorders'. The former are characterized by the absence of clear boundaries between disorder and non-disorder, while in the case of the latter there *are* clear boundaries. Haslam, Holland and Kuppens 2012 argue that the majority of frequently encountered disorders are dimensional. Examples of the latter include headaches, and according to DSM V at least, autism, with its extended category of autism spectrum disorder (ASD). A useful clear-cut case to note here is Down's Syndrome, which is taxonic as far as its biological basis is concerned. Yet *symptoms* of this disorder vary in their severity between one individual and another.

Is there a dividing line between the mildest symptoms and anything that might be manifested by an individual without this chromosomal abnormality?

Dyslexia *symptoms* present themselves with different levels of severity. Nevertheless, it does not immediately follow from this that dyslexia itself is a dimensional disorder. Compare it with measles. Either an individual has measles, or she does not. Presumably measles is a 'taxonic' disorder. Yet measles symptoms come in many strengths and sizes. Some of Nicolson's commentary suggests that he construes dyslexia as a taxonic disorder, especially his extensive discussion of neurological factors. However, he is never explicit about this, and he can argue that if his preferred option is to see dyslexia as 'dimensional', this does nothing to undermine the importance of neurological factors. It only counts against seeing the condition as having a natural kind type of status, and as I understand him, he is not committed to that. Elliott (this volume p. 80) claims that it 'is now widely accepted that reading ability (and disability) is dimensional and therefore there can be no clear-cut dyslexic/non-dyslexic distinction'.

Consider a classic question relating to these issues. Just how should the potential candidates for the dyslexia label be selected in the first instance? You could start with what you believed was a relevant neurological feature, and select subjects on that basis from the wider set of students with language difficulties. All the same, unless you were managing advanced scanning of multitudes of individuals, how would you ever get started? Moreover, how would you know what to look for in the brain?

Anyhow, just suppose that you could initiate such a project. If you succeeded you might, in effect, be constructing a taxonic feature for the dyslexia label. If, instead, you choose to classify as dyslexics those individuals whose difficulties are debilitating beyond a certain cut-off point, you might be building a 'dimensional' character into the label, and you might be less than surprised at being unable to pinpoint a specific neural feature common to all those labelled in this way.

Another option for labelling is to highlight a key feature of observable difficulties, such as poor phonological awareness. (I understand 'phonological awareness' in the standard way, as the capacity to grasp that words are made up from a variety of sound units.) Again, this looks as though it would build in a dimensional character for the label. Nevertheless, Nicolson observes that 'Dyslexia is associated with "delayed neural commitment" which will lead to delays not only in phonological processing but also in various other of the readiness capabilities' (this volume p. 59) Does this hint at a taxonic interpretation after all?

Even if dyslexia is dimensional rather than taxonic, this in turn fails to settle whether it is a 'real' condition. Nicolson holds (this volume p. 121) that one of the points of disagreement between him and Elliott is whether we can 'characterize differences between dyslexics and other poor readers'. He believes that we can characterize these differences, and that Elliott holds that we cannot. However, as I understand this, Nicolson is not insisting that the differences amount to a taxonic distinction. If it is not taxonic, it can still be 'real' in some sense, but it cannot then be appropriate to think of dyslexia in natural kind terms.

Cooper (2010) asks important questions about what it means to say a disorder is 'real'. Echoing J. L. Austin in *Sense and Sensibilia*, she makes the paradigmatic philosophical point that 'we should start by specifying what possible alternatives we have in mind' (p. 325). For instance, in asking whether a disorder is real we might be wondering whether it is tied to specific cultures or whether it is universal. Yet, observes Cooper, 'Disorders that are found only in certain places and times need not be fakes' (p. 333). It is interesting to note that neither Elliott nor Nicolson say much, if anything about this issue. Elliott makes brief reference to the challenging orthography of English. The main point here is that even if dyslexia is not universal, but only found within certain cultures or within certain communities speaking particular languages, it would not follow from this alone that it was not 'real' in some sense.

Cooper comments that only 'involuntary conditions are disorders; voluntary but undesirable behaviours are non-disorder forms of deviance' (p. 328). The 'reality' of the disorder would now be linked to the idea that it is something that happens to the individuals concerned, rather than something about which they can make choices.

Of course, whether a condition happens to an individual rather than being under their control is a necessary but not a sufficient condition for it being 'real'. For not all psychological processes falling into this passive category are disorders of any kind. The ancient word for emotion is 'passion'. This term identifies certain psychological phenomena that happen to an individual, as distinct from other psychological events and processes that are, at least to some degree, under that person's voluntary control. Arguably, few emotional states or 'passions' are real disorders in any sense. Inevitably, there are some tricky cases to consider here. If someone is overtaken by a very powerful emotion then, as we sometimes metaphorically observe, they are beside themselves. They are in a state at least akin to a 'disorder', albeit a temporary one.

Justice and equity again

The justice of accommodations, among other things assumes lack of control on the part of the student. He or she cannot help being limited by dyslexia, ADHD or other 'disorders'. It looks as though intuitions about fairness are closely linked to lack of control. Hence, so the story goes, it is 'fair' to make up for limitations that are 'undeserved' because they cannot be helped. In 2008, Cambridge University offered accommodations to students whose handwriting was bad, but only where the problem was 'caused by a disability or medical reason', and the University of Wales in 2006 considered that some students suffering from anxiety deserved 'additional exam arrangements' if they had 'an underlying health issue'. The subtext here is, apparently that where there is a 'medical' basis for a problem, the student cannot help having it and so is entitled to special support.

When such assumptions are made explicit, difficult questions immediately arise. Arguably, at least some aspects of cognitive function limitations *in general* are 'undeserved' by the students too, because they are not within their voluntary control. I say 'some', rather than 'all', to allow for the possibility that at any given time, a given level of cognitive functioning may in part result from previous efforts. A classic irritation experienced by musicians is hearing comments such as 'you are so lucky to have that talent', when they know perfectly well that their high functioning is largely a result of blood, sweat and tears. At any given moment the musician cannot summon up just any level of musical performance. Yet it is also true that they have a significant degree of responsibility for the performance standard that they can command at any one time. Why, then is it fair to offer accommodations to students in respect of some of their limitations that they cannot help, while no attention is paid to other constraints that they similarly cannot control?

Some forms of affirmative action on undergraduate recruitment might also be considered in this connection. Students cannot help attending inner-city comprehensive schools with scant history of sending pupils to universities, and it is no fault of theirs that they come from backgrounds affording low levels of social and cultural capital. Hence, or so it might be argued, it is 'fair' to make a special case for admitting such students. These policies are controversial, though in the UK the Office for Fair Access expects universities to charge full tuition fees to recruit along such lines.

However, once these kinds of policies are contemplated, it is difficult to know when to stop. If you believe in anything remotely like generic cognitive ability, or the 'intelligence' allegedly measured by traditional psychometric tests, then individuals are not responsible for how much of it they have. Obviously they can make choices about the extent to which they exploit it, but basically they cannot be said to 'deserve' what they have. Why is it not considered fair to 'accommodate' applicants with low IQs, when we are so certain that accommodation for people with disorders such as dyslexia is perfectly fair? Of course, a university could respond that it would be 'silly' to adopt policies that were inclusive of those with low IQs, since such applicants would be unable to follow the demanding academic courses to be found in higher education and would be unlikely to have any chance of achieving the relevant learning outcomes.

Current policies, designed to make sure that dyslexics are treated fairly, challenge responses of this kind. In theory, universities may be able to claim that a given academic course has certain learning outcomes at its very heart. So if they have reason to believe that applicants with certain learning disorders seem very unlikely to attain these outcomes, it is perfectly fair and reasonable not to accept them. Universities could offer the analogy with a colour blind applicant for driving a train: the applicant could not read the signals and hence would be disbarred from this type of employment.

In practice, universities seem unlikely to succeed in pursuing recruitment policies of this kind, given the current climate. I know of a university where the Disability Unit contended that one criterion for recognizing dyslexic students was a difficulty in 'generalizing'. Most higher education courses have 'generalizing' at the very heart of their learning outcomes, yet accommodations were *still* expected for certain students in the university concerned. (I am not for a moment implying that either Nicolson or Elliott would favour the use or application of this kind of dyslexia criterion.)

Does the 'constructed' status of some conditions mean that individuals cannot be passive victims in any sense? Hacking (2010) discusses a possible example of such a condition, called by at least one psychiatrist 'depressive devitalization syndrome'. This is thought of as a specific psychiatric disorder suffered by the children of refugees fleeing from dreadful situations in their countries of origin. The condition may have spread partly as a result of children imitating the behaviour of others, having obtained information about it through the media and by hearing gossip within the relevant communities. It turns out that once imitated, the behaviour becomes internalized. The children acquire a 'new psychic state' over which they lack complete control and which is distressing.

Does this example have any implications for the status of dyslexia? This is partly an empirical question. Social scientists would have to investigate whether and how students who acquire the dyslexia label could have imitated symptoms as a result of information available from their families and their broader social context, concerning how dyslexics are 'supposed' to behave. Such a line of inquiry might be greeted with hostility by defenders of the dyslexia label, on the grounds that it has a cynical, sceptical character. It is very clear from Nicolson's contribution that he would resist interpreting dyslexia as a condition resembling this Swedish example. Nevertheless, when discussing dyslexia as a 'reading disability', Nicolson does talk of it as an 'acquired disorder' (this volume p. 64) He believes that stress is one of the factors involved in the acquisition of the disorder. Elliott (this volume p. 84) comments that 'environmental experience in infancy can differentially affect subsequent brain structure and functioning'. Hacking is clear that some labels might involve both 'objective' features and the kind of interactions involved in looping effects.

It should be noted that some enduring psychological conditions such as the one Hacking cites in Sweden are very distressing to the people concerned. No one is claiming that they or their communities have 'made them up' in the sense of 'faking' something or pretending that they have a problem. Cooper (2010) suggests 'syndromes that are glued together by culture can be as scientifically respectable as those that are glued together by biology' (p. 330).

Cooper refers to common accounts of 'disorder' according to which a condition can only be a disorder if it is harmful. Conditions that cause no harm can be thought of straightforwardly as manifestations of human diversity. This point is largely tacit in the Elliott-Nicolson exchange: of the term 'disorder', Nicolson observes: 'The implicit assumption in referring to disorder is that there is some underlying brain difference that is intrinsic, and therefore unlikely to be *alleviated*' (my italics). The latter word implies that, understandably, Nicolson believes that the brain difference concerned is undesirable.

In judging whether something is harmful, the normative rears its head yet again. Homosexuality featured in early diagnostic and statistical manuals, and was only removed in 1973. Bingham and Banner (2014) comment: 'a scientifically robust description of the area in the brain governing sexuality would not permit the inference that homosexuality is a disorder any more than description of the neural correlates of falling in love or criminality would make these mental disorders' (p. 538). There are still societies that *would* deploy a neurological correlate of this kind, if any, to back claims that a disorder exists here.

It has already been noted that dyslexia symptoms are co-morbid with the symptoms of several other conditions such as ADHD and dyscalculia. In recent years, some controversial accounts of ADHD status have been developed. According to these, the use of the label reflects the norms of particular cultures about, for instance how pupils should behave in school. On this view, the label fails to identify an 'objective' identifiable neurological condition that causes certain symptoms in individuals over a period of time. We are told that in France, ADHD is thought of as a 'psycho-social' problem rather than a biologically based disorder. Given co-morbidity, is it possible for the

French to be 'right' about ADHD, and also possible for those who agree with Nicolson to be 'right' about dyslexia? I will not attempt to answer this question!

An additional contemporary twist, noted by Cooper, is afforded by groups who identify with conditions such as deafness or autism and refuse to count these as disabilities. Hacking (2013) observes that 'neurodiversity and autism pride movements hold that autism is a difference from neurotypicals, not a disorder'.

Dyslexia and methods for teaching reading

Both contributors refer to approaches to teaching early reading. Nicolson (this volume p. 49ff.) offers a brief history leading up to the 'reading wars', referring to 'look and say', 'systematic phonics' and other approaches. He believes that dyslexic children have problems with 'phonics-based instruction' (p. 63) because they are especially challenged by having to learn a 'bridging skill' that later has to be replaced by a 'more complete skill' (p. 63).

Elliott discusses the possibility that some pupils have reading difficulties because they have not been taught properly, rather than because they have dyslexia. Defenders of systematic synthetic phonics sometimes attempt to defend claims of this kind. It is difficult, if not impossible to falsify them, since they make a direct inference from the presence of difficulties to the inadequacy of the teaching, thereby excluding the possibility of a learning disorder by definitional fiat. A philosopher will suspect the presence of a vicious circularity in moves of these kinds. The teaching 'method' employed is afforded a shifting stipulative definition according to whether it 'works'. Nicolson (this volume p. 125) may be rejecting the accusation of vicious circularity here when he says, for instance: 'for a child still to be in need of support, the phonics learning experiences will not have been happy ones'. This may leave open the possibility that the phonics teaching could have been more 'effective' (and hence happier?). However, I am inclined to understand Nicolson here as leaving the door open for the possibility that 'effective' phonics teaching simply will not 'work' for *every* child, even if it does so for the majority.

Elliott may be closer to supporting this kind of argument from phonics enthusiasts when he says 'approaches to the teaching of reading that emphasize whole language approaches are particularly ineffective for those who experience difficulty in the acquisition of literacy skills' (this volume p. 85).

Nicolson offers a brief history of various methods of teaching reading and sketches what he calls 'theories of learning to read' (this volume p. 51). He opposes the 'reading wars' between those favouring different methods, and advocates adapting pedagogies to the needs of particular children at particular stages. Elliott tacitly assumes the 'existence' of various methods or interventions in his critique of a putative dyslexia marker, namely 'those who fail to make meaningful progress in reading even when provided with high-quality, evidence-based forms of intervention' (this volume p. 77).

This raises an important question about the extent to which it is actually possible to identify specific methods in a way that allows them to be researched. Understandably, neither Nicolson nor Elliott investigate these kinds of challenges. Nevertheless, I think it is appropriate to end this Afterword with a few remarks about the issue.

Suppose we see teaching as an *interactive* process, especially in the early years. Evidently this will be a matter of degree, but there would never be any occasions where the teacher failed in some way to monitor her pupils for their levels of understanding, motivation and attention and, as a consequence, modify her language, timing, level of questioning and task difficulty. Such monitoring might take place at the end of an episode of direct teaching, in order that the teacher might inform herself about how to handle the next lesson. Typically, in addition to this, there will be innumerable moments of diagnostic interaction during the teaching itself. This will be especially evident in lessons with children under eight years old. Older students, especially those in higher education, may be subjected to non-interactive lectures. Some wonder just how effective these are; be that as it may, the particular target of my comments here is the educational context in which primary-age children are schooled.

If the idea that teaching is necessarily *interactive* in the sense just outlined is right, lessons taught according to any given set of principles such as 'Reading Recovery' or 'Analytic Phonics' will cover a great multitude of sins and virtues. There will be no common essence to all the pedagogies coming under any one of these labels. So teachers using 'analytic phonics', 'synthetic phonics' or any other approach to the teaching of reading, do not afford researchers homogenous classroom processes over time that can be subjected to rigorous empirical research. Suppose, so as to circumvent this 'problem', 'teachers' and researchers were to come together and collaborate by making rigid pedagogical moves according to a detailed specification. It would then be arguable that whatever they *were* doing in the classroom, they would no longer be teaching.

Critics of this argument may assume that its conclusion, that certain alleged specifiable teaching methods do not exist, is clearly absurd, and hence there must be something wrong with the argument. Surely, they may urge, it is perfectly possible to outline the principles embodied in some of the various approaches to the teaching of reading. Teachers following these principles are obviously teaching according to the said approaches.

Yet such principles are, and must be open to a variety of interpretations. Accordingly, any teacher following them may, and probably should differ from her fellow professional. Hence, the pedagogical impact on any one child with, say a dyslexia label, will differ from that on her peer taught by another teacher. If the principles in question are open to a legitimate variety of interpretation, they can never have been researched 'rigorously' along the lines of a drug trial.

References

Abramson, L. Y., Seligman, M. E. P. and Teasdale, J. D. (1978), 'Learned Helplessness in Humans – Critique and Reformulation', *Journal of Abnormal Psychology* 87 (1): 49–74.

Adriaens, P. and De Block, A. (2013), 'Why We Essentialize Mental Disorders', *Journal of Medicine and Philosophy* 38: 107–27.

Agahi, A. S., Sepulveda, P. P. and Nicolson, R. I. (forthcoming), 'Careers, Talents and Dyslexia: Working to One's Strengths', *Dyslexia*.

Ahissar, M. (2007), 'Dyslexia and the Anchoring-deficit Hypothesis', *Trends in Cognitive Sciences* 11: 458–65.

Al Otaiba, S. and Fuchs, D. (2002), 'Characteristics of Children Who are Unresponsive to Early Literacy Intervention: A Review of the Literature', *Remedial and Special Education* 23: 300–16.

Al Otaiba, S. and Fuchs, D. (2006), 'Who Are the Young Children for Whom Best Practices in Reading are Ineffective?' *Journal of Learning Disabilities* 39: 414–31.

Aleci, C., Piana, G., Piccoli, M. and Bertolini, M. (2012), 'Developmental Dyslexia and Spatial Relationship Perception', *Cortex* 48 (4): 466–76.

Alloway, T. P., Gathercole, S. E., Kirkwood, H. J. and Elliott, J. G. (2009), 'The Cognitive and Behavioral Characteristics of Children with Low Working Memory', *Child Development* 80: 606–21.

American Academy of Pediatrics (Section on Ophthalmology and Council on Children with Disabilities, Ophthalmology, American Academy of Ophthalmology, American Association for Pediatric Ophthalmology and Strabismus and American Association of Certified Orthoptists. (2009), 'Learning Disabilities, Dyslexia, and Vision', *Pediatrics* 124: 837–44.

American Association of Intellectual and Developmental Disabilities (2010), *Intellectual Disability: Definition, Classification, and Systems of Supports*. Washington, DC: American Association of Intellectual and Developmental Disabilities.

American Psychiatric Association (2013), *Diagnostic and Statistical Manual of Mental Disorders* (5th edn), Arlington, VA: American Psychiatric Publishing.

Anderson, J. R. (1982), 'Acquisition of Cognitive Skill', *Psychological Review* 89: 369–406.

Anderson, J. R. (1983), *The Architecture of Cognition*, Cambridge, MA: Harvard University Press.

Arnoutse, C., van Leeuwe, J. and Verhoeven, L. (2005), 'Early Literacy from a Longitudinal Perspective', *Educational Review and Research* 11: 253–75.

Arrow, A. W. and Tunmer, W. E. (2012), 'Contemporary Reading Acquisition Theory: The Conceptual Basis for Differentiated Reading Instruction', in S. Suggate and E. Reese (eds), *Contemporary Debates in Childhood Education and Development*, pp. 241–9. London: Routledge.

Ashkenazi, S., Black, J. M., Abrams, D. A., Hoeft, F. and Menon, V. (2013), 'Neurobiological Underpinnings of Math and Reading Learning Disabilities', *Journal of Learning Disabilities* 46: 549–69.

Astle, D. E., Barnes, J. J., Baker, K., Colclough, G. L. and Woolrich, M. W. (2015), 'Cognitive Training Enhances Intrinsic Brain Connectivity in Childhood', *The Journal of Neuroscience* 35 (16): 6277–83.

Aylward, E., Richards, T., Berninger, V., Nagy, W., Field, K., Grimme, A. et al. (2003), 'Instructional Treatment Associated with Changes in Brain Activation in Children with Dyslexia', *Neurology* 61, 212–19.

Bach, S., Richardson, U., Brandeis, D., Martin, E. and Brem, S. (2013), 'Print-specific Multimodal Brain Activation in Kindergarten Improves Prediction of Reading Skills in Second Grade', *Neuroimage* 82: 605–15.

Baddeley, A. (2012), 'Working Memory: Theories, Models, and Controversies', *Annual Review of Psychology* 63: 1–29.

Banales, E., Kohnen, S. and McArthur, G. (2015), 'Can Verbal Working Memory Training Improve Reading?' *Cognitive Neuropsychology* 32 (3–4): 104–32.

Barkley, R. A. (1997), 'Behavioral Inhibition, Sustained Attention, and Executive Functions: Constructing a Unifying Theory of ADHD', *Psychological Bulletin* 121 (1): 65–94.

Barquero, L. A, Davis, N. and Cutting, L. E. (2014), 'Neuroimaging of Reading Intervention: A Systematic Review and Activation Likelihood Estimate Meta-analysis', *PLoS ONE*, 9 (1): e83668.

Barth, A. E., Denton, C. A., Stuebing, K. K., Fletcher, J. M., Cirino, P. T., Francis, D. J. et al. (2010), 'A Test of the Cerebellar Hypothesis of Dyslexia in Adequate and Inadequate Responders to Reading Intervention', *Journal of International Neuropsychological Society* 16: 526–36.

Bauer, P. J. and Zelazo, P. D. (2014), 'The National Institutes of Health Toolbox for the Assessment of Neurological and Behavioral Function: A Tool for Developmental Science', *Child Development Perspectives* 8 (3): 119–24.

Bellocchi, S., Muneaux, M., Bastien-Toniazzo, M. and Ducrot, S. (2013), 'I Can Read It in Your Eyes: What Eye Movements Tell Us about

Visuo-attentional Processes in Developmental Dyslexia', *Research in Developmental Disabilities* 34: 452–60.

Beneventi, H., Tønnessen, F. E., Ersland, L. and Hugdahl, K. (2010), 'Working Memory Deficit in Dyslexia: Behavioral and fMRI Evidence', *International Journal of Neuroscience* 120: 51–9.

Berent, I., Vaknin-Nusbaum, V., Balaban, E. and Galaburda, A. M. (2012), 'Dyslexia Impairs Speech Recognition but Can Spare Phonological Competence', *PLoS ONE* 7: e44875.

Berlin, R. (1887), *Eine besondre art der wortblindheit.* [A special type of wordblindness: Dyslexia]. Wiesbaden: Bergmann.

Berninger, V. W., Raskind, W., Richards, T., Abbott, R. and Stock, P. (2008), 'A Multidisciplinary Approach to Understanding Developmental Dyslexia within Working-memory Architecture: Genotypes, Phenotypes, Brain, and Instruction', *Developmental Neuropsychology* 33: 707–44.

Biancarosa, G. and Snow, C. E. (2006), *Reading Next: A Vision for Action and Research in Middle and High School Literacy: A Report to the Carnegie Corporation of New York*, 2nd edn. Washington, DC: Alliance for Excellent Education.

Bingham, R. and Banner, N. (2014), 'The Definition of Mental Disorder: Evolving but Dysfunctional?' *Journal of Medical Ethics* 40: 537–42.

Birmingham University (2015) http://www.birmingham.ac.uk/ undergraduate/support/disability/index.aspx (accessed 2 May 2015).

Bishop, D. V. M. (2001), 'Genetic Influences on Language Impairment and Literacy Problems in Children: Same or Different?' *Journal of Child Psychology and Psychiatry* 42: 189–98.

Bishop, D. V. M. (2006), 'Dyslexia: What's the Problem?' *Developmental Science* 9: 256–7.

Bishop, D. V. M. (2007), 'Curing Dyslexia and ADHD by Training Motor Coordination: Miracle or Myth?' *Journal of Paediatrics and Child Health* 43: 653–5.

Bishop, D. V. M. (2014), 'Ten Questions about Terminology for Children with Unexplained Language Problems', *International Journal of Language and Communication Disorders* 49: 381–15.

Black, J. and Hoeft, F. (2012), 'Prediction of Children's Reading Skills: Understanding the Interplay among Environment, Brain, and Behavior', in A. A. Benasich and R. H. Fitch (eds), *Developmental Dyslexia: Early Precursors, Neurobehavioral Markers, and Biological Substrates*, 191–207, Baltimore, MD: Paul H. Brookes Publishing.

Blair, C. (2002), 'School Readiness – Integrating Cognition and Emotion in a Neurobiological Conceptualization of Children's Functioning at School Entry', *American Psychologist* 57 (2): 111–27.

Boder, E. (1973), 'Developmental Dyslexia: A Diagnostic Approach

Based on Three Atypical Spelling-Reading Patterns', *Developmental Medicine and Child Neurology* 15: 663–87.

Boets, B. (2014), 'Dyslexia: Reconciling Controversies Within an Integrative Developmental Perspective', *Trends in Cognitive Sciences* 18 (10): 501–3.

Boets, B., De Smedt, B., Cleuren, L., Vandewalle, E., Wouters, J. and Ghesquire, P. (2010), 'Towards a Further Characterization of Phonological and Literacy Problems in Dutch-speaking Children with Dyslexia', *British Journal of Developmental Psychology* 28: 5–31.

Borella, E., Carretti, B. and Pelgrina, S. (2010), 'The Specific Role of Inhibition in Reading Comprehension in Good and Poor Comprehenders', *Journal of Learning Disabilities* 43: 541–52.

Bosse, M. L., Tainturier, M. J. and Valdois, S. (2007), 'Developmental Dyslexia: The Visual Attention Span Deficit Hypothesis', *Cognition* 104: 198–230.

Bradley, L. and Bryant, P. E. (1983), 'Categorizing Sounds and Learning to Read – A Causal Connection', *Nature* 301: 419–21.

Brandenburg, J., Klasczweski, J., Fishbach, A., Schucdart, K., Büttner, G., and Hasslehorn, M. (2015), 'Working Memory in Children with Learning Disabilities in Reading Versus Spelling: Searching for Overlapping and Specific Cognitive Factors', *Journal of Learning Disabilities* 48 (6): 622–34.

British Dyslexia Association (2015) Access Arrangements. Available online: http://www.bdadyslexia.org.uk/parent/access-arrangements [accessed 30 July 2015].

British Psychological Society (1999), *Dyslexia, literacy and psychological assessment: Report by a Working Party of the Division of Educational and Child Psychology of the British Psychological Society.* Leicester: Author.

Brookes, R. L., Nicolson, R. I. and Fawcett, A. J. (2007), 'Prisms Throw Light on Developmental Disorders', *Neuropsychologia* 45 (8): 1921–30.

Bryant, P. E. and Goswami, U. (1986), 'Strengths and Weaknesses of the Reading Level Design', *Psychological Bulletin* 100: 101–3.

Bryant, P. E., Maclean, L., Bradley, L. and Crossland, J. (1990), 'Rhyme and Alliteration, Phoneme Detection, and Learning to Read', *Developmental Psychology* 26: 429–38.

Buckingham, J., Wheldall, K. and Beaman-Wheldall, R. (2013), 'Why Poor Children are More Likely to Become Poor Readers: The School Years', *Australian Journal of Education* 57 (3): 190–213.

Bull, R. and Scerif, G. (2001), 'Executive Functioning as a Predictor of Children's Mathematics Ability: Inhibition, Switching and Working Memory', *Developmental Neuropsychology* 19 (3): 273–93.

Burt, C. (1937), *The Backward Child*, London: University of London Press.

Byrne, B. (2011), 'Evaluating the Role of Phonological Factors in Early Literacy Development: Insights from Experimental and Behavior-genetic Studies', in S. A. Brady, D. Braze and C. A. Fowler (eds), *Explaining Individual Differences in Reading: Theory and Evidence*, 175–95. New York: Psychology Press.

Byrne, B., Coventry, W. L., Olson, R. K., Samuelsson, S., Corley, R., Willcutt, E. G. et al. (2009), 'Genetic and Environmental Influences on Aspects of Literacy and Language in Early Childhood: Continuity and Change from Preschool to Grade 2', *Journal of Neurolinguistics* 22: 219–36.

Calfee, R. C. and Drum, P. (1986), 'Research on Teaching Reading', in M. C. Whittock (ed.), *Handbook of Research on Teaching*, 804–49. New York: Macmillan.

Callens, M., Tops, W. and Brysbaert, M. (2012), 'Cognitive Profile of Students Who Enter Higher Education with an Indication of Dyslexia', *PLoS One* 7 (6): e38081.

Camilli, G., Wolfe, P. M. and Smith, M. L. (2006), 'Meta-analysis and Reading Policy: Perspectives on Teaching Children to Read'. *Elementary School Journal* 107 (1): 27–36.

Canivez, G. L. (2013), 'Psychometric Versus Actuarial Interpretation of Intelligence and Related Aptitude Batteries', in D. H. Saklofske, C. R. Reynolds and V. L. Schwean (eds), *The Oxford Handbook of Child Psychological Assessment*, 84–112. New York: Oxford University Press.

Cantin, N., Polatajko, H. J., Thach, W. T. et al. (2007), 'Developmental Coordination Disorder: Exploration of a Cerebellar Hypothesis', *Human Movement Science* 26 (3): 491–509.

Caravolas, M., Lervag, A., Mousikou, P., Efrim, C., Litavsky, M., Onochie-Quintanilla, E., and Hulme, C. (2012), 'Common Patterns of Prediction of Literacy Development in Different Alphabetic Orthographies', *Psychological Science* 23: 678–86.

Carey, T. (2014), *Taming the Tiger Parent*, London: Robinson Press.

Carrion-Castillo, A., Franke, B. and Fisher, S. E. (2013), 'Molecular Genetics of Dyslexia: An Overview', *Dyslexia* 19 (4): 214–40.

Carroll, J. M., Snowling, M. J., Stevenson, J. and Hulme, C. (2003), 'The Development of Phonological Awareness in Preschool Children', *Developmental Psychology* 39: 913–23.

Castles, A. and Coulthart, M. (2004), 'Is There a Causal Link from Phonological Awareness to Success in Learning to Read?' *Cognition* 77–111.

Catts, H. W. and Adlof, S. (2011), 'Phonological and Other Language Deficits Associated with Dyslexia', in S. A. Brady, D. Braze and C. A. Fowler (eds), *Explaining Individual Differences in Reading: Theory and Evidence*, 137–51. New York: Psychology Press.

Catts, H. W. and Kamhi, A. (1999), *Language and Reading Disabilities*. Boston, MA: Allyn and Bacon.

Chacko, A., Bedard, A. C., Marks, D. J., Feirsen, N., Underman, J. Z., Chimiklis, A. et al. (2014), 'A Randomized Clinical Trial of Cogmed Working Memory Training in School-age Children with ADHD: A Replication in a Diverse Sample Using a Control Condition', *Journal of Child Psychology and Psychiatry* 55 (3): 247–55.

Chaix, Y., Albaret, J., Brassard, C., Cheuret, E., DeCastelnau, P., Benesteau, J. et al. (2007), 'Motor Impairment in Dyslexia: The Influence of Attention Disorders', *European Journal of Paediatric Neurology* 11: 368–74.

Chall, J. S. (1967), *Learning to Read: The Great Debate*. New York: McGraw-Hill.

Chall, J. S. (1996), *Learning to Read: The Great Debate*, 3rd edn, Orlando, FL: Harcourt Brace.

Chhabildas, N., Pennington, B. F. and Wilcutt, E. G. (2001), 'A Comparison of the Neuropsychological Profiles of the DSM-IV Subtypes of ADHD', *Journal of Abnormal Child Psychology* 29: 529–40.

Christopher, M. E., Miyake, A., Keenan, J. M., Pennington, B., DeFries, J. C., Wadsworth, S. J., Willcutt, E. and Olson, R. K. (2012), 'Predicting Word Reading and Comprehension with Executive Function and Speed Measures across Development: A Latent Variable Analysis', *Journal of Experimental Psychology: General* 141 (3): 470–88.

Clay, M. M. (1993), *An Observation Survey of Early Literacy Achievement*, Auckland, NZ: Heinemann.

Coles, G. (1998), *Reading Lessons: The Debate over Literacy*, New York: Hill and Wang.

Collis, N. L., Kohnen, S. and Kinoshita, S. (2013), 'The Role of Visual Spatial Attention in Adult Developmental Dyslexia', *The Quarterly Journal of Experimental Psychology* 66 (2): 245–60.

Connor, C. M. (2010), 'Child Characteristics-instruction Interactions: Implications for Students' Literacy Skills Development in the Early Grades', in S. B. Neuman and D. K. Dickinson (eds), *Handbook on Early Literacy*, 3rd edn, New York: Guilford.

Cooke, A. (2001), 'Critical response to "Dyslexia, Literacy and Psychological Assessment" (Report by a Working Party of the Division of Educational and Child Psychology of the British Psychological Society): A View from the Chalk Face.' *Dyslexia* 7: 47–52.

Cooper, R. (2010), 'Are Culture-bound Syndromes as Real as Universally-occurring Disorders?' *Studies in History and Philosophy of Science Part C: Studies in History and Philosophy of Biological and Biomedical Sciences* 41 (4): 325–32.

Corriveau, K. H., Goswami, U. and Thomson, J. M. (2010), 'Auditory Processing and Early Literacy Skills in a Preschool and Kindergarten Population', *Journal of Learning Disabilities* 43: 369–82.

Covington, M. V. (1992), *Making the Grade: A Self-worth Perspective on Motivation and School Reform*, New York: Cambridge University Press.

Cowan, N. and Alloway, T. P. (2008), 'The Development of Working Memory', in N. Cowan (ed.), *Development of Memory in Childhood*, 303–42, New York: Psychology Press.

Crombie, M. and Reid, G. (2009), 'The Role of Early Identification Research: Models from Research and Practice', in G. Reid (ed.), *The Routledge Companion to Dyslexia*, 71–9. London: Routledge.

Cutting, L. E. (2014), 'What is in a Word', *Science* 345 (6202): 1252.

Cutting, L. E. and Denckla, M. B. (2001), 'The Relationship of Rapid Serial Naming and Word Reading in Normally Developing Readers: An Exploratory Model', *Reading and Writing* 14: 673–705.

Davis, A. (2008), 'Ian Hacking, Learner Categories and Human Taxonomies', *Journal of Philosophy of Education* 42 (3): 441–55.

Davis, R. D. (1997), *The Gift of Dyslexia*, London: Souvenir Press.

De Clercq-Quaegebeur, M., Casalis, S., Lemaitre, M., Bourgois, B., Getto, M. and Vallée, L. (2010), 'Neuropsychological Profile on the WISC-IV of French Children with Dyslexia', *Journal of Learning Disabilities* 43: 563–74.

Dehaene, S. (2009), *Reading in the Brain*, New York: Viking.

Dehaene, S. and Cohen, L. (2011), 'The Unique Role of the Visual Word form Area in Reading', *Trends in Cognitive Sciences* 15 (6): 254–62.

Demonet, J. F., Taylor, M. J. and Chaix, Y. (2004), 'Developmental Dyslexia', *Lancet* 363 (9419): 1451–60.

Denckla, M. B. (1985), 'Motor Coordination in Children with Dyslexia: Theoretical and Clinical Implications', in F. H. Duffy and N. Geschwind (eds), *Dyslexia: A Neuroscientific Approach to Clinical Evaluation*, Boston, MA: Little Brown.

Department of Education and Science. (1975), '*A Language for Life (The Bullock Report)*', London: HMSO.

Desmond, J. E. and Fiez, J. A. (1998), 'Neuroimaging Studies of the Cerebellum: Language, Learning and Memory', *Trends in Cognitive Sciences* 2 (9): 355–62.

Diamond, A. (2012), 'Activities and Programs That Improve Children's Executive Functions', *Current Directions in Psychological Science* 21 (5): 335–41.

Diamond, A. (2013), 'Executive Functions', *Annual Review of Psychology*, 64: 135–68.

Diehl, J. J., Frost, S. J., Mencl, W. E., and Pugh, K. R. (2011), 'Neuroimaging and the Phonological Deficit Hypothesis', in S. A.

Brady, D. Braze and C. A. Fowler (eds), *Explaining Individual Differences in Reading: Theory and Evidence*, 217–37. New York: Psychology Press.

Dirks, E., Spyer, G., van Lieshout, E. C. D. M. and de Sonneville, L. (2008), 'Prevalence of Combined Reading and Arithmetic Disabilities', *Journal of Learning Disabilities* 41 (5): 460–73.

Doyon, J. and Benali, H. (2005), 'Reorganization and Plasticity in the Adult Brain during Learning of Motor Skills', *Current Opinion in Neurobiology* 15: 1–7.

Duff, F. J., Hayiou-Thomas, M. E. and Hulme, C. (2012), 'Evaluating the Effectiveness of a Phonologically Based Reading Intervention for Struggling Readers with Varying Language Profiles', *Reading and Writing* 25: 621–40.

Duncan, G. J., Dowsett, C. J., Claessens, A., Magnuson, K., Huston, A. C. et al. (2007), 'School Readiness and Later Achievement', *Developmental Psychology* 43: 1428–46.

Dunning, D. L., Holmes, J. and Gathercole, S. E. (2013), 'Does Working Memory Training Lead to Generalized Improvements in Children with Low Working Memory? A Randomized Controlled Trial', *Developmental Science* 16: 915–25.

Eckert, M. A., Leonard, C. M., Richards, T. L. et al. (2003), 'Anatomical Correlates of Dyslexia: Frontal and Cerebellar Findings', *Brain* 126: 482–94.

Eden, G. F., Stein, J. F., Wood, H. M. et al. (1994), 'Differences in Eye-movements and Reading Problems in Dyslexic and Normal-children', *Vision Research* 34: 1345–58.

Eden, G. F., VanMeter, J. W., Rumsey, J. M. et al. (1996), 'Abnormal Processing of Visual Motion in Dyslexia Revealed by Functional Brain Imaging', *Nature* 382: 66–9.

Ehri, L. C., Nunes, S. R., Willows, D. M., Schuster, B. V., Yaghoub-Zadeh, Z. and Shanahan, T. (2001), 'Phonemic Awareness Instruction Helps Children Learn to Read: Evidence from the National Reading Panel's Meta-analysis', *Reading Research Quarterly* 36: 250–87.

Eide, B. L. and Eide, F. F. (2011), *The Dyslexic Advantage: Unlocking the Hidden Potential of the Dyslexic Brain*, London: Hay House.

Eissa, M. (2010), 'Behavioral and Emotional Problems Associated with Dyslexia in Adolescence', *Current Psychiatry* 17 (1): 17–25.

Elbeheri, G. and Everatt, J. (2009), 'Dyslexia and IQ: From Research to Practice', in G. Reid (Ed.), *The Routledge Companion to Dyslexia*, 22–32, London: Routledge.

Elliott, J. G. (2003), 'Dynamic Assessment in Educational Settings: Realising Potential', *Educational Review* 55: 15–32.

Elliott, J. G. (2014a), 'Time to Rethink Dyslexia?' *Times Higher Education*, 6 March: 34.

Elliott, J. G. (2014b), 'The Dyslexia Debate: More Heat than Light?' *Learning Disabilities Australia Bulletin* 46 (1/2): 12–13.

Elliott, J. G., Gathercole, S. E., Alloway, T. P., Kirkwood, H. and Holmes, J. (2010), 'An Evaluation of a Classroom-based Intervention to Help Overcome Working Memory Difficulties', *Journal of Cognitive Education and Psychology* 9: 227–50.

Elliott, J. G. and Gibbs, S. (2008), 'Does Dyslexia Exist?' *Journal of Philosophy of Education* 42: 475–91.

Elliott, J. G. and Grigorenko, E. L. (2014), *The Dyslexia Debate*, New York: Cambridge University Press.

Elliott, J. G. and Place, M. (2012), *Children in Difficulty: A Guide to Understanding and Helping*, 3rd edn, London: Routledge.

Elliott, J. G. and Resing, W. C.M. (2015), 'Can Intelligence Testing Inform Educational Intervention for Children with Reading Disability?' *Journal of Intelligence* 3: 137–57.

Etmanskie, J. M., Partanen, M. and Siegel, L. S. (2016), 'A Longitudinal Examination of the Persistence of Late Emerging Reading Disabilities', *Journal of Learning Disabilities* 49: 21–35.

Facoetti, A., Lorusso, M. L., Paganoni, P., Umilta, C., Mascetti, G. G. et al. (2003), 'The Role of Visuospatial Attention in Developmental Dyslexia: Evidence from a Rehabilitation Study', *Cognitive Brain Research* 15 (2): 154–64.

Farmer, M. E. and Klein, R. M. (1995), 'The Evidence for a Temporal Processing Deficit Linked to Dyslexia: A Review', *Psychonomic Bulletin and Review* 2: 460–93.

Fawcett, A. J. and Nicolson, R. I. (1992), 'Automatisation Deficits in Balance for Dyslexic Children', *Perceptual and Motor Skills* 75 (2): 507–29.

Fawcett, A. J. and Nicolson, R. I. (1995), 'Persistence of Phonological Awareness Deficits in Older Children with Dyslexia', *Reading and Writing* 7: 361–76.

Fawcett, A. J. and Nicolson, R. I. (1999), 'Performance of Dyslexic Children on Cerebellar and Cognitive Tests', *Journal of Motor Behavior* 31: 68–78.

Fawcett, A. J., Nicolson, R. I. and Lee, R. (2004), *Ready to Learn*, San Antonio, TX: Harcourt Assessment.

Fawcett, A. J., Nicolson, R. and Maclagan, F. (2001), 'Cerebellar Tests Differentiate Between Groups of Poor Readers With and Without IQ Discrepancy', *Journal of Learning Disabilities* 34 (2): 119–35.

Finch, A. J., Nicolson, R. I. and Fawcett, A. J. (2002), 'Evidence for a Neuroanatomical Difference within the Olivo-cerebellar Pathway of Adults with Dyslexia', *Cortex* 38 (4): 529–39.

Fitzpatrick, C., McKinnon, R. D., Blair, C. B. et al. (2014), 'Do Preschool Executive Function Skills Explain the School Readiness Gap between

Advantaged and Disadvantaged Children?' *Learning and Instruction*,
30: 25–31.

Flavell, J. H. (1977), *Cognitive Development*, Englewood Cliffs, NJ:
Prentice-Hall.

Flesch, R. (1955), *Why Johnny Can't Read – And What You Can Do
About It*, New York: Harper and Brothers.

Fletcher, J. M. (2009), 'Dyslexia: The Evolution of a Scientific Concept',
Journal of the International Neuropsychological Society 15: 501–8.

Fletcher, J. M. (in press), 'Classification, Definition, and Identification
Frameworks for Dyslexia: A Historical Perspective', In Eden,
G. F (ed.), *The Wiley Handbook on the Cognitive Neuroscience of
Developmental Dyslexia*. London: John Wiley & Sons, Ltd.

Fletcher, J. M., Lyon, G. R., Fuchs, L. S. and Barnes, M. A. (2007),
Learning Disabilities, New York: Guilford.

Fletcher, J. M., Stuebing, K. K., Barth, A. E., Denton, C. A., Cirino,
P. T., Francis, D. J. et al. (2011), 'Cognitive Correlates of Inadequate
Response to Reading Intervention', *School Psychology Review* 40:
3–22.

Flowers, L., Meyer, M., Lovato, J., Wood, F., and Felton, R. (2001),
'Does Third Grade Discrepancy Status Predict the Course of Reading
Development?' *Annals of Dyslexia* 51: 49–71.

Fodor, J. A. (1983), *The Modularity of Mind*, Cambridge, MA: MIT Press.

Franceschini, S., Gori, S., Ruffino, M. et al. (2013), 'Action Video Games
Make Dyslexic Children Read Better', *Current Biology* 23 (6): 462–6.

Frederickson, N. (1999), 'The ACID Test – Or Is It?' *Educational
Psychology in Practice* 15: 2–8.

Frith, U. (1986), 'A Developmental Framework for Developmental
Dyslexia', *Annals of Dyslexia* 36 (1): 67–81.

Froyen, D. J. W., Willems, G. and Blomert, L. (2011), 'Evidence
for a Specific Cross-modal Association Deficit in Dyslexia: An
Electrophysiological Study of Letter Speech Sound Processing',
Developmental Science 14 (4): 635–48.

Fuchs, D., McMaster, K. L., Fuchs, L. S. and Al Otaiba, S. (2013),
'Data-based Individualization as a Means of Providing Intensive
Instruction to Students with Serious Learning Disorders', in H. L.
Swanson, K. R. Harris and S. Graham (eds), *Handbook of Learning
Disabilities*, 526–44. New York: Guilford Press.

Fuchs, L. S., Fuchs, D. and Compton, D. L. (2010), 'Commentary:
Rethinking Response to Intervention at Middle and High School',
School Psychology Review 39: 22–8.

Furnes, B. and Samuelsson, S. (2010), 'Predicting Reading and Spelling
Difficulties in Transparent and Opaque Orthographies: A Comparison
between Scandinavian and US/Australian Children', *Dyslexia* 16:
119–42.

Gabay, Y., Schiff, R. and Vakil, E. (2012), 'Dissociation Between the Procedural Learning of Letter Names and Motor Sequences in Developmental Dyslexia', *Neuropsychologia* 50 (10): 2435–41.

Galaburda, A. M., Sherman, G. F., Rosen, G. D., Aboitiz, F. and Gerschwin, N. (1985), 'Developmental Dyslexia: Four Consecutive Patients with Cortical Anomalies', *Annals of Neurology* 18, 222–33.

Galaburda, A. M., LoTurco, J. J., Ramus, F., Fitch, R. H. and Rosen, G. D. (2006), 'From Genes to Behavior in Developmental Dyslexia', *Nature Neuroscience* 9: 1213–17.

Gathercole, S. E., Pickering, S. J., Knight, C. and Stegmann, Z. (2004), 'Working Memory Skills and Educational Attainment: Evidence from National Curriculum Assessments and 7 and 14 Years of Age', *Applied Cognitive Psychology* 18: 1–16.

Georgiou, G. K. and Parrila, R. (2013), 'Rapid Automatized Naming and Reading: A Review', in H. L. Swanson, K. R. Harris, and S. Graham (eds), *Handbook of Learning Disabilities*, 169–85, New York: Guilford Press.

Gervain, J. and Mehler, J. (2010), 'Speech Perception and Language Acquisition in the First Year of Life', *Annual Review of Psychology* 61: 191–18.

Geschwind, N. and Levitsky, W. (1968), 'Human Brain: Left-right Asymmetries in Temporal Speech Region', *Science* 161: 186–7.

Giedd, J. N. and Rapoport, J. L. (2010), 'Structural MRI of Pediatric Brain Development: What have We Learned and Where Are We Going? *Neuron* 67: 728–34.

Gilger, J. W. and Kaplan, B. J. (2001), 'Atypical Brain Development: A Conceptual Framework for Understanding Developmental Learning Disabilities', *Developmental Neuropsychology* 20 (2): 465–81.

Gillingham, A. and Stillman, B. (1960), *Remedial Training for Children with Specific Difficulties in Reading, Writing and Penmanship*, Cambridge, MA: Educators Publishing.

Goetz, T., Bieg, M., Luedtke, O. et al. (2013), 'Do Girls Really Experience More Anxiety in Mathematics?' *Psychological Science* 24 (10): 2079–87.

Goldston, D. B., Walsh, A., Mayfield-Arnold, E., Reboussin, B., Daniel, S. S., Erkanli, A. et al. (2007), 'Reading Problems, Psychiatric Disorders and Functional Impairment from Mid- to Late Adolescence', *Journal of the American Academy of Child and Adolescent Psychiatry* 46: 25–32.

Goodman, K. S. (1967), 'Reading: A Psycholinguistic Guessing Game', *Journal of the Reading Specialist* 6: 126–35.

Goodman, K. S. (1986), *What's Whole in Whole Language?* Portsmouth, NH: Heinemann.

Goswami, U. and Bryant, P. E. (1990), *Phonological Skills and Learning to Read*, Hillsdale, NJ: Lawrence Erlbaum Associates.

Goswami, U., Thomson, J., Richardson, U., Stainthorp, R., Hughes, D., Rosen, S. et al. (2002), 'Amplitude Envelope Onsets and Developmental Dyslexia: A New Hypothesis', *Proceedings of the National Academy of Sciences of the United States of America* 99 (16): 10911–16.

Goswami, U., Mead, N., Fosker, T., Huss, M., Barnes, L. and Leong, V. (2013), 'Impaired Perception of Syllable Stress in Children with Dyslexia: A Longitudinal Study', *Journal of Memory and Language* 69: 1–17.

Gresham, F. M. and Vellutino, F. R. (2010), 'What is the Role of Intelligence in the Identification of Specific Learning Disabilities? Issues and Clarifications', *Learning Disabilities Research & Practice* 25: 194–206.

Grigorenko, E. L. (2006), 'Learning Disabilities in Juvenile Offenders', *Child and Adolescent Psychiatric Clinics of North America* 15: 353–71.

Grills-Taquechel, A. E., Fletcher, J. M., Vaughn, S. R. and Stuebing, K. K. (2012), 'Anxiety and Reading Difficulties in Early Elementary School: Evidence for Unidirectional- or Bi-directional Relations?' *Child Psychiatry & Human Development* 43: 35–47.

Guttorm, T. K., Leppanen, P. H. T., Hamalainen, J. A. et al. (2010), 'Newborn Event-Related Potentials Predict Poorer Pre-Reading Skills in Children at Risk for Dyslexia' *Journal of Learning Disabilities* 43 (5): 391–401.

Hacking, I. (2006), 'Kinds of People: Moving Targets', British Academy Lecture. Available from http://www.britac.ac.uk/pubs/src/_pdf/hacking.pdf (accessed 4 May 2015).

Hacking, I. (2010), 'Pathological Withdrawal of Refugee Children Seeking Asylum in Sweden', *Studies in History and Philosophy of Science Part C: Studies in History and Philosophy of Biological and Biomedical Sciences* 41 (4): 309–17.

Hacking, I. (2013), 'Lost in the Forest', *London Review of Books* 35. Available from http://www.lrb.co.uk/v35/n15/ian-hacking/lost-in-the-forest (accessed 4 May 2015).

Hackman, D. A. and Farah, M. J. and Meaney, M. J. (2010), 'Socioeconomic Status and the Brain: Mechanistic Insights from Human and Animal Research', *Nature Reviews Neuroscience* 11: 651–9.

Hackman, D. A., Gallop, R., Evans, G. W. and Farah, M. J. (2015), 'Socioeconomic status and Executive Function: Developmental Trajectories and Mediation', *Developmental Science* 18: 686–702.

Handler, S. M., Fierson, W. M., the Section of Opthalmology and Council on Children with Disabilities, American Academy of Opthalmology, American Association for Pediatric Opthalmology and Strabismus and American Association of Certified Orthoptists. (2011), 'Joint Technical Report – Learning Disabilities, Dyslexia, and Vision', *Pediatrics* 127: e818–e56.

Hardy, I. and Woodcock, S. (2014), 'Contesting the Recognition of Specific Learning Disabilities in Educational policy: Intra- and International insights', *International Journal of Educational Research* 66: 113–24.

Hari, R. and Renvall, H. (2001), 'Impaired Processing of Rapid Stimulus Sequences in Dyslexia', *Trends in Cognitive Sciences* 5: 525–32.

Hart, B. and Risley, T. (2003), 'The Early Catastrophe', *American Educator* 27: 6–9.

Hart, S. A., Logan, J. A., Soden-Hensler, B., Kershaw, S., Taylor, J. and Schatschneider, C. (2013), 'Exploring How Nature and Nurture Affect the Development of Reading: An Analysis of the Florida Twin Project on Reading', *Developmental Psychology* 49: 1971–81.

Hart, S. A., Petrill, S. A., DeThorne, L. S., Deater-Deckard, K., Thompson, L. A., Schatschneider, C. et al. (2009), 'Environmental Influences on the Longitudinal Covariance of Expressive Vocabulary: Measuring the Home Literacy Environment in a Genetically Sensitive Design', *Journal of Child Psychology and Psychiatry* 50: 911–19.

Hartas, D. (2011), 'Families' Social Backgrounds Matter: Socioeconomic Factors, Home Learning and Young Children's Language, Literacy and Social Outcomes', *British Educational Research Journal* 37: 893–914.

Haslam, N., Holland, E. and Kuppens, P. (2013), 'Categories Versus Dimensions in Personality and Psychopathology: A Quantitative Review of Taxometric Research', *Psychological Medicine* 42: 903–20.

Haslum, M. (1989), 'Predictors of Dyslexia?' *Irish Journal of Psychology* 10 (4): 622–30.

Heaton, P. and Winterton, P. (1996), *Dealing with Dyslexia*, 2nd edn, London: Whurr Publishers.

Hedenius, M., Ullman, M. T., Alm, P. et al. (2013), 'Enhanced Recognition Memory after Incidental Encoding in Children with Developmental Dyslexia', *Plos One*, 8(5).

Henderson, S. E., Sugden, D. A. and Barnett, A. L. (2007), *Movement Assessment Battery for Children (Examiner's Manual)*, 2nd edn, London: Pearson Assessment.

Herbers, J. E., Cutuli, J. J., Supkoff, L. M., Heistad, D., Chan, C., Hinz, E. and Masten, A. S. (2012), 'Early Reading Skills and Academic Achievement Trajectories of Students Facing Poverty, Homelessness, and High Residential Mobility', *Educational Researcher* 41 (9): 366–74.

Herrington, M. and Hunter-Carsch, M. (2001), 'A Social Interactive

Model of Specific Learning Difficulties', in M. Hunter-Carsch (ed.), *Dyslexia: A Psycho-social Perspective*, 107–33, London: Whurr.

Hills, A. E., Newhart, M., Heidler, J. et al. (2005), 'The Roles of the "Visual Word Form Area" in reading', *Neuroimage* 24 (2): 548–59.

Hinshelwood, J. (1895), 'Word-blindness and Visual Memory', *Lancet* 146: 1564–70.

Hinshelwood, J. (1902), 'Congenital Word-blindness, with Reports of Two Cases', *Ophthalmology Review* 21: 91–9.

Hinshelwood, J. (1907), 'Four Cases of Congenital Word-blindness Occuring in the Same Family', *British Medical Journal* 1: 608–9.

Hinshelwood, J. (1917), *Congenital Word Blindness*, London: H. K. Lewis & Co.

Hoeft, F., McCandliss, B. D., Black, J. M., Gantman, A., Zakerani, N., Hulme, C. et al. (2011), 'Neural Systems Predicting Long-term Outcome in Dyslexia', *Proceedings of the National Academy of Sciences of the United States of America* 108: 361–6.

Hoff, E. (2003), 'The Specificity of Environmental Influence: Socioeconomic Status Affects Early Vocabulary Development via Maternal Speech', *Child Development* 74 (5): 1368–78.

Holmes, J., Gathercole, S. E. and Dunning, D. L. (2009), 'Adaptive Training Leads to Sustained Enhancement of Poor Working Memory in Children', *Developmental Science* 12: 9–15.

Holmes-Smith, P. (2006), *Socioeconomic Density and Its Effect on School Performance*, Sydney: New South Wales Department of Education and Training.

Holt, J. (1964), *How Children Fail*, New York: Pitman.

Huey, E. B. (1908), *The Psychology and Pedagogy of Reading*, New York: Macmillan.

Hulme, C. and Snowling, M. J. (1992), 'Deficits in Output Phonology: An Explanation of Reading Failure?' *Cognitive Neuropsychology* 9: 47–72.

Hutton, U. M. Z. and Towse, J. N. (2001), 'Short-term Memory and Working Memory as Indices of Children's Cognitive Skills', *Memory* 9: 383–94.

Hyatt, K. J., Stephenson, J. and Carter, M. (2009), 'A Review of Three Controversial Educational Practices: Perceptual Motor Programs, Sensory Integration, and Tinted Lenses', *Education and Treatment of Children* 32: 313–42.

Inhelder, B. and Piaget, J. (1958), *The Growth of Logical Thinking from Childhood to Adolescence*, New York: Basic Books.

Jacob, R. and Parkinson, J. (2015), 'The Potential for School-based Interventions that Target Executive Function to Improve Academic Achievement: A Review', *Review of Educational Research* 85: 512–52.

Le Jan, G., R., L. B.-J., Costet, N., Trolès, N., Scalart, P., Pichancourt, D., et al. (2011). Multivariate predictive model for dyslexia diagnosis. *Annals of Dyslexia, 61*, 1–20.

Jednoróg, K., Altarelli, I., Monzalvo, K., Fluss, J., Dubois, J., Billard, C., Dehaene-Lambertz, G. and Ramus, F. (2012), 'The Influence of Socioeconomic Status on Children's Brain Structure', *PLoS ONE* 7 (8): e42486.

Johnson, E. S., Humphrey, M., Mellard, D. F., Woods, K. and Swanson, H. L. (2010), 'Cognitive Processing Deficits and Students with Specific Learning Disabilities: A Selective Meta-analysis of the Literature', *Learning Disability Quarterly* 33: 3–18.

Juel, C. and Minden-Cupp, C. (2000), 'Learning to Read Words: Linguistic Units and Instructional Strategies', *Reading Research Quarterly* 35: 458–92.

Juul, H., Poulsen, M. and Elbro, C. (2014), 'Separating Speed From Accuracy in Beginning Reading Development', *Journal of Educational Psychology* 106 (4): 1096–6.

Kaiser, M-L., Schoemake, M. M., Albaret, J-M. et al. (2015), 'What is the Evidence of Impaired Motor Skills and Motor Control Among Children with Attention Deficit Hyperactivity Disorder (ADHD)? Systematic Review of the Literature', *Research in Developmental Disabilities* 36: 338–57.

Kaplan, B. J., Wilson, N. B., Dewey, D. and Crawford, S. G. (1998), 'DCD May Not Be a Discrete Disorder', *Human Movement Science* 17: 471–90.

Karmiloff-Smith, A. (1995), *Beyond Modularity: A Developmental Perspective on Cognitive Science*, Cambridge, MA: MIT Press.

Kaufman, A. S. (1975), 'Factor Analysis of the WISC-R at 11 Age Levels between 6½ and 16½ Years', *Journal of Consulting and Clinical Psychology* 43 (2): 135–47.

Kavale, K. A. and Mattson, P. D. (1983), '"One Jumped off the Balance Beam": Meta-analysis of Perceptual-motor Training', *Journal of Learning Disabilities* 16: 165–73.

Kearns, D. and Fuchs, D. (2013), 'Does Cognitively Focused Instruction Improve the Academic Performance of Low-achieving Students?' *Exceptional Children* 79 (3): 263–90.

Kibby, M. Y., Marks, W., Morgan, S. and Long, C. J. (2004), 'Specific Impairment in Developmental Reading Disabilities: A Working Memory Approach', *Journal of Learning Disabilities* 37: 349–63.

Kingma, E. (2014), 'Naturalism about Health and Disease: Adding Nuance for Progress', *Journal of Medicine and Philosophy* 39: 590–608.

Kirk, H. E., Gray, K., Riby, D. M. and Cornish, K. M. (2015), 'Cognitive Training as a Resolution for Early Executive Function Difficulties in

Children with Intellectual Disabilities', *Research in Developmental Disabilities* 38: 145–60.

Kirk, J. and Reid, G. (2001), 'An Examination of the Relationship between Dyslexia and Offending in Young People and the Implications for the Training System', *Dyslexia* 7: 77–84.

Koponen, T., Salmi, P., Eklund, K. and Aro, T. (2013), 'Counting and RAN: Predictors of Arithmetic Calculation and Reading Fluency', *Journal of Learning Disabilities* 105 (1): 162–75.

Kovas, Y., Voronin, I., Kaydalov, A., Malykh, S. B., Dale, P. S. and Plomin, R. (2013), 'Literacy and Numeracy Are More Heritable than Intelligence in Primary School', *Psychological Science* 24 (10): 2048–56.

Krafnick, A. J., Flowers, D. L., Luetje, M. M., Napoliello, E. M. and Eden, G. F. (2014), 'An Investigation into the Origin of Anatomical Differences in Dyslexia', *The Journal of Neuroscience* 34 (3): 901–8.

Krapohl, E., Rimfeld, K., Shakeshaft, N. G., Trzaskowski, M., McMillan, A., Pingault, J., Asbury, K., Harlaar, N., Kovas, Y., Dale, P. S. and Plomin, R. (2014), 'The High Heritability of Educational Achievement Reflects Many Genetically Influenced Traits, not Just Intelligence', *Proceedings of the National Academy of Sciences of the United States of America* 111: 15273–8.

Kronbichler, M., Hutzler, F. and Wimmer, H. (2002), 'Dyslexia: Verbal Impairments in the Absence of Magnocellular Impairments', *Cognitive Neuroscience And Neuropsychology* 13: 617–20.

Kuhl, P. K. (2004), 'Early Language Acquisition: Cracking the Speech Code. Nature Reviews', *Neuroscience* 5 (11): 831–43.

LaBerge, D. and Samuels, S. J. (1974), 'Toward a Theory of Automatic Information Processing in Reading', *Cognitive Psychology* 6: 293–323.

Ladd, G. W. and Dinella, L. M. (2009), 'Continuity and Change in Early School Engagement: Predictive of Children's Achievement Trajectories from First to Eighth Grade?', *Journal of Educational Psychology* 101: 190–206.

Lajiness-O'Neill, R., Akamine, Y. and Bowyer, S. M. (2007), 'Treatment Effects of Fast ForWord (R) Demonstrated by Magnetoencephalography (MEG) in a Child with Developmental Dyslexia', *Neurocase* 13 (5–6): 390–401.

Lallier, M., Tainturier, M., Dering, B., Donnadieu, S., Valdois, S. and Thierry, G. (2010), 'Behavioral and ERP Evidence for Amodal Sluggish Attentional Shifting in Developmental Dyslexia', *Neuropsychologia* 48: 4125–35.

Landerl, K. and Moll, K. (2010), 'Comorbidity of Learning Disorders: Prevalence and Familial Transmission', *Journal of Child Psychology and Psychiatry* 51: 287–94.

Landerl, K. and Wimmer, H. (2000), 'Deficits in Phoneme Segmentation Are Not the Core Problem in Dyslexia: Evidence from German and English Children', *Applied Psycholinguistics* 21: 243–62.

Landerl, K. and Wimmer, H. (2008), 'Development of Word Reading Fluency and Spelling in a Consistent Orthography: An 8-year Follow-up', *Journal of Educational Psychology* 100: 150–61.

Landerl, K., Ramus, F., Moll, K., Lyytinen, H., Leppänen, P. et al. (2013), 'Predictors of Developmental Dyslexia in European Orthographies with Varying Complexity', *Journal of Child Psychology and Psychiatry* 54 (6): 686–94.

Leiner, H. C., Leiner, A. L. and Dow, R. S. (1989), 'Reappraising the Cerebellum: What does the Hindbrain Contribute to the Forebrain', *Behavioural Neuroscience* 103: 998–1008.

Leonard, H. C. and Hill, E. L. (2014), 'Review: The Impact of Motor Development on Typical and Atypical Social Cognition and Language: A Systematic Review', *Child and Adolescent Mental Health* 19: 163–70.

Lervåg, A., Bråten, I. and Hulme, C. (2009), 'The Cognitive and Linguistic Foundations of Early Reading Development: A Norwegian Latent Variable Longitudinal Study', *Developmental Psychology* 45: 764–81.

Liberman, A. M. (1999), 'The Reading Researcher and the Reading Teacher Need the Right Theory of Speech', *Scientific Studies of Reading* 3: 95–111.

Liberman, I. Y. and Shankweiler, D. P. (1985), 'Phonology and the Problems of Learning to Read and Write', *Remedial and Special Education* 6: 8–17.

Lindamood, P. and Lindamood, P. (2011), *The Lindamood Phoneme Sequencing® Program for Reading, Spelling, and Speech*, 4th edn, Avila Beach, CA: Gander Publishing.

Loras, H., Sigmundsson, H., Stensdotter, A. and Talcott, J. B. (2014), 'Postural Control is not Systematically Related to Reading Skills: Implications for the Assessment of Balance as a Risk Factor for Developmental Dyslexia', *PLOS One* 9 (6): e98224.

Lovett, B. and Hood, S. B. (2014), 'Comorbidity in Child Psychiatric Diagnosis: Conceptual Complications', in C. Perring and L. Wells, (eds), *Diagnostic Dilemmas in Child and Adolescent Psychiatry: Philosophical Perspectives*, Oxford: Oxford University Press.

Lum, J. A. G., Ullman, M. T. and Conti-Ramsden, G. (2013), 'Procedural Learning is Impaired in Dyslexia: Evidence from a Meta-analysis of Serial Reaction Time Studies', *Research in Developmental Disabilities* 34 (10): 3460–76.

Lum, J. A. G., Conti-Ramsden, G., Morgan, A. T. et al. (2014), 'Procedural Learning Deficits in Specific Language Impairment (SLI):

A Meta-analysis of Serial Reaction Time Task Performance', *Cortex* 51: 1–10.

Lundberg, I., Olofsson, A. and Wall, S. (1980), 'Reading and Spelling Skills in the First School Years Predicted from Phonetic Awareness Skills in Kindergarten', *Scandinavian Journal of Psychology* 21: 159–73.

Lyon, G. R. (1996), 'Learning Disabilities', *Future of Children* 6: 54–76.

Lyon, G. R. and Weiser, B. (2013), 'The State of the Science in Learning Disabilities: Research Impact on the Field from 2001 to 2011', in H. L. Swanson, K. R. Harris and S. Graham (eds), *Handbook of Learning Disabilities*, 118–51, New York: Guilford Press.

Lyon, G. R., Shaywitz, S. E. and Shaywitz, B. A. (2003), 'A Definition of Dyslexia', *Annals of Dyslexia* 53: 1–14.

Lyons, I. M. and Beilock, S. L. (2012), 'When Math Hurts: Math Anxiety Predicts Pain Network Activation in Anticipation of Doing Math', *Plos One* 7 (10).

Lyytinen, H., Erskine, J., Tolvanen, A., Torppa, M., Poikkeus, A. and Lyytinen, P. (2006), 'Trajectories of Reading Development: A Follow-up from Birth to School Age of Children With and Without Risk for Dyslexia', *Merrill-Palmer Quarterly: Journal of Developmental Psychology* 52: 514–46.

Machek, G. R. and Nelson, J. M. (2007), 'How Should Reading Disabilities be Operationalized? A Survey of Practicing School Psychologists', *Learning Disabilities Research & Practice* 22: 147–57.

Maier, S. F. and Seligman, M. E .P. (1976), 'Learned Helplessness – Theory and Evidence', *Journal of Experimental Psychology-General* 105 (1): 3–46.

Maloney, E. A. (2012), 'Math Anxiety: Who Has It, Why it Develops, and How to Guard Against It', *Trends in Cognitive Science* 16: 404–6.

Martinussen, R. (2015), 'The Overlap of ADHD, Reading Disorders, and Language Impairment', *Perspectives on Language and Literacy* 41 (1): 9–14.

Mazzocco, M. M. and Grimm, J. J. (2013), 'Growth in Rapid Automatized Naming from Grades K to 8 in Children with Math or Reading Disabilities', *Journal of Learning Disabilities* 46 (6): 517–33.

McArthur, G. (2007), 'Test-retest Effects in Treatment Studies of Reading Disability: The Devil is in the Detail', *Dyslexia* 13: 240–52.

McCardle, P. D. and Chhabra, V. (eds) (2004), *The Voice of Evidence in Reading Research*, Baltimore, MD: Brookes.

McEwen, B. S. (2012), 'Brain on Stress: How the Social Environment Gets Under the Skin', *Proceedings of the National Academy of Sciences of the United States of America* 109: 17180–5.

McIntosh, K., Sadler, C. and Brown, J. A. (2012), 'Kindergarten

Reading Skill Level and Change as Risk Factors for Chronic Problem Behavior', *Journal of Positive Behavior Interventions* 14: 17–28.

McPhillips, M., Hepper, P. G. and Mulhern, G. (2000), 'Effects of Replicating Primary-reflex Movements on Specific Reading Difficulties in Children: A Randomised, Double-blind, Controlled Trial', *Lancet* 355 (9203): 537–41.

Mehan, H. (2014), 'The Prevalence and Use of the Psychological-medical Discourse in Special Education', *International Journal of Educational Research* 63: 59–62.

Melby-Lervåg, M. and Hulme, C. (2013), 'Is Working Memory Training Effective? A Meta-analytic Review', *Developmental Psychology* 49 (2): 270–91.

Melby-Lervåg, M., Lyster, S. and Hulme, C. (2012), 'Phonological Skills and Their Role in Learning to Read: A Meta-analytic Review', *Psychological Bulletin* 138: 322–52.

Meltzoff, A. N., Kuhl, P. K., Movellan, J. et al. (2009), 'Foundations for a New Science of Learning', *Science* 325 (5938): 284–8.

Menghini, D., Finzi, A., Benassi, M. et al. (2010), 'Different Underlying Neurocognitive Deficits in Developmental Dyslexia: A Comparative Study', *Neuropsychologia* 48 (4): 863–72.

Menghini, D., Finzi, A., Carlesimo, G. A. and Vicari, S. (2011), 'Working Memory Impairment in Children with Developmental Dyslexia: Is it Just a Phonological Deficit?' *Developmental Neuropsychology* 36: 199–213.

Miciak, J., Fletcher, J. M., Stuebing, K. K., Vaughn, S. and Tolar, T. D. (2013), 'Patterns of Cognitive Strengths and Weaknesses: Identification Rates, Agreement, and Validity for Learning Disabilities Identification', *School Psychology Quarterly* 29 (1): 21–37.

Miles, T. R. (1983), *Dyslexia: The Pattern of Difficulties*, Oxford: Blackwell.

Miller, A. C., Fuchs, D., Fuchs, L. S., Compton, D., Kearns, D., Zhang, W. and Kirchner, D. P. (2014), 'Behavioral Attention: A Longitudinal Study of Whether and How It Influences the Development of Word Reading and Reading Comprehension Among At-risk Readers', *Journal of Research on Educational Effectiveness* 7 (3): 232–49.

Molfese, D. L. (2000), 'Predicting Dyslexia at 8 years of Age Using Neonatal Brain Responses', *Brain and Language* 72 (3): 238–45.

Moll, K., Göbel, S. M., Gooch, D., Landerl, K. and Snowling, M. J. (forthcoming), 'Cognitive Risk Factors for Specific Learning Disorder: Processing Speed, Temporal Processing, and Working Memory', *Journal of Learning Disabilities*. DOI:10.1177/0022219414547221.

Moores, E., Cassim, R. and Talcott, J. B. (2011), 'Adults with Dyslexia Exhibit Large Effects of Crowding, Increased Dependence on Cues, and Detrimental Effects of Distractors in Visual Search Tasks', *Neuropsychologia* 49 (14): 3881–90.

Morgan, P. L., Farkas, G., Tufis, P. A. and Sperling, R. A. (2008), 'Are Reading and Behaviour Problems Risk Factors for Each Other?' *Journal of Learning Disabilities* 41: 417–36.

Morgan, W. P. (1896), 'A Case of Congenital Word-blindness (Inability to Learn to Read)', *British Medical Journal* 2: 1543–4.

Morton, J. and Frith, U. (1995), 'Causal Modelling: A Structural Approach to Developmental Psychopathology', in D. Cicchetti and D. J. Cohen (eds), *Manual of Developmental Psychopathology*, vol. 2, 274–98, New York: Wiley.

Moura, O., Simões, M. R. and Pereira, M. (2014), 'WISC-III Cognitive Profile in Children with Developmental Dyslexia: Specific Cognitive Disability and Diagnostic Utility', *Dyslexia* 20: 19–37.

Mugnaini, D., Lassi, S., La Malfa, G. and Albertini, G. (2009), 'Internalizing Correlates of Dyslexia', *World Journal of Pediatrics* 5: 255–64.

Myers, C. A., Vandermosten, M., Farris, E. A., Hancock, R., Gimenez, P., Black, J. M., Casto, B., Drahos, M., Tumber, M., Hendren, R., Hulme, C. and Hoeft, F. (2014), 'White Matter Morphometric Changes Uniquely Predict Children's Reading Acquisition', *Psychological Science* 25 (10): 1870–83.

Naples, A. J., Chang, J. T., Katz, L. and Grigorenko, E. L. (2009), 'Same or Different? Insights into the Etiology of Phonological Awareness and Rapid Naming', *Biological Psychology* 80: 226–39.

National Early Literacy Panel. (2008), *Developing Early Literacy: Report of the National Early Literacy Panel*, Washington, DC: National Institute for Literacy.

Nayfield, I., Fuccillo, J. and Greenfield, D. B.(2013), 'Executive Functions in Early Learning: Extending the Relationship between Executive Functions and School Readiness to Science', *Learning and Individual Differences* 26: 81–8.

Nelson, J. R., Benner, G. J. and Gonzalez, J. (2003), 'Learner Characteristics that Influence the Treatment of Effectiveness of Early Literacy Interventions: A Meta-analytic Review', *Learning Disabilities Research and Practice* 18: 255–67.

NICHD. (2000), *Report of the National Reading Panel: Teaching Children to Read*, Washington, DC: National Institute for Child Health and Human Development.

Nicolson, R. I. (2005), 'Dyslexia: Beyond the Myth', *The Psychologist*, 18: 658–9.

Nicolson, R. I. (2015), *Positive Dyslexia*, Sheffield: Rodin Books.

Nicolson, R. I. and Fawcett, A. J. (1990), 'Automaticity: A New Framework for Dyslexia Research?' *Cognition* 35 (2): 159–82.

Nicolson, R. I. and Fawcett, A. J. (1994), 'Reaction Times and Dyslexia', *Quarterly Journal of Experimental Psychology* 47A: 29–48.

Nicolson, R. I. and Fawcett, A. J. (1995), 'Dyslexia is More than a Phonological Disability', *Dyslexia: An International Journal of Research and Practice* 1: 19–37.

Nicolson, R. I. and Fawcett, A. J. (1996), *The Dyslexia Early Screening Test*, London: The Psychological Corporation.

Nicolson, R. I. and Fawcett, A. J. (2000), 'Long-term Learning in Dyslexic Children', *European Journal of Cognitive Psychology* 12: 357–93.

Nicolson, R. I. and Fawcett, A. J. (2004), *Dyslexia Early Screening Test (DEST)*, Oxford: Pearson Education.

Nicolson, R. I. and Fawcett, A. J. (2006), 'Do Cerebellar Deficits Underlie Phonological Problems in Dyslexia?' *Developmental Science* 9: 259–62; discussion 265–9.

Nicolson, R. I. and Fawcett, A. J. (2007), 'Procedural Learning Difficulties: Reuniting the Developmental Disorders?' *Trends in Neurosciences* 30 (4): 135–41.

Nicolson, R. I. and Fawcett, A. J. (2008), *Dyslexia, Learning and the Brain*, Boston, MA: MIT Press.

Nicolson, R. I., Fawcett, A. J. and Dean, P. (1995), 'Time-estimation Deficits in Developmental Dyslexia – Evidence of Cerebellar Involvement', *Proceedings of the Royal Society of London Series B-Biological Sciences* 259 (1354): 43–7.

Nicolson, R. I., Fawcett, A. J., Berry, E. L. et al. (1999), 'Association of Abnormal Cerebellar Activation with Motor Learning Difficulties in Dyslexic Adults', *Lancet*, 353: 1662–7.

Nicolson, R. I., Fawcett, A. J. and Dean, P. (2001), 'Developmental Dyslexia: The Cerebellar Deficit Hypothesis', *Trends in Neurosciences* 24 (9): 508–11.

Nicolson, R. I., Daum, I., Schugens, M. M. et al. (2002), 'Eyeblink Conditioning Indicates Cerebellar Abnormality in Dyslexia', *Experimental Brain Research* 143 (1): 42–50.

Nicolson, R. I., Fawcett, A. J., Brookes, R. L. et al. (2010), 'Procedural Learning and Dyslexia', *Dyslexia* 16 (3): 194–212.

Nicolson, R. I., Fawcett, A. J. and Dean, P. (2012), 'Dyslexia, Development and the Cerebellum', *Trends in Neurosciences* 24: 515–16.

Norton, E. S. and Wolf, M. (2012), 'Rapid Automatized Naming (RAN) and Reading Fluency: Implications for Understanding and Treatment of Reading Disabilities', *Annual Review of Psychology* 63: 427–52.

Norton, E. S., Beach, S. D. and Gabrieli, J. D. (2015), 'Neurobiology of Dyslexia', *Current Opinion in Neurobiology* 30: 73–8.

O'Donnell, P. S. and Miller, D. N. (2011), 'Identifying Students with Specific Learning Disabilities: School Psychologists' Acceptability of the Discrepancy Model Versus Response to Intervention', *Journal of Disability Policy Studies* 22: 83–94.

OECD. (2010), *Programme for International Student Assessment: Reading*, Organisation for Economic Cooperation and Development, Paris: OECD.

Olson, R. K. (2002), 'Nature and Nurture', *Dyslexia* 8 (3): 143–59.

Olson, R. K. (2011), 'Genetic and Environmental Influences on Phonological Abilities and Reading Achievement', in S. A. Brady, D. Braze and C. A. Fowler (eds), *Explaining Individual Differences in Reading: Theory and Evidence*, 197–216. New York: Psychology Press.

Orton, J. L. (1966), 'The Orton-Gillingham Approach', in J. Money (ed.), *The Disabled Reader: Education of the Dyslexic Child*, Baltimore, MD: Johns Hopkins Press.

Pan, B. A., Rowe, M. L., Singer, J. D. and Snow, C. E. (2005), 'Maternal Correlates of Growth in Toddler Vocabulary Production in Low-Income Families', *Child Development* 76 (4): 763–82.

Papert, S. (1980), *Mindstorms: Children, Computers and Powerful Ideas*, New York: Basic Books.

Papineau, D. (1994), 'Mental Disorder, Illness and Biological Dysfunction', *Royal Institute of Philosophy Supplement* 37: 73–82.

Pennington, B. F., Gilger, J. W., Pauls, D. et al. (1991), 'Evidence for Major Gene Transmission of Developmental Dyslexia', *Jama – Journal of the American Medical Association*, 266: 1527–34.

Penolazzi, B., Spironelli, C., Vio, C. and Angrilli, A. (2010), 'Brain Plasticity in Developmental Dyslexia after Phonological Treatment: A Beta EEG Band Study', *Behavioural Brain Research* 209: 179–82.

Pernet, C. R., Poline, J. B., Demonet, J. F. et al. (2009), 'Brain Classification Reveals the Right Cerebellum as the Best Biomarker of Dyslexia', *BMC Neuroscience*, 10: 67.

Peterson, R. L. and Pennington, B. F. (2012), 'Developmental Dyslexia', *Lancet* 379 (9830): 1997–2007.

Petty, M. C. (1939), 'An Experimental Study of Certain Factors Influencing Reading Readiness', *Journal of Educational Psychology* 30: 215–30.

Pfeiffer, S. I., Reddy, L. A., Kletzel, J. E., Schmelzer, E. R. and Boyer, L. M. (2000), 'The Practitioner's View of IQ Testing and Profile Analysis', *School Psychology Quarterly* 15 (4): 376–85.

Pham, A. V. and Hasson, R. M. (2014), 'Verbal and Visuospatial Working Memory as Predictors of Children's Reading Ability', *Archives of Clinical Neuropsychology* 29: 467–77.

Poulsen, M., Juul, H. and Elbro, C. (2015), 'Multiple Mediation Analysis of the Relationship between Rapid Naming and Reading', *Journal of Research in Reading* 38: 124–40.

Pressley, M. (2006), *Reading Instruction that Works: The Case for Balanced Teaching*, New York: The Guilford Press.

Price, C. J. (2012), 'A Review and Synthesis of the First 20 years of PET and fMRI Studies of Heard Speech, Spoken Language and Reading', *Neuroimage* 62 (2): 816–47.

Pringle-Morgan, W. (1896), 'A Case of Congenital Word Blindness', *British Medical Journal* 2: 178.

Prochnow, J. E., Tunmer, W. E. and Chapman, J. W. (2013), 'A Longitudinal Investigation of the Influence of Literacy-related Skills, Reading Self-perceptions, and Inattentive Behaviours on the Development of Literacy Learning Difficulties', *International Journal of Disability, Development and Education* 60 (3): 185–207.

Rabiner, D. L., Murray, D. W., Skinner, A. T. and Malone, P. S. (2010), 'A Randomized Trial of Two Promising Computer-based Interventions for Students with Attention Difficulties', *Journal of Abnormal Child Psychology* 38: 131–42.

Rack, J. P. (2003), 'The Who, What, Why and How of Intervention Programmes: Comments on the DDAT Evaluation', *Dyslexia* 9: 137–9.

Rack, J. P., Snowling, M. J., Hulme, C. and Gibbs, S. (2007), 'No Evidence that an Exercise-based Treatment Programme (DDAT) has Specific Benefits for Children with Reading Difficulties', *Dyslexia* 13: 97–104.

Ramus, F. (2014a), 'Neuroimaging Sheds New Light on the Phonological Deficit in Dyslexia', *Trends in Cognitive Sciences* 18 (6): 274–5.

Ramus, F. (2014b), 'Should There Really Be a "Dyslexia Debate"?', *Brain* 137 (12): 3371–4.

Ramus, F. and Ahissar, M. (2012), 'Developmental Dyslexia: The Difficulties of Interpreting Poor Performance, and the Importance of Normal Performance', *Cognitive Neuropsychology* 29 (1–2): 104–22.

Ramus, F. and Szenkovits, G. (2008), 'What Phonological Deficit?' *The Quarterly Journal of Experimental Psychology* 61: 129–41.

Ramus, F., Marshall, C. R., Rosen, S. and van der Lely, H. K. J. (2013), 'Phonological Deficits in Specific Language Impairment and Developmental Dyslexia: Towards a Multidimensional Model', *Brain* 136: 630–45.

Ramus, F., Pidgeon, E. and Frith, U. (2003), 'The Relationship Between Motor Control and Phonology in Dyslexic Children', *Journal of Child Psychology and Psychiatry and Allied Disciplines* 44 (5): 712–22.

Rashotte, C. A., MacPhee, K. and Torgesen, J. K. (2001), 'The Effectiveness of a Group Reading Instruction Program with Poor Readers in Multiple Grades', *Learning Disability Quarterly* 24: 119–34.

Rawls, J. (1955), 'Two Concepts of Rules', *The Philosophical Review* 64: 3–32.

Rawls, J. (1999), *A Theory of Justice,* revised edn, Cambridge, MA: Harvard University Press.

Redick, T. S. (2015), 'Working Memory Training and Interpreting Interactions in Intelligence Interventions', *Intelligence* 50: 14–20.

Regtvoort, A., Zijlstra, H. and van der Leij, A. (2013), 'The Effectiveness of a 2-year Supplementary Tutor-assisted Computerized Intervention on the Reading Development of Beginning Readers at Risk for Reading Difficulties: A Randomized Controlled Trial', *Dyslexia* 19 (4): 256–80.

Reynolds, D. and Nicolson, R. I. (2007), 'Follow-up of an Exercise-based Treatment for Children with Reading Difficulties', *Dyslexia* 13: 78–96.

Reynolds, D., Nicolson, R. I. and Hambly, H. (2003), 'Evaluation of an Exercise-based Treatment for Children with Reading Difficulties', *Dyslexia,* 9: 48–71.

Rice, M. and Brooks, G. (2004), *Developmental Dyslexia in Adults: A Research Review,* London: NRDC.

Richards, T. L. and Berninger, V. W. (2008), 'Abnormal fMRI Connectivity in Children with Dyslexia During a Phoneme Task: Before but Not After Treatment', *Journal of Neurolinguistics* 21: 294–304.

Richardson, U., Leppanen, P. H. T., Leiwo, M. and Lyytinen, H. (2003), 'Speech Perception of Infants with High Familial Risk for Dyslexia Differ at the Age of 6 Months', *Developmental Neuropsychology* 23: 385–97.

Riddick, B. (2010), *Living with Dyslexia: The Social and Emotional Consequences of Specific Learning Difficulties/Disabilities,* Oxford: Routledge.

Ritchie, S. J., Bates, T. C. and Plomin, R. (2015), 'Does Learning to Read Improve Intelligence? A Longitudinal Multivariate Analysis in Identical Twins from age 7 to 16', *Child Development* 86: 23–36.

Rochelle, K. S. and Talcott, J. B. (2006), 'Impaired Balance in Developmental Dyslexia? A Meta-analysis of the Contending Evidence', *Journal of Child Psychology and Psychiatry* 47, 1159–66.

Rose, J. (2009), *Identifying and Teaching Children and Young People with Dyslexia and Literacy Difficulties (the Rose Report),* Nottingham: DCSF Publications.

Rudel, R. G. (1985), 'The Definition of Dyslexia: Language and Motor Deficits', in F. H. Duffy and N. Geschwind (eds), *Dyslexia: A Neuroscientific Approach to Clinical Evaluation.* Boston, MA: Little Brown.

Rutter, M. (1978), 'Prevalence and Types of Dyslexia', in A. Benton and D. Pearl (eds), *Dyslexia: An Appraisal of Current Knowledge,* 5–28, New York: Oxford University Press.

Rutter, M. and Maughan, B. (2005), 'Dyslexia: 1965–2005', *Behavioural and Cognitive Psychotherapy* 33: 389–402.

Rutter, M. and Yule, W. (1975), 'The Concept of Specific Reading Retardation', *Journal of Child Psychology and Psychiatry* 139: 21–33.

Rutter, M., Kim-Cohen, J. and Maughan, B. (2006), 'Continuities and Discontinuities in Psychopathology between Childhood and Adult Life', *Journal of Child Psychology and Psychiatry* 47: 276–95.

Sasser, T. R., Bierman, K. L. and Heinrichs, B. (2015), 'Executive Functioning and School Adjustment: The Mediational Role of Pre-kindergarten Learning-related Behaviors', *Early Childhood Research Quarterly*, 30: 70–9.

Savage, R. S. (2004), 'Motor Skills, Automaticity and Developmental Dyslexia: A Review of the Research Literature', *Reading and Writing* 17: 301–24.

Savage, R. S. and Frederickson, N. (2005), 'Evidence of a Highly Specific Relationship between Rapid Automatic Naming of Digits and Text-reading Speed', *Brain and Language* 93: 152–9.

Savage, R. S., Frederickson, N., Goodwin, R., Patni, U., Smith, N. and Tuersley, L. (2005), 'Relationships among Rapid Digit Naming, Phonological Processing, Motor Automaticity, and Speech Perception in Poor, Average, and Good Readers and Spellers', *Journal of Learning Disabilities* 38: 12–28.

Savage, R. S., Lavers, N. and Pillay, V. (2007), 'Working Memory and Reading Difficulties: What We Know and What We Don't Know about the Relationship', *Educational Psychology Review* 19: 185–221.

Scammacca, N., Roberts, G., Vaughn, S. and Stuebing, K. (2015), 'A Meta-analysis of Interventions for Struggling Readers in Grades 4–12: 1980–2011', *Journal of Learning Disabilities* 48: 369–90.

Scarborough, H. S. (1998), 'Predicting the Future Achievement of Second Graders with Reading Disabilities: Contributions of Phonemic Awareness, Verbal Memory, Rapid Naming, and IQ', *Annals of Dyslexia* 48: 115–36.

Scarborough, H. S and Brady, S. A. (2002), 'Toward a Common Terminology for Talking about Speech and Reading: A Glossary of the "Phon" Words and Some Related Terms', *Journal of Literacy Research* 34: 299–336.

Schatschneider, C., Fletcher, J. M., Francis, D. J., Carlson, C. D. and Foorman, B. R. (2004), 'Kindergarten Prediction of Reading Skills: A Longitudinal Comparative Analysis', *Journal of Educational Psychology* 96: 265–82.

Schlaggar, B. L. and McCandliss, B. D. (2007), 'Development of Neural Systems for Reading', *Annual Review of Neuroscience* 30: 475–503.

Schneider, W. and Shiffrin, R. M. (1977), 'Controlled and Automatic

Human Information Processing I: Detection, Search and Attention', *Psychological Review* 84: 1–66.

Schneps, M. H., Thomson, J. M., Chen, C. et al. (2013), 'E-Readers Are More Effective than Paper for Some with Dyslexia', *Plos One* 8 (9).

Schwabe, L. and Wolf, O. T. (2013), 'Stress and Multiple Memory Systems: from "Thinking" to "doing", *Trends in Cognitive Sciences* 17 (2): 60–8.

Searle, J. (1995), *The Construction of Social Reality*, London: Penguin Books.

Selye, H. (1946), 'The General Adaptation Syndrome and the Diseases of Adaptation', *Journal of Clinical Endocrinology & Metabolism* 6 (2): 117–230.

Shankweiler, D. and Crain, S. (1986), 'Language Mechanisms and Reading Disorders: A Modular Approach', *Cognition* 24: 139–68.

Shankweiler, D. and Fowler, A. E. (2004), 'Questions People Ask About the Role of Phonological Processes in Learning to Read', *Reading and Writing: An Interdisciplinary Journal* 17: 483–515.

Share, D. L. (1996), 'Word Recognition and Spelling Processes in Specific Reading Disabled and Garden-variety Poor Readers', *Dyslexia* 2: 167–74.

Share, D. L. (2008), 'On the Anglocentricities of Current Reading Research and Practice: The Perils of Overreliance on an "Outlier" Orthography', *Psychological Bulletin* 134: 584–615.

Shaywitz, S. (1996), 'Dyslexia', *Scientific American* (November): 78–84.

Shaywitz, S. E. (2005), *Overcoming Dyslexia*, New York: Alfred Knopf.

Shaywitz, S. E. and Shaywitz, B. A. (2008), 'Paying Attention to Reading: The Neurobiology of Reading and Dyslexia', *Development and Psychopathology* 20: 1329–49.

Simpson, J. and Everatt, J. (2005), 'Reception Class Predictors of Literacy Skills', *British Journal of Educational Psychology* 75: 171–88.

Singleton, C. H. (2009a), 'Visual Stress and Dyslexia', in G. Reid (ed.), *The Routledge Companion to Dyslexia*, 43–57, New York: Routledge.

Smith, F. (1971), *Understanding Reading: A Psycholinguistic Analysis of Reading and Learning to Read*, New York: Holt, Rinehart & Winston.

Snow, C. E. and Juel, C. (2005), 'Teaching Children to Read: What Do We Know About How to Do It?' in M. J. Snowling and C. Hulme (eds), *The Science of Reading: A Handbook*, 501–20, Oxford: Blackwell.

Snowling, M. J. (2000), *Dyslexia*, Oxford: Blackwell.

Snowling, M. J. (2008), 'Specific Disorders and Broader Phenotypes: The Case of Dyslexia', *Quarterly Journal of Experimental Psychology* 61: 142–56.

Snowling, M. J. (2013), 'Early Identification and Interventions for

Dyslexia: A Contemporary View', *Journal of Research in Special Educational Needs* 13 (1): 7–14.

Snowling, M. J. and Hulme, C. (1994), 'The Development of Phonological Skills in Children', *Philosophical Transactions of the Royal Society* B, 346: 21–6.

Snowling, M. J. and Hulme, C. (2003), 'A Critique of Claims from Reynolds, Nicolson and Hambly (2003) that DDAT Is an Effective Treatment for Reading Problems: "lies, damned lies and (inappropriate) statistics"', *Dyslexia* 9: 1–7.

Southampton University (2015) http://www.southampton.ac.uk/edusupport/study_support/index.page [accessed 4 May 2015]

Spencer, M., Quinn, J. M. and Wagner, R. K. (2014), 'Specific Reading Comprehension Disability: Major Problem, Myth, or Misnomer?' *Learning Disabilities Research & Practice* 29 (1): 3–9.

Spironelli, C., Penolazzi, B., Vio, C., and Angrilli, A. (2010), 'Cortical Reorganization in Dyslexic Children after Phonological Training: Evidence from Early Evoked Potentials', *Brain* 133, 3385–95.

Squire, L. R. (1987), *Memory and Brain*, Oxford: Oxford University Press.

Stainthorp, R., Stuart, M., Powell, D., Quinlan, P. and Garwood, H. (2010), 'Visual Processing Deficits in Children with Slow RAN Performance', *Scientific Studies of Reading* 14: 266–92.

Stanovich, K. E. (1980), 'Towards an Interactive Compensatory Model of Individual Differences in the Development of Reading Fluency', *Reading Research Quarterly* 16 (1): 32–71.

Stanovich, K. E. (1986), 'Matthew Effects in Reading: Some Consequences of Individual Differences in the Acquisition of Literacy', *Reading Research Quarterly* 21: 360–407.

Stanovich, K. E. (1988), 'Explaining the Differences between the Dyslexic and the Garden-Variety Poor Reader: The Phonological-Core Variable-Difference Model', *Journal of Learning Disabilities* 21 (10): 590–604.

Stanovich, K. E. (2005), 'The Future of a Mistake: Will Discrepancy Measurement Continue to Make the Learning Disabilities Field a Pseudoscience?' *Learning Disability Quarterly* 28: 103–6.

Steacy, L. M., Kirby, J. R., Parrila, R., and Compton, D. L. (2014), 'Classification of Double Deficit Groups Across Time: An Analysis of Group Stability from Kindergarten to Second Grade', *Scientific Studies of Reading* 18: 255–73.

Stein, J. F. (1989), 'Visuospatial Perception and Reading Problems', *Irish Journal of Psychology* 10 (4): 521–33.

Stein, J. F. (2001), 'The Magnocellular Theory of Developmental Dyslexia', *Dyslexia* 7: 12–36.

Stein, J. F. (2012), 'The Magnocellular Theory of Dyslexia', in A. A. Benasich and R. H. Fitch (eds), *Developmental Dyslexia: Early Precursors, Neurobehavioral Markers, and Biological Substrates*, 32–45. Baltimore, MD: Paul H. Brookes Publishing.

Stein, J. F. and Kapoula, Z. (eds) (2012), *Visual Aspects of Dyslexia*, Oxford: Oxford University Press.

Stein, J. F. and Walsh, V. (1997), 'To See but Not to Read: The Magnocellular Theory of Dyslexia', *Trends in Neurosciences* 20: 147–52.

Stevens, C., Fanning, J., Coch, D. et al. (2008), 'Neural Mechanisms of Selective Auditory Attention are Enhanced by Computerized Training: Electrophysiological Evidence from Language-impaired and Typically Developing Children', *Brain Research* 1205: 55–69.

Stuebing, K. K., Fletcher, J. M., LeDoux, J. M., Lyon, R. G., Shaywitz, S. E. and Shaywitz, B. A. (2002), 'Validity of IQ-discrepancy Classifications of Reading Disabilities: A Meta-analysis', *American Educational Research Journal* 39: 469–518.

Stuebing, K. K., Barth, A. E., Cirino, P. T. et al. (2008), 'A Response to Recent Reanalyses of the National Reading Panel Report: Effects of Systematic Phonics Instruction are Practically Significant', *Journal of Educational Psychology* 100 (1): 123–34.

Stuebing, K. K., Barth, A. E., Molfese, P. J., Weiss, B. and Fletcher, J. M. (2009), 'IQ is not Strongly Related to Response to Reading Instruction: A Meta-analytic Interpretation', *Exceptional Children* 76: 31–51.

Stuebing, K. K., Barth, A. E., Trahan, L. H., Reddy, R. R., Miciak, J. and Fletcher, J. M. (2015), 'Are Child Characteristics Strong Predictors of Response to Intervention? A Meta-analysis', *Review of Educational Research* 85: 395–429.

Suggate, S. P., Schaughency, E. A. and Reese, E. (2013), 'Children Learning to Read Later Catch Up to Children Reading Earlier', *Early Childhood Research Quarterly* 28 (1): 33–48.

Swanson, H. L. (2006), 'Working Memory and Reading Disabilities: Both Phonological and Executive Processing Deficits are Important', in T. P. Alloway and S. E. Gathercole (eds), *Working Memory and Neurodevelopmental Disorders*, 59–88. New York: Psychology Press.

Swanson, H. L., Ashbaker, M. H. and Lee, C. (1996), 'Learning Disabled Readers' Working Memory as a Function of Processing Demands', *Journal of Experimental Child Psychology* 61: 242–75.

Szazs, T. (1960), 'The Myth of Mental Illness', *American Psychologist*, 15: 113–18.

Szwed, M., Ventura, P., Querido, L., Cohen, L. and Dehaene, S. (2012), 'Reading Acquisition Enhances an Early Visual Process of Contour Integration', *Developmental Science* 15: 139–49.

Tallal, P. (1980), 'Auditory Temporal Perception, Phonics, and Reading Disabilities in Children', *Brain and Language* 9: 182–98.

Tallal, P. and Gaab, N. (2006), 'Dynamic Auditory Processing, Musical Experience and Language Development', *Trends in Neurosciences* 29: 382–90.

Tallal, P., Miller, S. and Fitch, R. H. (1993), 'Neurobiological Basis of Speech – A Case for the Pre-eminence of Temporal Processing', *Annals of the New York Academy of Sciences* 682: 27–47.

Tamboer, P., Vorst, H. C. and Oort, F. J. (forthcoming), 'Five Describing Features of Dyslexia', *Journal of Learning Disabilities*. DOI: 10.1177/0022219414558123.

Taylor, J., Roehrig, A. D., Soden Hensler, B., Connor, C. M. and Schatschneider, C. (2010), 'Teacher Quality Moderates the Genetic Effects on Early Reading', *Science* 328, 512–14.

Teicher, M. H., Samson, J. A., Polcari, A. et al. (2006), 'Sticks, Stones, and Hurtful Words: Relative Effects of Various Forms of Childhood Maltreatment', *American Journal of Psychiatry*, 163 (6): 993–1000.

Thompson, P. A., Hulme, C., Nash, H. M., Gooch, D., Hayiou-Thomas, E. and Snowling, M. J. (2015), 'Developmental Dyslexia: Predicting Individual Risk', *Journal of Child Psychology and Psychiatry* 56: 976–87.

Thomson, M. (2002), 'Dyslexia and Diagnosis', *The Psychologist* 15: 151.

Thomson, M. (2003), 'Monitoring Dyslexics' Intelligence and Attainments: A Follow-up Study', *Dyslexia* 9: 3–17.

Thomson, M. (2009), *The Psychology of Dyslexia: A Handbook for Teachers*, 2nd edn, Oxford: Wiley-Blackwell.

Thomson, S. and De Bortoli, L. (2010), *Challenges for Australian Education: Results from PISA 2009*. Melbourne: ACER.

Torgerson, C. J., Brooks, G. and Hall, G. (2006), *A Systematic Review of the Research Literature on the Use of Systematic Phonics in the Teaching of Reading and Spelling*, London: Department for Education and Skills.

Torgesen, J. K. (2004), 'Lessons Learned from Research on Interventions for Students Who Have Difficulty Learning to Read', in P. McCardle and V. Chhabra (eds), *The Voice of Evidence in Reading Research*, 355–82. Baltimore, MD: Brookes.

Torgesen, J. K. (2001), 'Theory and Practice of Intervention', in A. J. Fawcett (ed.), *Dyslexia: Theory and Good Practice*. London: Whurr.

Torgesen, J. K., Wagner, R. K., Rashotte, C. A. et al. (1999), 'Preventing Reading Failure in Young Children with Phonological Processing Disabilities: Group and Individual Responses to Instruction', *Journal of Educational Psychology* 91 (4): 579–93.

Torgesen, J. K., Alexander, A. W., Wagner, R. K. et al. (2001), 'Intensive

Remedial Instruction for Children with Severe Reading Disabilities: Immediate and Long-term Outcomes from Two Instructional Approaches', *Journal of Learning Disabilities* 34 (1): 33–58.

Torppa, M., Parrila, R., Niemi, P., Lerkkanen, M-K., Poikkeus, A-M. and Nurmi, J-E. (2013), 'The Double Deficit Hypothesis in the Transparent Finnish Orthography: A Longitudinal Study from Kindergarten to Grade 2', *Reading and Writing* 26: 1353–80.

Touwen, B. C. L. and Sporrel, T. (1979), 'Soft Signs and MBD', *Developmental Medicine and Child Neurology* 21: 1097–1105.

Tunmer, W. E. (2015), *Excellence and Equity in Literacy Education* (Palgrave Studies in Excellence and Equity in Global Education), London: Palgrave.

Tunmer, W. E. and Nicholson, T. (2011), 'The Development and Teaching of Word Recognition Skill', in M. L. Kamil, P. D. Pearson, E. B. Moje and P. Afflerbach (eds), *Handbook of Reading Research*, vol. 4, 405–31, London: Routledge.

Ullman, M. T. (2004), 'Contributions of Memory Circuits to Language: The Declarative/procedural Model', *Cognition* 92 (1–2): 231–70.

Ullman, M. T. and Pierpont, E. I. (2005), 'Specific Language Impairment is Not Specific to Language: The Procedural Deficit Hypothesis', *Cortex* 41 (3): 399–433.

Underwood, E. (2013), 'Faulty Brain Connections in Dyslexia?' *Science* 342 (6163): 1158.

U.S. Office of Education (1977), 'Assistance to States for Education for Handicapped Children: Procedures for Evaluating Specific Learning Disabilities', *Federal Register* 42: G1082–5.

Vaessen, A. and Blomert, L. (2010), 'Long-term Cognitive Dynamics of Fluent Reading Development', *Journal of Experimental Child Psychology* 105: 213–31.

Vaessen, A., Gerretsen, P. and Blomert, L. (2009), 'Naming Problems Do Not Reflect a Second Independent Core Deficit in Dyslexia: Double Deficits Explored', *Journal of Experimental Child Psychology* 103: 202–21.

Van Daal, V., van der Leij, A. and Ader, H. (2013), 'Specificity and Overlap in Skills Underpinning Reading and Arithmetical Fluency', *Reading and Writing* 26 (6): 1009–30.

Van der Leij, A., van Bergen, E., van Zuijen, T., de Jong, P., Maurits, N. and Maassen, B. (2013), 'Precursors of Developmental Dyslexia: An Overview of the Longitudinal Dutch Dyslexia Programme Study', *Dyslexia* 19: 191–213.

Van der Mark, S., Bucher, K., Maurer, U. et al. (2009), 'Children with Dyslexia Lack Multiple Specializations along the Visual Word-form (VWF) System', *Neuroimage*, 47 (4): 1940–9.

Van Dyke, J. A., Johns, C. L. and Kukona, A. (2014), 'Low

Working Memory is Only Spuriously Related to Poor Reading Comprehension', *Cognition* 131(3): 373–403.

Vargo, F. E., Grossner, G. S. and Spafford, C. S. (1995), 'Digit Span and Other WISC-R Scores in the Diagnosis of Dyslexic Children', *Perceptual and Motor Skills* 80: 1219–29.

Varvara, P., Varuzza, C., Sorrentino, A. C. P. et al. (2014), 'Executive Functions in Developmental Dyslexia', *Frontiers in Human Neuroscience* 8 Article 120.

Vaughn, S., Wanzek, J., Murray, C. S., Scammacca, N., Linan-Thompson, S. and Woodruff, A. L. (2009), 'Response to Early Reading Intervention: Examining Higher and Lower Responders', *Exceptional Children* 75: 165–83.

Vaughn, S., Cirino, P. T., Wanzek, J., Wexler, J., Francis, D. J., Fletcher, J. M. et al. (2010), 'Response to Intervention for Middle School Students with Reading Difficulties: Effects of a Primary and Secondary Intervention', *School Psychology Review* 39: 3–21.

Vaughn, S., Wexler, J., Roberts, G., Barth, A., Cirino, P. T., Romain, M. A. et al. (2011), 'Effects of Individualized and Standardized Interventions on Middle School Students with Reading Disabilities', *Exceptional Children* 77: 391–407.

Vaughn, S., Wexler, J., Leroux, A, Roberts, G., Denton, C., Barth, A. and Fletcher, J. (2012), 'Effects of Intensive Reading Intervention for Eighth-Grade Students With Persistently Inadequate Response to Intervention', *Journal of Learning Disabilities* 45 (6): 515–25.

Vellutino, F. R. (1979), *Dyslexia: Theory and Research*, Cambridge, MA: MIT Press.

Vellutino, F. R. (1987), 'Dyslexia', *Scientific American* 256: 34–41.

Vellutino, F. R., Scanlon, D. M. and Spearing, D. (1995), 'Semantic and Phonological Coding in Poor and Normal Readers', *Journal of Experimental Child Psychology* 59: 76–123.

Vellutino, F. R., Fletcher, J. M., Snowling, M. J. and Scanlon, D. M. (2004), 'Specific Reading Disability (Dyslexia): What Have We Learned in the Past Four Decades?' *Journal of Child Psychology & Psychiatry* 45: 2–40.

Vellutino, F. R., Scanlon, D. M., Zhang, H. and Schatschneider, C. (2008), 'Using Response to Kindergarten and First Grade Intervention to Identify Children At-risk for Long-term Reading Difficulties', *Reading and Writing* 21: 437–80.

Vidyasagar, T. R. and Pammer, K. (2010), 'Dyslexia: A Deficit in Visuo-spatial Attention, Not in Phonological Processing', *Trends in Cognitive Science* 14: 57–63.

Vukovic, R. K. and Siegel, L. S. (2006), 'The Double-deficit Hypothesis: A Comprehensive Analysis of the Evidence', *Journal of Learning Disabilities* 39: 25–47.

Vukovic, R. K., Lesaux, N. K. and Siegel, L. S. (2010), 'The Mathematics Skills of Children with Reading Difficulties', *Learning and Individual Differences* 20: 639–43.

Wagner, R. K. (2005), 'Understanding Genetic and Environmental Influences on the Development of Reading: Reaching for Higher Fruit', *Scientific Studies of Reading*, 9 (3): 317–26.

Wagner, R. K. (2008), 'Rediscovering Dyslexia: New Approaches for Identification and Classification', in G. Reid, A. Fawcett, F. Manis and L. Siegel (eds), *The Sage Handbook of Dyslexia*, 174–91, London, UK: Sage.

Wagner, R. K. and Muse, A. (2006), 'Short-term Memory Deficits in Developmental Dyslexia', in T. P. Alloway and S. E. Gathercole (eds), *Working Memory and Neurodevelopmental Disorders*, New York: Psychology Press.

Wagner, R. K., Torgesen, J. K., Rashotte, C. A., Hecht, S. A., Barker, T. A., Burgess, S. R. et al. (1997), 'Changing Relations between Phonological Processing Abilities and Word-level Reading as Children Develop from Beginning to Skilled Readers: A Five-year Longitudinal Study', *Developmental Psychology* 33: 468–79.

Wang, S. and Gathercole, S. E. (2013), 'Working Memory Deficits in Children with Reading Difficulties: Memory Span and Dual Task Coordination', *Journal of Experimental Child Psychology* 115 (1): 188–97.

Wanzek, J., Vaughn, S., Scammacca, N. K., Metz, K., Murray, C. S., Roberts, G. and Danielson, L. (2013), 'Extensive Reading Interventions for Students with Reading Difficulties after Grade 3', *Review of Educational Research* 83 (2): 163–95.

Ward, S. B., Ward, T. J., Hatt, C. V., Young, D. L. and Molner, N. R. (1995), 'The Incidence and Utility of the ACID, ACIDS and SCAD Profiles in a Referred Population', *Psychology in the Schools* 32: 267–76.

Washburn, E. K., Joshi, R. M. and Cantrell, E. B. (2011), 'Are Preservice Teachers Prepared to Teach Struggling Readers?' *Annals of Dyslexia* 61: 21–43.

Wass, S. (2015), 'Applying Cognitive Training to Target Executive Functions During Early Development', *Child Neuropsychology* 21 (2): 150–66.

Watkins, M. W., Kush, J. C. and Glutting, J. J. (1997), 'Discriminant and Predictive Validity of the WISC-III ACID Profile Among Children with Learning Disabilities', *Psychology in the Schools*, 34: 309–19.

Wechsler, D. (2003), *Wechsler Intelligence Scale for Children® – Fourth Edition (WISC®-IV)*, San Antonio, TX: Pearson.

Wender, P. (1978), 'Minimal Brain Dysfunction: An Overview', in M. A. Lipton, A. Di Mascio and K. F. Killam (eds), *Psychopharmacology: A Decade of Progress*, New York: Raven Press.

Westerndorp, M., Hartman, E., Houwen, S., Smith, J. and Visscher, C. (2011), 'The Relationship between Gross Motor Skills and Academic Achievement in Children with Learning Disabilities', *Research in Developmental Disabilities* 32: 2773–9.

White, S., Milne, E., Rosen, S., Hansen, P., Swettenham, J., Frith, U. et al. (2006), 'The Role of Sensorimotor Impairments in Dyslexia: A Multiple Case Study of Dyslexic Children', *Developmental Science* 9: 237–69.

Whitebread, D. and Bingham, S. (2013), 'Too Much, Too Young: Should Schooling Start at Age 7?' *New Scientist* 2943: 28–9.

Willcutt, E. G., Betjemann, R. S., McGrath, L. M., Chhabildas, N. A., Olson, R. K., DeFries, J. C. et al. (2010), 'Etiology and Neuropsychology of Comorbidity between RD and ADHD: The Case for Multiple-deficit Models', *Cortex* 46: 1345–61.

Wilkins, A. J. (1995), *Visual Stress*, Oxford: Oxford University Press.

Willcutt, E. G., Doyle, A. E., Nigg, J. T. et al. (2005), 'Validity of the Executive Function Theory of Attention-deficit/hyperactivity Disorder: A Meta-analytic Review', *Biological Psychiatry* 57 (11): 1336–46.

Willcutt, E. G. and Pennington, B. F. (2000), 'Comorbidity of Reading Disability and Attention-deficit/hyperactivity Disorder: Differences by Gender and Subtype', *Journal of Learning Disabilities* 33 (2): 179–91.

Willcutt, E. G., Pennington, B. F., Olson, R. K. and DeFries, J. C. (2007), 'Understanding Comorbidity: A Twin Study of Reading Disability and Attention-deficit/hyperactivity Disorder', *American Journal of Medical Genetics Part B: Neuropsychiatric Genetics* 144B: 709–14.

Willcutt, E. G., Petrill, S. A., Wu, S., Boada, R., DeFries, J. C., Olson, R. K. and Pennington, B. F. (2013), 'Comorbidity between Reading Disability and Math Disability: Concurrent Psychopathology, Functional Impairment, and Neuropsychological Functioning', *Journal of Learning Disabilities* 46 (6): 500–16.

Wolf, M. (2007), *Proust and the Squid: The Story and Science of the Reading Brain*, New York: HarperCollins.

Wolf, M. and Bowers, P. G. (1999), 'The Double-deficit Hypothesis for the Developmental Dyslexia', *Journal of Educational Psychology* 91: 415–38.

Wolf, M., Bowers, P. G. and Biddle, K. (2000), 'Naming-speed Processes, Timing, and Reading: A Conceptual Review', *Journal of Learning Disabilities* 33: 387–407.

Wolf, M., Gottwald, S., Galante, W., Norton, E. and Miller, L. (2009), 'How the Origins of the Reading Brain Instruct our Knowledge of Reading Intervention', in K. Pugh and P. McCardle (eds), *How Children Learn to Read: Current Issues and New Directions in the Integration of Cognition, Neurobiology and Genetics of Reading and Dyslexia Research and Practice*, 289–99, New York: Psychology Press.

Wolff, P. H., Melngailis, I., Obregon, M. and Bedrosian, M. (1995), 'Family Patterns of Developmental Dyslexia, Part II: Behavioral Phenotypes', *American Journal of Medical Genetics* 60: 494–505.

Young, C. B., Wu, S. S. and Menon, V. (2012), 'The Neurodevelopmental Basis of Math Anxiety', *Psychological Science* 23 (5): 492–501.

Yule, W. (1976), Dyslexia. *Psychological Medicine,* 6: 165–7.

Zachar, P. (2000), 'Psychiatric Disorders are not Natural Kinds', *Philosophy, Psychiatry and Psychology* 7 (3), 167–82.

Zeffiro, T. and Eden, G. (2001), 'The Cerebellum and Dyslexia: Perpetrator or Innocent Bystander? Comment', *Trends in Neurosciences* 24 (9): 512–13.

Zelazo, P. D. and Carlson, S. M. (2012), 'Hot and Cool Executive Function in Childhood and Adolescence: Development and Plasticity', *Child Development Perspectives* 6 (4): 354–60.

Ziegler, J. C., Bertrand, D., Tóth, D., Csépe, V., Reis, A., Faísca, L. et al. (2010), 'Orthographic Depth and Its Impact on Universal Predictors of Reading', *Psychological Science* 21: 551–9.

Zovkic, I. B. and Sweatt, J. D. (2013), 'Epigenetic Mechanisms in Learned Fear: Implications for PTSD', *Neuropsychopharmacology* 38 (1): 77–93.

Index